CONTEMPORARY
CHINA

A HISTORY OF THE CONTEMPORARY WORLD

General Editor: Keith Robbins

This series offers an historical perspective on the development of the contemporary world. Each of the books examines a particular region or a global theme as it has evolved in the recent past. The focus is primarily on the period since the 1980s but authors provide deeper context wherever necessary. While all the volumes offer an historical framework for analysis, the books are written for an interdisciplinary audience and assume no prior knowledge on the part of readers.

Published

Contemporary America
M. J. Heale

Contemporary Global Economy
Alfred E. Eckes, Jr.

Contemporary Japan, Second Edition
Jeff Kingston

Contemporary Latin America
Robert H. Holden & Rina Villars

Contemporary China
Yongnian Zheng

CONTEMPORARY
CHINA
A HISTORY SINCE 1978

YONGNIAN ZHENG

A John Wiley & Sons, Ltd., Publication

This edition first published 2014
© 2014 John Wiley & Sons Ltd

Wiley-Blackwell is an imprint of John Wiley & Sons, formed by the merger of Wiley's global
Scientific, Technical and Medical business with Blackwell Publishing.

Registered Office
John Wiley & Sons Ltd, The Atrium, Southern Gate, Chichester, West Sussex, PO19 8SQ, UK

Editorial Offices
350 Main Street, Malden, MA 02148-5020, USA
9600 Garsington Road, Oxford, OX4 2DQ, UK
The Atrium, Southern Gate, Chichester, West Sussex, PO19 8SQ, UK

For details of our global editorial offices, for customer services, and for information about how
to apply for permission to reuse the copyright material in this book please see our website at
www.wiley.com/wiley-blackwell.

The right of Yongnian Zheng to be identified as the author of this work has been asserted in
accordance with the UK Copyright, Designs and Patents Act 1988.

Library of Congress Cataloging-in-Publication Data
Zheng, Yongnian.
  Contemporary China : a history since 1978 / Yongnian Zheng.
    pages cm
  Includes bibliographical references and index.
  ISBN 978-0-470-65579-5 (cloth) – ISBN 978-0-470-65580-1 (pbk.)
  1. China–History–1976–2002.   2. China–History–2002–   I. Title.
  DS779.2.Z4364 2012
  951.05–dc23
                          2012043027

A catalogue record for this book is available from the British Library.

Cover image: A man rides an electric tricycle past a truck loaded with new Volkswagen cars on a
street in Nanjing. © Sean Yong / Reuters.
Cover design by www.simonlevyassociates.co.uk

Set in 10/12.5 pt Minion by Toppan Best-set Premedia Limited
Printed in Singapore by Ho Printing Singapore Pte Ltd

1   2014

Contents

Figures and Tables

Series Editor's Preface

The contemporary world frequently presents a baffling spectacle: "New world orders" come and go; "Clashes of civilizations" seem imminent if not actual; "Peace dividends" appear easily lost in the post; terrorism and "wars on terror" occupy the headlines. "Mature" states live alongside "failed" states in mutual apprehension. The "rules" of the international game, in these circumstances, are difficult to discern. What "international law" is, or is not, remains enduringly problematic. Certainly it is a world in which there are still frontiers, borders, and boundaries but both metaphorically and in reality they are difficult to patrol and maintain. "Asylum" occupies the headlines as populations shift across continents, driven by fear. Other migrants simply seek a better standard of living. The organs of the "international community," though frequently invoked, look inadequate to deal with the myriad problems confronting the world. Climate change, however induced, is not susceptible to national control. Famine seems endemic in certain countries. Population pressures threaten finite resources. It is in this context that globalization, however understood, is both demonized and lauded.

Such a list of contemporary problems could be amplified in detail and almost indefinitely extended. It is a complex world, ripe for investigation in this ambitious new series of books. "Contemporary," of course, is always difficult to define. The focus in this series is on the evolution of the world since the 1980s. As time passes, and as the volumes appear, it no longer seems sensible to equate "the world since 1945" with "contemporary history." The legacy of the "Cold War" lingers on but it is emphatically "in the background." The fuzziness about "the 1980s" is deliberate. No single year ever carries the same significance across the globe. Authors are therefore establishing their own precise starting points, within the overall "contemporary" framework.

The series treats the history of particular regions, countries or continents but does so in full awareness that such histories, for all their continuing distinctiveness, can only rarely be considered apart from the history of the world as a whole. Economic, demographic, environmental and religious issues transcend state, regional or continental boundaries. Just as the world itself struggles to reconcile diversity and individuality with unity and common purpose, so do the authors of these volumes. The concept is challenging. Authors have been selected who sit loosely on their disciplinary identity – whether that be as historians, political scientists or students of international relations. The task is to integrate as many aspects of contemporary life as possible in an accessible manner.

The analysis of "Contemporary China" in this volume reflects these ambitions. It combines its account of extraordinary economic development with an acute awareness of shifting political alignments and ideological formulations. It does not ignore social tensions. It knows that China is not uniform and the balance between city and country, littoral and hinterland, "province" and Beijing is unstable and needs to be understood. Even so, it is "one China" that makes its mark on the world. The strength of this account, too, is that "contemporary China" is situated firmly in pasts, long pasts, which overhang into the present. Here is no simple presentation of a country traveling a predictable path to "modernization" and "democracy" but rather one whose transition has its internal constraints and imperatives. An author based in Singapore and with first-hand experience of China today understands both present "Western" questions and "Chinese" answers. The outcome is a distinctive and distinguished assessment.

Keith Robbins

Preface

China today is the second largest economy in the world. Its integration with the world system has great implications for not only business but also the lives of ordinary people in other parts of the world. A simple case could be seen in Chinese consumption. What and how much the Chinese people consume will immediately impact on commodity prices outside China. This age of interdependency has made China increasingly relevant to everyone. To understand the country better, a great number of works on China have been produced by not only the scholarly community, but also businesspersons, journalists, politicians, and travelers.

Yet the world continues to feel uncertain about China as a fast changing China requires close watching. In many aspects, understanding China remains a difficult task. The degree of institutionalization is still low in areas such as power succession, decision-making, intra-Party competition, and Beijing's relations with the provinces. This is vividly exemplified by the Bo Xilai affair in Chongqing, an event which has not only cast a shadow over Chinese citizens but also created uncertainties outside China.

New sources and data have however emerged, which could throw light on China's realities. The open-door policy initiated by the late Deng Xiaoping had made it possible for scholars to conduct fieldwork, interviews, and even participatory observation inside China. Although China remains a sensitive subject in many research areas such as politics, religions, and human rights, Chinese citizens are becoming more open and bold when talking to scholars. More importantly, in the past decades, hundreds of volumes by mainland authors have been published in Hong Kong. Many were written by retired high ranking Party cadres and government officials. Even ousted leaders such as Zhao Ziyang published their memoirs in the Special Administrative Region (SAR), often, with others' help, in the form of interviews. All these writings have provided China scholars with not only rich information but also different perspectives on what has happened in China. Another change is associated with the spread of information and communication technologies among Chinese citizens. Despite tight control on the part of the Chinese government, Chinese citizens are able to publish their personal stories, experiences, and opinions online. This book takes all these newly available advantages and draws information from both English and Chinese writings, from both inside and outside China.

In understanding China, some scholars tend to take a state-centered or elitist approach while others focus on a society-centered approach. This book endeavors to present a balanced view by looking at the interactions between different actors, such as between the center and the provinces, and between the state and society. Chinese society is so vast and complicated that no single actor can determine its development. In reality, more often than not, changes are consequences of the interplay of multiple forces. Therefore, this book looks at different actors such as the elite, the provinces, the bureaucracy, civil society, and different political, economic, and cultural forces to examine how they play and interplay in the making of contemporary Chinese history.

A book on history will usually document the main events during a particular period of history. This book focuses on analyzing the unfolding of contemporary Chinese history. It covers the key aspects of economic, political, and social development from the onset of reform to the present. The basic goal of the book is to offer a comprehensive, systematic, and analytical narrative on developments and changes in the contemporary era.

The book begins with the reform and open-door policy initiated by the late Deng Xiaoping in 1978 when he regained power in the aftermath of the Cultural Revolution and tracks how the country has progressed and thrived alongside worldwide movements toward globalization, market economy, and democratization. China has not only responded to these movements, but proactively made use of them to remake itself. For China, the reform and opening is for not only economic development, but also the "second revolution" as termed by Deng Xiaoping in the rebuilding of the country's economic and political institutions.

The 1970s were crucial for the initiation of the reform and opening policy. After the People's Republic of China was established in 1949, the Maoist regime embarked on social engineering programs to build a new China. In the first decade, the system was rather successful in transforming China. However, the system soon proved unsustainable. By the 1970s, the leadership was in endless power struggles while the economy was in bad shape and Chinese living standards were very low.

The reform and opening policy was thus the answer to building a new system while promoting socioeconomic development. The popular perception that China is a model of "economic reform without political reform" is not accurate. While the Chinese leadership has placed overwhelming emphasis on economic reform, it has also made efforts and attempts to reform its increasingly outdated social and political institutions. The reform and opening has created an economic miracle for China. Rapid economic growth, however, has also generated both positive and negative consequences. It has brought about an equally rapid social transformation. The open economy has laid down a solid foundation for an increasingly open society, and witnessed the rise of middle classes and various forms of civil organizations demanding more political participation. On the other hand, China's economic miracle has been mired by widening income disparities, environmental degradation, corruption, ethnic conflict, and social decay. China has evolved from an equal society under Mao to an extremely unequal one with an increasingly high degree of social injustice, which has led to the frequent rise of social protests of different magnitudes and natures. The rise of the Internet in China has enabled social forces to actively take part in political participation on one hand and to effectively organize protests on the other.

To meet the demands for political participation and to cope with the various social issues, the Chinese leadership has to engage actively in institutional and political reforms. However, that process has not been easy and smooth. In the 1980s, the leadership under Deng Xiaoping and Zhao Ziyang had laid down a grand plan for China's political reform. That reform movement ended with the crack-down on the pro-democracy movement in 1989. The leadership has since been very resistant to any Western type of political liberalization. Nevertheless, China has also practiced different types of so-called "democracy with Chinese characteristics," such as intra-Party democracy, village and township democracy, and deliberative democracy. However, the communist regime has always been able to accommodate different democratic elements without changing itself into a Western type of democracy.

To reflect these developments in China, this book is structured to encompass firstly a comprehensive overview of the background of the reform and opening policy in the first two chapters. Chapter 1 highlights the legacy of the Maoist era, since the post-Mao reform and opening policy was a reaction to the Maoist policy. This chapter discusses how the old system was built, and how it constrained China's socioeconomic development and became unsustainable by the 1970s. The chapter also discusses the various crises that the Maoist system had generated and demonstrates the self-destruction nature of the old system.

Chapter 2 provides an overview of the post-Mao reform from the perspective of elite politics and policy. The post-Mao reform is divided into three main eras represented by the three generations of leadership from Deng Xiaoping (1978–1989) through Jiang Zemin (1989–2002) to Hu Jintao (2002–12). The narratives are structured to reflect the international environment, changing domestic political landscape, major shifts in reform strategy, crisis-management, and the elite politics. During the Deng period, China began its rural reform before expanding it to the urban areas. When economic reform became stunted, the leadership turned to political reform, which led to the 1989 Tiananmen crisis. The Jiang period focused overwhelmingly on economic reform, and political reform was not on the agenda of the leadership. In the Hu Jintao era, the leadership has turned to social reform.

The next six chapters comprise the main body of this book, covering key aspects of economic reform and social transformation. Chapter 3 discusses the evolution of the post-Mao economic reform and its associated economic growth and structural changes. Chapter 4 discusses how globalization affects China's economic transformation. It examines the development of China from a long period of opening up to a new stage of "going global." China's reform has unfolded in the context of China's interaction with the world. While China has been one of the major driving forces of globalization, its domestic development has also been affected by its integration with the world system.

Chapter 5 examines how economic reform and globalization have led to drastic social changes, including the rise of civil society, middle classes, NGOs, and netizens. The market-oriented reform has transformed China from a Maoist ideology-based society to an interest-based society. The rise of new social forces has changed the fabric of Chinese society, impacting especially on its political development. Chapter 6 singles out the various undesirable consequences of economic reform, such as income inequality and social injustice. These consequences often lead to social protests of various forms, greatly constraining the sustainability of China's development. This discussion also covers China's ethnic conflicts, especially in Xinjiang and Tibet, and addresses key issues such as ethnic nationalism, protests, and challenges to China's national integration. Chapter 7 focuses on cultural and ideological changes. The reform period has witnessed the decline of the traditional communist ideology and the revival of other ideologies such as nationalism and Confucianism. Meanwhile, pluralist social interests have also led different social groups to look at other ideologies such as liberalism and the new leftism. This chapter discusses how different intellectual groups came to be associated with the rise of different ideologies.

Chapter 8 addresses an important issue which is frequently ignored in contemporary Chinese history, namely, relations between Beijing and other provinces. China's economic reform has been characterized by drastic decentralization in the initial stage followed by waves of efforts to recentralize on the part of the central government. This chapter scrutinizes China's evolvement into a *de facto* federal system and analyzes how this system affects different aspects of power relations between central and local governments. It also draws implications of *de facto* federalism for China's foreign relations.

The last three chapters focus on the question of "whither China" by examining how the communist regime has responded to the diverse consequences of the economic reform and social transformation. Chapter 9 discusses social policy reform and its dynamics. The market-oriented economic reform has effectively undermined China's social fabric. Old institutions in the areas of social security, health care, and education have lost their ground, but new ones are hard to build. While this often leads to the rise of social grievances, it has also generated pressure for the Party-state to engage in social reforms. Since the early twenty-first century, social reforms have topped the agenda of the top leadership. Chapter 10 examines how the Party-state has continuously reformed its bureaucratic institutions to promote market-oriented economic development on one hand and adjust itself to the changing socioeconomic environment on the other. The bureaucratic system established by Mao to support the planned economy has been transformed into one which underpins the market-oriented economy. Meanwhile, the Party-state has also made efforts to establish a regulatory regime to govern a market-oriented economy and an increasingly pluralistic and complicated society.

Finally, Chapter 11 looks at a key relationship in contemporary China, namely, the communist regime and democracy. An increasingly open economy and society has generated pressure for democratization. While democratization is not on the agenda of the Chinese leadership, this does not mean that the country will not be democratized. In fact, the Party-state has been quite accommodating in coping with democratic pressure. In the early stages, bottom-up democracy such as village and township elections and various forms of social participation came into existence. Since the late 1990s and after China passed the strong-man age, intra-Party democracy has surfaced and intra-Party competition has become important. This chapter also highlights the mutual transformative nature of state and societal relations in China.

Acknowledgments

During the process of planning, research, and writing of this book, I had the privileged assistance of several research assistants at the East Asian Institute (EAI): Huang Yanjie, Chapters 3 and 9, Weng Cuifen, Chapter 2, and Yao Jielu, Chapter 4. I have also benefited from the many discussions and sharing of information with my other colleagues in EAI, including Wang Gungwu, John Wong, Zhao Litao, Bo Zhiyue, Yang Mu, Qi Dongtao, Sarah Tong, Shan Wei, Chen Gang, Zhao Hong, Lye Liang Fook, Qian Jiwei, Pan Rongfang, Yang Mu, Yang Jing, and Yu Hong.

I must also thank EAI for providing such an excellent platform for intellectual exchanges. The wealth of information from visiting scholars from China and the world over, such as Kjeld Erik Brødsgaard, Lowell Dittmer, Gilbert Rozman, Wu Guoguang, Tang Wenfang, Tong Yanqi, Huang Yanzhong, Liu Yawei, Guo Xiajuan, Pan Wei, Min Ye, Xie Yue, and Meng Na has added value to this book, not to mention the various international conferences and workshops on different subjects of contemporary China that EAI and others have organized. The intellectual exchanges with other participants, such as David Shambaugh, Bruce Dickson, Lynn White, Joseph Fewsmith, Kelly Brown, and Denial Bell, have been most enlightening.

On the editorial side, I would also like to thank Lye Liang Fook and Jessica Loon for providing effective editorial assistance, and my daughter Katherine and my son Nevin, who have been a great motivating force during the writing process. They were approaching their college year during the preparatory stage of this work and had suggested that a book of this nature could be the best way for them to understand China better. They were very involved in the process of my writing and were an excellent source of inspiration as they made me feel that producing such a book was my responsibility for the next generation. Katherine, who is now a college student, has helped in the reading of the entire manuscript.

My thanks also go to Series Editor Keith Robbins and Tessa Harvey at Wiley-Blackwell, who have both played a big part in the birth of this book.

Last but not least, I would like to dedicate this book specially to Yang Lijun, who is always behind me providing both moral and intellectual support.

Chapter 1

The Maoist Legacy

Contemporary Chinese history began when the late Deng Xiaoping initiated the reform and open-door policy in 1978. These policy initiatives had their roots in the pre-reform Mao era. After the People's Republic of China (PRC) was established in 1949, Mao embarked on one of the largest experiments in human history to bring forth a total transformation to Chinese politics, economy, and society. In the early decades of his rule, the Chinese Communist Party (CCP) and its state (hereafter, the Party-state) successfully undertook a number of far-reaching social changes. But the Maoist development model was soon found to be unsustainable as it came at extremely high human costs. By the late 1970s, all signs indicated a collapse of the system, and reforms were imperative. The Maoist experiment was a great lesson for the post-Mao leadership and became an integral part of contemporary Chinese history. After Mao, Chinese leaders introduced enormous reforms to remedy Mao's errors and to make institutional innovations and renewals.

While drastic economic changes have taken place in the post-Mao era, China's political structure remains intact. The post-Mao reform has been seriously constrained by the Maoist legacy. While the system was a product of the twentieth-century revolution, both Nationalist and Communist, it is also linked to China's deep imperial history and carries powerful imperial traditions that influence basic ideas and practices.[1] Many features of institutions and policies of historical patterns adopted during the Maoist rule have reappeared in the post-Mao era.

This chapter identifies the main institutional features and policy orientations during the Maoist era. It first traces the origins of the system to China's transformation since the late nineteenth century. It also shows how Maoist rule further transformed the country with its establishment of new state

Contemporary China: A History since 1978, First Edition. Yongnian Zheng.
© 2014 John Wiley & Sons, Ltd. Published 2014 by John Wiley & Sons, Ltd.

institutions which penetrated Chinese society, mobilizing social forces and constraining China's socioeconomic development. Finally, it discusses how the system led to the post-Mao reform. To a great degree, Maoist communism met its end not because of the post-Mao reform but because of its self-destructive nature.

Political System

The political system that Mao established was a product of China's long struggles with a modern state system since the late Qing dynasty.[2] China's modern history began with the coming of Western powers. For a country with a long history of established civilization, it was hard for China to become modernized under external forces. China was defeated repeatedly by Western powers, first by the British during the two Opium Wars and then by the alliances of Western powers. It was also thoroughly defeated by its own modernized neighbor Japan.

These defeats had set Chinese political and intellectual elites thinking of the need to rebuild and revamp the Chinese state, which was no match to the Western form of modern state.[3] Nationalism, an idea which China imported from Japan and other Western powers, played a crucial role in the country's long search for a modern state. In its later years, the Qing court made attempts to introduce various measures toward a constitutional monarchy, much in line with the successful Japanese model. With the rise of nationalism, however, Chinese elites began to doubt whether the Qing state had an adequate foundation on which to build a modern state. For political radicals, particularly nationalists, China should be not only a strong state, but also a state of Chinese ethnicity rather than the Manchurian ethnicity on which the Qing state was built. A constitutional monarchy or reforms within the existing Qing state would not be able to help save China and its people. This version of nationalism was shared by many Chinese political activists at home and abroad and even prevailed among Chinese officials. For nationalistic revolutionaries, constitutional monarchy was not enough; only a republic purged of all traces of the self-serving and inept Manchurians could make the state strong and bring about their patriotic goals. Only nationalism could forestall racial destruction by foreign powers and build a strong China.

Dr Sun Yat-sen and his revolutionary followers employed two principles of nationalism – statehood based on ethnicity and popular sovereignty based on democracy – to rebuild China, and their efforts eventually led to the 1911 revolution and the establishment of the Republic of China in 1912.[4] Central to the new republican state was the parliamentary system. Nevertheless, the revolution itself was a product of decentralization of political power. State-making, which required a centralized political force, became very difficult. During and after the revolution, the forces for decentralization became dominant in Chinese politics. Provincial officials, who had acted autonomously during the revolution, sought to strengthen their autonomy and block the resurgence of an all-powerful and autocratic center. The state itself was no longer monolithic, but composed of competing levels of authority. Below the provincial level, local elites dominated the self-government organs that proliferated after 1911, expanded control over local finances, and held sway over the appointment of local officials.[5]

Great political liberalization convinced Yuan Shikai, the most powerful military man, that "the devolution of power from the center to the provinces and localities was inimical to the restoration of Chinese national strength."[6] Following the advice of his American advisor Frank Goodnow[7] and others that a constitutional monarchy was more appropriate to China's tradition than republicanism, Yuan attempted to re-establish the political dominance of the center. Yet Yuan's various efforts to restore the monarchy failed because of political opposition from all sides. By the early 1920s, the republican state began to disintegrate as a constitutional and parliamentary entity and as a bureaucratic force. This trend soon brought chaos and warlordism to China.

Dr Sun Yat-sen initiated a long process to establish a new political order. In his early days, Sun placed much emphasis on popular sovereignty and believed that a republican government, based on the Western European and North American multiparty model, would provide a channel for popular political participation and make China strong. But this was not to be. Indeed, the new democratic political arrangement "failed to bring unity and order, not to mention legitimacy. Representative government degenerated rapidly into an autocracy hostile to popular participation and ineffective in foreign policy."[8] Sun came to the conclusion that without strong political institutions, no democratic regime would be stable and China would not become a strong state. Consequently, he turned to the organizational side of state-building. His new strategy was "state-building through party organization," a concept he adapted from the Russian revolution.

According to Sun, Russians placed the Communist Party above the state; the Russian model was more appropriate to China's modernization and state-making than the liberal European and American model. China should follow the strategy of "governing the state through the party" whose first priority was to establish a new state structure. He argued that "[w]e now do not have a state to be ruled. What we need to do is to construct a state first. After the construction of the state, we can govern it."[9] Only after a strong and highly organized party had been built could China begin to make a strong state, and only a strong state could lead to a working democracy. He also categorized China's political development into three stages: first, military government; second, authoritarian government; and third, constitutional government.[10]

With Sun's great efforts, the Nationalist Party was reformed and became highly organized and centralized. Sun's successor Chiang Kai-shek kept to the same course and used the party to restore unity and order, end foreign humiliation, abolish unequal treaties, regain lost territory, and ultimately restore China's lost grandeur. After the Northern Expedition (1926–28), China was recentralized under the Nationalist Party regime. The new state was established through two primary methods. In the military sphere, the regime maximized the center's control over the instruments of force; in the civilian sector it extended and deepened the national government's penetration of local society by quasi-fascist projects such as the Blue Shirts and the New Life movements and self-government reforms like new country campaigns. However, the Nationalist regime put much emphasis on the control of urban areas, and failed to realize that "in a predominantly rural society the sphere of influence of cities was much more severely circumscribed than in the West where such a strategy might well have proved successful."[11] Local elites, on whom the regime heavily relied, were not able to succeed in fundamentally transforming the lives of the peasants.[12]

More importantly, the Nationalist government failed to arrive at a viable state idea.[13] As the ruling party, the Nationalist Party stressed a centralized state structure and limited political participation. However, the idea of popular sovereignty was spreading in the country, and was very appealing at that societal level. By contrast, the CCP was able to transform the idea of popular sovereignty and use it to mobilize urban people and intellectuals against the Nationalist regime. Joseph Levenson showed that the Communist version of the state idea was more appealing to Chinese intellectuals than the Nationalist version.[14] Furthermore, the Nationalist regime lacked effective means to spread its nation-state ideas among the Chinese. The regime's urban-centered modernization strategy left rural areas untouched. In contrast, by sending its officials to rural areas, the CCP successfully transmitted its nation-state ideas to the peasants. The rise of peasant nationalism during the anti-Japanese war (1937–45) finally led to the downfall of the Nationalist government and the triumph of the CCP in 1949.

The CCP quickly established a highly centralized political system by placing much emphasis on organizational and ideological control. The new state system until today has the following unique institutional features.[15]

The nomenklatura system

The CCP's most powerful instrument in structuring its domination over the state is a system called the *nomenklatura* system.[16] It was based on the Soviet model, with little changes made from time to time.[17] Within this system, the two most important principles are Party control of the government and Party management of cadres.[18] The CCP selects all government officials; almost all government officials and all top officials are Party members; and in each government agency, Party members are organized under a Party committee that is subordinate to the Party committee at the higher administrative level. The hierarchy of government organs is overlaid by a parallel hierarchy of Party committees that enables Party leaders to supervise Party members in the government and lead the work of the government from within.

From the mid-1950s until 1984, the *nomenklatura* system allowed the CCP leadership to appoint officials two levels down in the system, that is, each level of the Party structure is responsible for political appointments that are two levels down. For example, all positions above vice-ministerial level (such as State President, Vice State President, Premier, Vice Premiers, State Councillors, and others) fall under the jurisdiction of the Political Bureau of the Central Committee (more specifically the Standing Committee). In this case, the Political Bureau first selects the candidates, then passes the nominations to the National People's Congress (NPC), China's parliament, for approval.

This "Party management of cadres" system is also the most effective means for the CCP to constrain localism. The Political Bureau and its Department of Organization keep a tight rein on the selection and appointment of provincial Party secretaries and governors. The CCP leadership exercises the "cadre exchange system" or "term limits" to prevent the latter from having local vested interests.

Central leading small groups (CLSGs)

There are two types of leading small groups (LSGs), namely, Central Leading Small Groups (CLSGs) and State Council Leading Small Groups. Both types are ad hoc supra-ministerial coordinating and consulting bodies formed to build consensus on issues that concern the entire Party, the government, and military system when the existing bureaucratic structure is unable to do so. The two groups have radically different functions. While the State Council Leading Small Groups focus on coordinating policy implementation for the government, the CLSGs focus on initiating and managing policy for the Political Bureau, thus enabling the CCP to effectively exercise its domination over the government.

CLSGs do not formulate concrete policies; instead, they often focus on setting up guiding principles for concrete policies. Any recommendations of leading groups are likely to be reflected in the policy-making process because they represent the consensus of the leading members of the relevant Party, government, and military agencies. In some cases, the policy-making body may simply adopt a CLSG recommendation in its entirety.

CLSGs covers a wide range of important issue areas, including foreign affairs, financial and economic affairs, rural work, Party building work, publicity and ideological work, overseas publicity, Party history work, and other emerging important issues. CLSGs do not have permanent staff, and often have to rely on their offices to manage daily operations and to make research and policy recommendations. While the effectiveness of a CLSG often depends on the effectiveness of its office, the way it operates also gives individual leaders, usually the head of a given CLSG, room to influence policy recommendations.

Xitong

Another mechanism which performs similar functions to the CLSGs is the *xitong*. CLSGs exist only at the central level, but *xitong*s also function at local levels such as the province and city. The purpose of *xitong*s is to enable the Party to exercise its domination over the government. Under it, society is divided into different functional spheres supervised and controlled by the corresponding functional Party organs and cadres.[19]

A *xitong* is different from its counterpart administrative department in the Party. These departments are part of the formal and legal structure and have limited capacity in overseeing a specific administrative agency. By contrast, the Party leadership in the *xitong*s is usually not part of the formal, legal organizational structure, since in general Party leaders' names are not publicized here, and also a *xitong* often oversees several related governmental ministries, departments, and agencies.

After it came into power, the CCP established a set of Party departments at the central and provincial levels such as the Industrial and Transportation Department, Trade and Financial Department, Education and Cultural Department, Agricultural Work Department, and City Planning Department. These departments performed the same functions as the government at the same level. In this way, there is little distinction between Party and government departments, with the latter's governmental functions taken over by Party departments.

Today, each *xitong* is usually headed by a member of the Political Bureau Standing Committee at the central level. At the provincial level, this function is performed by a member of the Provincial Party Committee. The main *xitong*s include:

- The military system which covers the entire armed forces.
- The political and legal system that covers the ministries of State Security, Public Security, Justice, and Civil Affairs, the Supreme Court and Procuratorate, the National People's Congress, and People's Armed Police Force.
- The administrative system which is divided into various smaller, secondary systems such as foreign affairs, science and technology, sport and public health, and finance and economy.

- The propaganda system which covers the State Council's ministries of Education, Culture, State Administration of Radio, Film, and Television, State Administration of Press and Publication, Chinese Academy of Social Sciences, the Xinhua News Agency, the *People's Daily* and *Qiu Shi* (Seeking Truth) journal.
- The United Front system that covers the Chinese People's Political Consultant Conference (CPPCC), the eight "democratic parties," the All-China Federation of Industry and Commerce, the State Council's Commission for Nationalities Affairs, the Religious Affairs Bureau, and the Offices for Overseas Chinese, Taiwan, Hong Kong, and Macao Affairs.
- The mass organization system which covers the All-China Trade Union Federation, the Communist Youth League, the All-China Women's Federation, and various subordinate trade unions, youth, and women's organizations.
- The organizational and personnel system, mainly Party organization departments and the government personnel ministry or department at each level, which manage cadres of all the organizations mentioned earlier.

Dangzu

If CLSGs are mechanisms through which the Party exercises its domination over the government at the top, then Party groups (*dangzu*) are Party vehicles set up for the same purpose. The fact that China is a one-party system does not mean that there is no conflict between the Party and the government. Conflict frequently arises when the Party makes key decisions, and the government implements them.

Party groups are sometimes called Party "core groups" and should not be confused with another important body, "Party committees" or "unit Party affairs committees" (*jiguan dangwei*). Both Party groups and Party committees in all government agencies in China were established by the CCP. While Party committees existed in all other communist states, Party groups were unique to the CCP. Party committees belong to the Party organizational system and not to the governmental agencies to which they are appended. Their members are at least in principle elected by Party members working in the same government body. They focus on Party affairs, such as supervising the behavior of Party members within the same agency, recruiting new Party members, directing political studies and ideological work, and collecting membership fees. Party committees answer to the next higher Party committee.[20]

By contrast, the Party group within a government agency is more powerful than the Party committee. The Party committee is under the direction of the Party group in the same governmental agency. In other words, the Party group has the responsibility of actually administering the work of the whole governmental agency. Party group members are not elected by Party members in the same organization, but appointed by the next higher level Party committees. For example, at the national level, all Party groups in different ministries are appointed by the CCP Organization Department and the Central Secretariat. Below that, Party groups are appointed by the relevant provincial and local Party committees. The Party group at each level answers to the Party committee one level above, to which they owe their appointments.[21]

A Party group in a governmental agency is usually made up of four to five Party members who hold senior positions in that agency. The secretary of the Party group always has the final say in all the agency's important affairs and approves and issues important documents. The main purpose of the Party group is to oversee the important activities (e.g., policy-making, policy implementation, and personnel appointment) of the governmental agency to which it belongs. The Party group has to ensure that the preference of the Party is reflected in all such activities. Indeed, without the Party's endorsement, no important activities can take place in that governmental agency. By doing so, "the Party actually took over administrative power."[22]

The party and the military

The Party–military relationship merits particular attention as it shows how the Party maintains its domination over the government. However, the People's Liberation Army (PLA) does not form an integral part of the government, or vice versa. The Party–military relationship has long been defined as symbiotic.[23] The close ties between these two most powerful political institutions can be seen in the many defining shared features such as ideology and personnel structure and a nearly equal political status.

The role of the military is visible in many key areas of Chinese politics ranging from leadership succession to control over the government and social stability. Thanks to his revolutionary experience, the command of Mao Zedong over the military was unshakable. Until his death, Mao relied on his revolutionary ideological and personnel network to exercise a tight control over the military. When China was in political chaos during the Cultural Revolution (CR), Mao relied on the support of Defense Minister Lin Biao to work against other senior civilian leaders such as Peng Zhen, Liu Shaoqi, and Deng Xiaoping. During the last years of the CR, Lin Biao and his lieutenants attempted to institutionalize the role of the military in civilian affairs. Although Lin died in 1971, after allegedly plotting against Mao, the military remained an essential part of China's political system. When Mao died in 1976, the military's support was essential to Hua Guofeng, Mao's successor, in arresting Jiang Qing and the other members of the "Gang of Four," namely, Zhang Chunqiao, Wang Hongwen, and Yao Wenyuan.

State–Society Relations

In traditional China, the reach of the emperor was very limited and hardly went beyond the county level. Since each county had only one official member of the national bureaucracy (the *zhixian*, or county magistrate), the emperor made extensive use of intermediate elites, particularly the gentry class,[24] or "individuals who held official degrees gained normally by passing examinations, or sometimes by recommendation or purchase."[25] When the Nationalist Party attempted to build a new state, it left the structure of governance unchanged. The county was still at the lowest level of administration, and the government was still highly dependent on local elites and centered in cities. Simply put, its power did not penetrate the rural society.

The CCP on the other hand was able to penetrate every corner of society and dominate social forces through various mechanisms.[26] The so-called "multiparty cooperation" was the most important part of the United Front developed by the CCP in its long struggle for power. With this system, the CCP was able to exercise control over the so-called "democratic parties" (*minzhu dangpai*) through state institutions such as the People's Congress and the CPPCC. Furthermore, the CCP divided the whole society into various functional groups which are incorporated into the regime as in the case of the "democratic parties."[27] Altogether, China today has 32 functional groups.

The household registration (*hukou*) system was used to control population movement and bind people to their place of birth and work. Without a household registration booklet, no one could obtain food, clothing, housing, employment, schooling for children, marry, or enlist in the army. The system thus created a spatial hierarchy of urban places.[28] A related institution for controlling population was the work unit (*danwei*) system for ideological indoctrination and administrative disciplining such as warning, open criticism, and negative records in the dossier.[29] The *danwei* system was also a mechanism for ensuring political compliance and allegiance from individual citizens by providing them with economic and social security such as inexpensive housing, free medical care, generous retirement pensions, and a wide range of subsidies for everything from transportation to nutrition.

A highly organized society, together with a planned economy, enabled the Party-state to mobilize numerous social groups into the political arena, thus creating new power resources within Chinese society to implement profound tasks of social engineering such as land reform, collectivization, and nationalization of business and commerce. Nevertheless, over time, the highly organized and efficacious Party-state gradually degenerated into a regime obsessed with ideology and lacking in almost any genuine social base beyond its Party-state apparatus.[30]

Economic System

The economic system that the CCP built had a new structural dimension, namely, planned economy, which was based on the then Soviet model.[31] Central planners controlled all major sectors of the economy and made all decisions relating to the use of resources and the distribution of output. They would decide on the products to be produced and direct lower-level enterprises to produce those goods in accordance with national and social objectives.

The novelty of this system can be exaggerated. There was a dimension of continuity. China's state-led economic development and industrial modernization began in the late nineteenth century and early twentieth century. The system of "official supervision and merchant management" (*guandu shangban*) was developed in the early industrialization stages before it gradually developed into a system of "bureaucratic capitalism."[32] The Nationalist government continued this tradition and played an important role in directing economic development. Under Mao's planned economy, however, the role of the state became excessive, even though Mao eventually found that a highly centralized Soviet-style economy did not work well for China, and initiated waves of decentralization. China's economic system was also different from that of other East Asian economies such as Japan and the "four dragons" (South Korea, Singapore, Hong Kong, and Taiwan). In these economies, the issue is about the role of the state and the market in the process of economic development; in China, it is about the role of the central government and local governments since all market mechanisms had been eliminated under the planned economy. The absence of market forces led to another characteristic of the Maoist economic system: political campaigning as the main driving force behind economic development.

The Chinese economy before 1949 was predominantly pre-industrial agrarian. When the European powers came to China in the mid-nineteenth century, China was already in a state of decline, and the economy had been in stagnation for a long time. Indeed, the CCP inherited an economy which was not only backward but also badly ravaged by a long period of war and internal turmoil. After the CCP took power, it immediately moved to consolidate its control by launching several campaigns, including the suppression of counter-revolutionaries and implementing land reform. In the rural areas, the process of socialist transformation started with a comprehensive land reform which redistributed land from landlords and rich peasants to the poor and landless peasants. After the land reform, peasant households were organized first into agricultural cooperatives and then, in 1956, into the Soviet-type collectives. In 1958, the collectives were further merged to form people's communes. In urban areas, the nationalization of trade and industry started with the "three-anti" (*sanfan*) and "five-anti" (*wufan*) campaigns. By 1956, most private enterprises had been transformed into cooperatives or joint state–private enterprises operating under the umbrella of the state sector.

Through such socialist transformation the CCP was able to consolidate its control in both rural and urban areas. The mobilization of resources for maximum economic growth under central planning was through the Five-Year Plan (FYP) system. The Soviet model, however, was biased against small industry and labor-intensive technology, as it was against agriculture and rural development. Mao came to realize that the Soviet model was not in congruence with China's basic resources, its large population, and its low level of technology. He went on to experiment with his own development model by launching the Great Leap Forward (GLF) movement from 1958 to 1960, which called for a simultaneous development of agriculture and industry, both small and large industries. Mass mobilization was to replace the more systematic centralized planning as the main development strategy. The purpose of the GLF was to surpass Britain in 15 years. Mao believed that by mass mobilization, the country could achieve unlimited economic growth. In the urban areas, the industrial GLF was marked by a rise of a new industrial front made up of numerous small to medium labor-intensive enterprises. The agricultural GLF was centered on the people's communes which mobilized peasants en masse for large-scale rural capital construction projects such as building dams and irrigation work, and making iron and steel.

With such all-out mobilization of resources for economic development, the first year of GLF brought 22% economic growth. But the excesses soon surfaced as chaos, waste of resources, and increasing neglect of farming mounted. Precipitated by bad weather and followed by bad harvests, the GLF collapsed in 1959. The economic crisis deepened in 1961 with economic growth plunging by as much as 30%. For the first time after the Communist revolution, China had to import wheat from the West to avert mass starvation. Radical decentralization soon led to the decline of the central government's control of China's overall economy. Decentralization resulted in a deficit crisis due to the decline of the central government's capacity to collect revenue. Within four years (1958–61), the central government suffered a deficit of more than 18 billion *yuan*.[33]

The GLF also led to the great famine which cost millions of human lives.[34] The period 1962–65 marked a retreat from the GLF, emphasizing economic retrenchment and recovery. Mao was criticized by some pragmatic leaders, particularly Marshall Peng Dehuai.[35] After the collapse of the GLF, the Soviet model of development was totally discarded.

However, Mao was undaunted and unconvinced by the setback of the GLF. In 1966, he started the CR which gave him an opportunity to carry forward his own development strategy which emphasized economic self-reliance.

Decentralization was to be further expanded, while rural development and labor-intensive industries were to be given top priority. The CR did not disrupt production in the same way or to the same degree as the GLF because most CR activities were mainly confined to major cities, leaving the agricultural sector basically intact. In urban areas, though the main targets of the CR were the Party and government organizations, industrial production also suffered as factory management everywhere came under attack and workers got embroiled in incessant political campaigns. The overall adverse effects of the CR on the economy were not as serious as the GLF. The economy plunged into negative growth in 1967 and 1968, but bounced back in the 1970s.

Both Mao Zedong and Zhou Enlai died in 1976. Immediately after Mao's death, Premier Hua Guofeng together with other more moderate leaders staged a putsch against leading CR radicals led by Mao's wife, Jiang Qing, in what was often termed the downfall of the "Gang of Four." When Hua was in control during the immediate post-Mao years, he strived to continue with developing the Chinese economy under a modified form of central planning. He launched the Ten-Year Plan in 1978, which was, however, soon scrapped for being too ambitious. Power eventually returned to the pragmatic old guards led by Deng Xiaoping in 1978. By that time, Deng had realized that there was something fundamentally wrong with the Chinese economic system. He was thus determined to open a new chapter in China's modern economic history by the launching of economic reform and the open-door policy.

Elite Politics

Mao's experiments in state building, economic development, and social transformation took place in the context of China's elite politics. Under Mao, elite politics were complicated. He wanted the Party-state machinery to achieve his personal vision of state building and social transformation. The state Mao envisioned was one without a strong bureaucracy. He tended to regard all his colleagues as mere tools for the realization of his utopian state. He took disagreements between him and his colleagues as challenges to his authority. Mao was ruthless to dissenters, and power struggles, more often than not, paralyzed the system.[36]

Mao's authority was absolute in the post-1949 period until his death in 1976; he did not allow his colleagues to challenge his utopian visions, let alone his political authority. He also frequently emphasized the importance of unity of the Party since it was unity that led the CCP to its success. Nevertheless, in his perceptions, the unity of the Party had to be achieved by various mechanisms through which his colleagues and his people demonstrated their loyalty to himself. It is also worth noting that Mao did not engage in power struggle for the sake of power itself; rather, he did it purposefully. Surrounding each power succession, Mao would situate himself between radicals and pragmatic leaders, and maneuvered political forces toward his goal.

Elite politics in Mao's era was characterized by repeated political purges.[37] The first major leadership purge was the Gao Gang Affairs of 1953–54.[38] Around 1953, Mao wanted to implement the "two-front" leadership by which he would retreat to the "second front" to consider large questions of policy and direction while other younger leaders would run the daily affairs of the Party and stay on the "first front." Liu Shaoqi, who had been Mao's chosen successor since at least the Seventh Party Congress in 1945, was expected to become the leader on the "first front." Nevertheless, by that time, Mao had become critical of Liu and made his disenchantment known to Gao, who was also a Political Bureau member and Mao's personal favorite. Gao was not satisfied with his position in the Party, and the new policy initiative gave him an opportunity to challenge Liu's position. Gao launched an effort to undermine Liu with the clear aim of becoming the new successor. Mao was aware of the damage Gao's actions were causing to Party unity, and turned decisively against his favorite. This only resulted in solidifying Liu's status as successor further.

In the early 1960s, Mao began to have serious doubts about Liu. The "two-front" leadership arrangement led to a situation in which Mao perceived that he was increasingly marginalized in decision-making. By 1965, Mao had completely lost confidence in Liu and decided to have him removed. In 1966, Mao managed to install Lin Biao as the new successor with the support of another personal favorite whom he seemingly regarded as totally loyal, and the support of the army for the unprecedentedly disruptive CR. Once reluctantly installed as the successor, Lin essentially adopted the passive tactic of echoing whatever positions Mao adopted. This involved fulsome praise of the CR. Nevertheless, by 1970, Mao had come to doubt and took precautionary measures against his successor. Conflicts involving turf warfare and petty personal frictions unfolded between civilian radicals led by Madam Mao (Jiang Qing) and a group involving Lin's household, particularly his wife and son, and top central military officials from among his revolutionary colleagues. Sensing that the military had gathered too much power, Mao sided with his wife at the 1970 Lushan Plenum and demanded self-criticisms from Lin's group, which he found inadequate. This eventually forced a showdown with Lin that led to the latter's fateful flight from China in September 1971.

In the post-Lin Biao conflict of the radicals around Jiang Qing against the remaining pre-CR elite represented by Zhou Enlai, and after his 1973 rehabilitation by Deng Xiaoping, Mao considered a range of younger leaders as eventual successors, particularly the radical Wang Hongwen, and eventually Hua Guofeng, who also had support from veteran revolutionaries for such a role.

Mao used power struggle as an incentive for other leaders in order to achieve his political goal. As a major player in all these power struggles, he was able to manipulate these political factions. He frequently changed his political alliances to eliminate any perceived political threat to his authority and move toward his goal. He was able to maneuver since his authority was absolute. With his passing, his political enterprise faded with him.

Maoism: Experiment and Failure

Maoism is undoubtedly one of the greatest experiments in human history. Like Dr Sun Yat-sen and Chiang Kai-shek before him, Mao was aware of the importance of having a strong state. Nonetheless, it was never clear what form of a strong state Mao had attempted to build. He was never satisfied with the form of the state his revolution had brought about. Whereas states rest on bureaucratic systems, Mao's form of the state was one without a bureaucratic system. He thus called for a continuous revolution to consistently remake the state.

The Party-state was successful in establishing a hegemonic regime and an overall control over local society through its coercive organization and ideology. The domination of the state, however, does not necessarily mean that the state is able to modernize the country. The state's capacity to develop the economy and society depends on not only the will and skill of the top leadership, but also the lower-level state organizations and social institutions. Without the initiative of social institutions and the cooperation of lower-level organizations, leaders will have difficulties mobilizing people and getting them to rally behind them.

The planned economy was in opposition to such initiatives since the system met collective objectives by individual sacrifice. Under such a system, rewards, whether wages or perquisites, were to be distributed according to the value that the state ascribed to the service performed. The planned economy eliminated the profit motives of the individuals and placed production decisions in the hands of state planners. Maoism thus allowed ideology to take precedence over economics. Without material incentives, Mao turned to other means to facilitate the transformation of the country, such as political campaigns, decentralization, and power struggles.

All political movements were initiated from above, particularly by Mao himself, and with multiple purposes. Until the late 1950s, political movements were targeted at the consolidation of the new regime, and the transformation of society. The success of the early movements had given Mao undue confidence in social engineering. He became increasingly ambitious, and believed that he could wield political power to achieve his utopian version of the socialist state. He thus initiated the GLF, and then the CR. While Mao wanted continuous revolutions to sustain his version of the state, in the later years of his life political movements had lost their great momentum. Political campaigns came at great costs, both physical and human. While the leftists sided with Mao in political campaigning, many other leaders became pragmatic and lost their confidence in the Maoist version of the state and society. The Chinese also lost their enthusiasm. In the early years of the PRC, the Chinese genuinely believed that Mao could lead the way to a new society. But in reality, endless political movements undermined society, and made the lives of ordinary folks increasingly difficult. Chinese society, particularly the younger generations, began to reflect on and doubt the Maoist system. This became apparent during the spontaneous social movement after the death of Zhou Enlai in 1976. Urban citizens and university students in Beijing and elsewhere gathered at Tiananmen Square to pay their condolences to Zhou and to protest against the leftists. While the movement was finally clamped down by the government, it was an indicator of a decline in the legitimacy of Maoism.

Mao's political movements left behind positive legacies. Many old guards like Deng Xiaoping who had survived these movements came to realize the folly of too much political and ideological contention, as manifested in numerous mass movements and campaigns, and that political and social stability was crucial to economic development. The post-Mao leadership thus placed an overwhelming emphasis on social stability. The fear of social chaos has been a major driving force behind most policy initiatives in the post-Mao era.

The Deng leadership thus abandoned political campaigning and prioritized stability. This meant avoiding power struggles and eventual social chaos. Deng thus reiterated the importance of collective leadership and regarded social order as the minimum prerequisite for economic development. To regain its legitimacy, the leadership no longer relied on ideological education but turned to performance, namely, delivering economic goods to society. When rapid economic development gave rise to a divided society, the post-Deng leadership introduced social policies to address the issues of social injustice. Needless to say, changes in policy agendas have also led to great changes in terms of state–society relations in the contemporary era.

Notes

1 Lieberthal (2004: xvii).
2 For the complexity of China's history from imperial days down to the reforms, see Spence (1990) and Fairbank and Goldman (1998).
3 For discussions of the nature of the Chinese traditional state, see Schram (1985, 1987).
4 For an examination of Sun Yat-sen's role in the Chinese revolution, see Bergère (1998).

5   Kuhn (1975) and Young (1977).
6   Cohen (1988: 522).
7   Frank J. Goodnow (1859–1939) was one of the principal founders of the American Political Science Association and became its first president in 1903. From 1914 to his retirement in 1929, he was the president of Johns Hopkins University. He also served on President Taft's commission on economy and efficiency in 1911–12. In 1913, Goodnow was invited by Yuan Shikai to be his legal advisor.
8   Hunt (1993: 68).
9   Sun (1986: 103).
10   Chen (1988).
11   Whitney (1970: 71).
12   Averill (1981).
13   Whitney (1970: Chapter 2).
14   Levenson (1964).
15   Schurmann (1968) provided a classic analysis of the interrelationship of the role of ideology and organization in China. Lieberthal (2004) analyzed how China is governed from an institutional perspective.
16   Burns (1989: ix).
17   For the development of the *nomenklatura* system, see Burns (1989, 1994).
18   For discussions of these two principles, see Lieberthal (2004: Chapter 6); Huang (1996: Chapter 4); and Shirk (1993).
19   Huai (1995).
20   Pen (1995).
21   Ibid., 159–60.
22   Ibid., 160.
23   For the changing role of the PLA under Mao and in the post-Mao era, see Gittings (1965); Joffe (1987); Finkelstein and Gunness (2007); Mulvenon and Yang (1999); Shambaugh (2002); and Bickford (1999).
24   Fairbank (1983: 32–39).
25   Ibid., 33.
26   For analysis of state–society relations in the context of Chinese tradition, see Tsou (1986); Womack (1991); Shue (1988); and Walder (1986).
27   China has eight "democratic parties," namely Revolutionary Committee of the Chinese Kuomintang, China Democratic League, China National Democratic Construction Association, China Association for Promoting Democracy, Chinese Peasants and Workers Democratic Party, China Zhi Gong Dang, Jiu San Society, and Taiwan Democratic Self-Government League. See Information Office of the State Council (2007).
28   Cheng and Selden (1997).
29   All organizations in urban China where people worked such as enterprises, retail shops, hospitals, schools, civil associations, and government organs were called *danwei*. Roughly speaking, three types of *danwei* can be identified: 1) enterprise units, including all units engaged in making profit; 2) non-profit units, including scientific, educational, professional, cultural, athletic, and health care organizations; and 3) administrative units or governmental organs. For analysis of the *danwei* system, see Bray (2005); Wang (2005); and Lü and Perry (1997).

30 Shue (1994).
31 For a review of China's economic development from 1949 to 1985, see Riskin (1987).
32 Feuerwerker (1968).
33 *Statistical Yearbook of China 1991*, p. 12.
34 On China's great famine, see Dikötter (2010); Yang (1996); and Yang (2008).
35 Peng Dehuai (1898–1974) was a prominent military leader of the CCP, and China's Defense Minister from 1954 to 1959. In June 1959, he tried to tell Chairman Mao that the Great Leap Forward was a dramatic mistake. Peng was criticized by Mao and other members of the Political Bureau and was disgraced. He was arrested in 1966 during the Cultural Revolution. He died of cancer on November 29, 1974.
36 R. MacFarquhar provided a detailed analysis of China's elite politics from 1949 to 1966, see his trilogy (1974, 1983, 1997). For elite politics during the Cultural Revolution, see MacFarquhar and Schoenhals (2006).
37 Teiwes (1993).
38 Teiwes (1990).

References

Averill, S. C. 1981. "The New Life in Action: The Nationalist Government in South Jiangxi." *The China Quarterly* 88: 594–628.
Bergère, M.-C. 1998. *Sun Yat-sen*, translated by Janet Lloyd. Stanford, CA: Stanford University Press.
Bickford, T. 1999. "A Retrospective on the Study Chinese Civil–Military Relations since 1979." Paper to CAPS/RAND Conference. Washington, DC.
Bray, D. 2005. *Social Space and Governance in Urban China: The Danwei System from Origins to Reform*. Stanford, CA: Stanford University Press.
Burns, J. P., ed. 1989. *The Chinese Communist Party's Nomenklatura System*. Armonk, NY: M. E. Sharpe.
Burns, J. P. 1994. "Strengthening Central CCP Control of Leadership Selection: The 1990 *Nomenklatura*." *The China Quarterly* 138: 458–91.
Chen, Runyun. 1988. *Xiandai Zhongguo zhengfu* (Modern Chinese Government). Jilin: Jilin wenshi chubanshe.
Cheng, Tiejun and Mark Selden. 1997. "The Construction of Spatial Hierarchies: China's Hukou and Danwei System." In Timothy Cheek and Tony Saich, eds., *New Perspectives on State Socialism in China*. Armonk, NY: M. E. Sharpe, pp. 23–50.
Cohen, P. A. 1988. "Post-Mao Reforms in Historical Perspective." *Journal of Asian Studies* 47, 3: 519–41.
Dikötter, F. 2010. *Mao's Great Famine: The History of China's Most Devastating Catastrophe, 1958–62*. London: Bloomsbury.
Fairbank, J. K. 1983. *The United States and China*, 4th edn. Cambridge, MA: Harvard University Press.
Fairbank, J. K. and M. Goldman. 1998. *China: A New History*. Cambridge, MA: Harvard University Press.

Feuerwerker, A. 1968. *China's Early Industrialization: Sheng Hsuan-Huai (1844–1916) and Mandarin Enterprises.* Cambridge, MA: Harvard University Press, reprint.

Finkelstein, D. M. and K. Gunness, eds. 2007. *Civil–Military Relations in Today's China: Swimming in a New Sea.* Armonk, NY: M. E. Sharpe.

Gittings, J. 1965. *The Role of the Chinese Army.* Oxford: Oxford University Press.

Huai, Yan. 1995. "Organizational Hierarchy and the Cadre Management System." In Carol Lee Hamrin and Suisheng Zhao, eds., *Decision-Making in Deng's China: Perspectives from Insiders.* Armonk, NY: M. E. Sharpe, pp. 39–50.

Huang, Yasheng. 1996. *Inflation and Investment Controls in China: The Political Economy of Central–Local Relations during the Reform Era.* Cambridge: Cambridge University Press.

Hunt, M. 1993. "Chinese National Identity and the Strong State: The Late Qing-Republic Crisis." In Lowell Dittmer and Samuel S. Kim, eds., *China's Quest for National Identity.* Ithaca, NY: Cornell University Press, pp. 62–79.

Information Office of the State Council. 2007. *White Paper on China's Political Party System.* Beijing, November 15.

Joffe, E. 1987. *The Chinese Army after Mao.* Cambridge, MA: Harvard University Press.

Kuhn, P. A. 1975. "Local Self-Government under the Republic: Problems of Control, Autonomy, and Modernization." In Frederic Wakeman, Jr. and Carolyn Grant, eds., *Conflict and Control in Late Imperial China.* Berkeley, CA: University of California Press, pp. 257–98.

Levenson, J. 1964. *Modern China and Its Confucian Past: The Problem of Intellectual Continuity.* New York: Anchor Books.

Lieberthal, K. 2004. *Governing China: From Revolution through Reform,* 2nd edn. New York and London: W.W. Norton & Company.

Lü, Xiaobo and Elizabeth J. Perry, eds. 1997. *Danwei: The Changing Chinese Workplace in Historical and Comparative Perspective.* Armonk, NY: M. E. Sharpe.

MacFarquhar, R. 1974. *The Origins of the Cultural Revolution 1: Contradictions among the People, 1956–1957.* Oxford: Oxford University Press.

MacFarquhar, R. 1983. *The Origins of the Cultural Revolution 2: The Great Leap Forward 1958–1960.* Oxford: Oxford University Press.

MacFarquhar, R. 1997. *The Origins of the Cultural Revolution 3: The Coming of the Cataclysm, 1961–1966.* Oxford: Oxford University Press.

MacFarquhar, R. and M. Schoenhals. 2006. *Mao's Last Revolution.* Cambridge, MA: Harvard University Press.

Mulvenon, J. C. and R. H. Yang, eds. 1999. *The People's Liberation Army in the Information Age.* Santa Monica, CA: Rand.

Pen, Hsiao. 1995. "Separating the Party from the Government." In Carol Lee Hamrin and Suisheng Zhao, eds., *Decision-Making in Deng's China: Perspectives from Insiders.* Armonk, NY: M. E. Sharpe, pp. 163–64.

Riskin, C. 1987. *China's Political Economy: The Quest for Development since 1949.* Oxford: Oxford University Press.

Schram, S. R., ed. 1985. *The Scope of State Power in China.* Hong Kong: The Chinese University of Hong Kong Press.

Schram, S. R., ed. 1987. *Foundations and Limits of State Power in China.* Hong Kong: The Chinese University of Hong Kong Press.

Schurmann, F. 1968. *Ideology and Organization in Communist China.* Berkeley, CA: University of California Press.

Shambaugh, D. 2002. *Modernizing China's Military: Progress, Problems and Prospects.* Berkeley, CA: University of California Press.

Shirk, S. 1993. *The Political Logic of Economic Reform in China.* Berkeley, CA: University of California Press.

Shue, V. 1988. *The Reach of the State: Sketches of the Chinese Body Politics.* Stanford, CA: Stanford University Press.

Shue, V. 1994. "State Power and Social Organization in China." In Joel S. Migdal, Atul Kohli, and Vivienne Shue, eds., *State Power and Social Forces: Domination and Transformation in the Third World.* Cambridge: Cambridge University Press, pp. 65–88.

Spence, J. D. 1990. *The Search for Modern China.* London: Hutchinson.

Statistical Yearbook of China 1991. Beijing: Zhongguo tongji chubanshe.

Sun, Yat-sen. 1986. *Sun Zhongshan quanji* (Collected Works of Sun), vol. 9. Beijing: Zhonghua shuju.

Teiwes, F. C. 1990. *Politics at Mao's Court: Gao Gang and Party Factionalism in the Early 1950s.* Armonk, NY: M. E. Sharpe.

Teiwes, F. C. 1993. *Politics and Purges in China: Rectification and the Decline of Party Norms, 1950–1965.* Armonk, NY: M. E. Sharpe.

Tsou, T. 1986. *The Cultural Revolution and Post-Mao Reforms: A Historical Perspective.* Chicago, IL: University of Chicago Press.

Walder, A. 1986. *Communist Neo-Traditionalism: Work and Authority in Chinese Industry.* Berkeley, CA: University of California Press.

Wang, Feiling. 2005. *Organization through Division and Exclusion: China's Hukou System.* Stanford, CA: Stanford University Press.

Whitney, J. 1970. *China: Area, Administration, and Nation Building.* Chicago, IL: Department of Geography, University of Chicago.

Womack, B., ed. 1991. *Contemporary Chinese Politics in Historical Perspective.* Cambridge: Cambridge University Press.

Yang, Dali. 1996. *Calamity and Reform in China: State, Rural Society and Institutional Change since the Great Leap Famine.* Stanford, CA: Stanford University Press.

Yang, Jisheng. 2008. *Tombstone* (Mu bei – Zhongguo liushi niandai dajihuang jishi). Hong Kong: Cosmos Books.

Young, E. P. 1977. *The Presidency of Yuan Shih-K'ai: Liberalism and Dictatorship in Early Republican China.* Ann Arbor, MI: University of Michigan Press.

Chapter 2

Elite Politics

Though the post-Mao reform and open-door policy was called China's "second revolution,"[1] it is not free from the constraints of the Mao legacy. While Deng drastically departed from the Maoist class struggle, his "second revolution" toward economic modernization operated within the political system that Mao had established. New reform initiatives are subject to elite politics before they can be translated into actual policies. Elite politics and power struggles therefore determine the progress of the reform.

Moreover, both society and local governments have provided many reform initiatives. Many reform experiments are conducted at local levels before they become national initiatives. However, not all local reforms can become national ones as they are subject to elite politics at the top.

This chapter focuses on elite politics to provide the political backgrounds of the reform and opening up since 1978. The reform era can be divided into three phases, namely, the Deng Xiaoping era (1978–89),[2] the Jiang Zemin era (1989–2002), and the Hu Jintao era (2002–12). The focus of reform policies varies significantly under different generations of leadership. Policy shifts in different periods have taken place in the context of elite politics. In examining elite politics, this chapter highlights several interrelated aspects of elite politics, including leadership succession, power consolidation, ideological change, and elite recruitment, which are political prerequisites for policy shifts to take place.

Contemporary China: A History since 1978, First Edition. Yongnian Zheng.
© 2014 John Wiley & Sons, Ltd. Published 2014 by John Wiley & Sons, Ltd.

Elite Politics after Mao

Factional politics

After Mao's death in 1976, three political factions among Chinese leaders emerged: the radicals, the victims of the Cultural Revolution (CR), and the beneficiaries of the CR. The radicals, who were the extreme leftists, were led by the "Gang of Four," namely, Zhang Chunqiao, Jiang Qing, Wang Hongwen, and Yao Wenyuan. The victims, or the moderates, were primarily senior leaders such as Deng Xiaoping, Chen Yun, Li Xiannian, and Ye Jianying. The beneficiaries were those who were promoted in the political hierarchy during the CR, who included Premier Hua Guofeng and his supporters such as Chen Xilian, Wang Dongxing, and Ji Dengkui. Among these three factions, the leftists and the moderates were more powerful and the conflicts between them were the fiercest.

Immediately after Mao's death, the "Gang of Four" moved to usurp the Party leadership, including establishing their own operational office, fighting for the right to succeed to Mao's legacy, mobilizing the propaganda machinery to attack the moderates, and even arming the so-called "Second Arms" which consisted of militiamen.[3] The moderates and the beneficiaries of the CR worked in alliance to fight against the "Gang of Four." On October 5, 1976, a Political Bureau meeting held by Hua decided to arrest the "Gang of Four." Wang Dongxing successfully arrested the "Gang of Four" the next day. On October 7, the Central Committee (CC) of the CCP named Hua as successor to Mao, chairman of the CC, and chairman of the Central Military Commission (CMC).

Hua, however, lacked the political power base. With the arrest of the "Gang of Four," the loose coalition of the moderates and the beneficiaries of the CR fell apart. They could not agree on the best way to assess the Maoist legacy, whether Deng should be reinstated, and how to redress the grievances of victims of the CR. The moderates advocated a departure from Mao's radicalism to a normal political and economic life and redressing of all the problems. Senior revolutionaries such as Chen Yun and Li Xiannian called for the restoration of Deng to lead the resolution of the historical issues.[4] Understandably, Deng's comeback was important for the senior Party veterans in restoring their pre-CR positions.

Hua chose to retain the Maoist political and ideological lines. He perceived Deng's potential reinstatement as a great threat, for it would imply that Mao had made mistakes and thus would erode the legitimacy of Hua's leadership.[5] To consolidate his power base, Hua first took actions to ensure that he was the only legitimate leader to inherit Mao's legacy. He guided the building of Mao's Memorial Hall on Tiananmen Square, and approved Wang Dongxing's proposal of the ideological slogan of "Two Whatevers," that is, "whatever deci-

sions Chairman Mao had made we would firmly support, and whatever directives Chairman Mao had given we would persistently follow."[6] He and his
supporters were thus called the "whateverists." In terms of economic policies,
Hua attempted to restore the old Soviet planned system by launching an ambitious 1976–85 Ten-Year Plan which emphasized heavy industrial development
through large-scale investments.[7]

However, Hua's efforts failed to address the widespread public disappointment in the poor economic performance. Facing mounting disenchantment
and the increasingly strong cry for the reinstatement of Deng, Hua was forced
to comply. In August 1977, Deng was restored to all his previous positions: Vice
Chairman of the Party, member of the Standing Committee of the Political
Bureau, Vice Chairman of the CMC, and Chief of Staff of the PLA. After reinstatement, Deng started to weaken Hua's power by launching an ideological
campaign, the "First Liberation of Thought" in opposition to the "Two
Whatevers."[8] Meanwhile, he also established his own ideological slogan of
"Practice is the sole criterion for testing truth." This new ideology received
overwhelming support from all directions.[9] Without a convincing ideological
foundation, Hua and his allies were forced to give up their positions in the
following years.

The Third Plenum

After the removal of the ideological obstacles to reform, Deng and his supporters began to search for solutions to the serious problems China faced. The most
urgent task was to establish a strong and reform-minded leadership. To meet
this end, a 36-day-long Central Working Conference of the CCP was held in
November 1978 before the Third Plenum of the Eleventh Central Committee
in December. At the conference, Hua was forced to make an apology for his
mistakes. Deng made an important political speech, "Liberate Thought, Seek
Truth from Facts, and Unite to Look Forward," paving the way to the Third
Plenum. At the historic Plenum, the leadership formally announced the shift-
ing of policy priority from Maoist class struggles to economic modernization.
Major personnel reshuffling took place. Chen Yun, Deng Yingchao, Wang Zhen,
and Hu Yaobang (one of Deng's protégés) were appointed to the Political
Bureau. Chen also entered the Standing Committee and became the First
Secretary of the newly established Central Committee of Discipline Inspection
(CCDI). One of Hua's main supporters Wang Dongxing, former head of Mao's
personal security force, was removed from his post.

The Third Plenum was a watershed in China's political, economic, and social
development. Deng became the *de facto* head of the Party leadership, and
started his reform and opening up policy which led to China's rapid economic
development in the following three decades.

Deng Xiaoping Era, 1978–89

Power politics

Deng consolidated his power base by promoting his protégés to critical positions. Immediately after the Third Plenum, Hu Yaobang was promoted to Secretary General and Minister of Propaganda. In 1980, Hua was replaced by Zhao Ziyang, another of Deng's protégés, as the Premier. In June 1981, an important political document titled the "Resolution of Certain Problems in the History of the CCP since the Establishment of People's Republic of China" was issued, indicating the end of the Hua era. Hua resigned from his two top positions as chairman of the CC and chairman of the CMC. Hu took over the position of chairman of the CC and Deng became the new chairman of the CMC.[10] The office of CC chairman was abolished in the 1982 Party Constitution, and since then the Secretary General has become the top position in the Party.

This arrangement had Hu and Zhao at the first front administering daily work, while Deng, Chen, Ye, and Li were the major decision-makers at the second front. Deng was the paramount leader, while Chen was the second in charge. In the early years of the reform, the working relationship between Deng and Chen was smooth, with Deng in charge of major political issues and Chen on major economic policies. They were able to reach consensus on a series of issues such as the reassessment of Mao, the removal of Hua, the change from "politics-in-command" to "economics-in-command," and the need to adjust economic policies, despite their different stance on other issues such as the pace of development and opening up.[11] Tensions however soon surfaced.

The group of leaders led by Chen insisted that China maintain the Leninist political system and restore the planned economic system. Chen formulated a conservative economic reform policy as reflected in the slogan of the "planned economy as primary, and market economy as supplementary." Key members of this conservative camp were mainly senior revolutionaries such as Li Xiannian, Song Renqiong, Yao Yilin, Song Ping, Wang Zhen, Yu Qiuli, Hu Qiaomu, and Deng Liqun.[12]

Deng and his group on the other hand were known as the reformists. While Deng agreed with the conservatives on the need to maintain the Leninist political system, he differed on the issue of economic reform. Deng believed that abandoning the planned economic system was necessary and that socialism could also accommodate a market economy.[13] Members of Deng's camp included Hu Yaobang, Zhao Ziyang, Wan Li, and others who were more than a decade younger than Deng.

Deng also supported political reform. In the early 1980s, he repeatedly reminded Chinese leaders of the need for political reform when engaging in economic reform. Many believed then that Deng would lead China toward a free market economy and democratic politics.[14] However, Deng had never wanted any Western type of multiparty system, insisting that the process of political opening should be administrated to improve the rule of the CCP.

While Deng was a moderate reformist, many of his younger protégés were more radical, believing that both economic and political reforms were needed. Unfortunately, these younger leaders did not have a clear vision of where political reform would lead China, and how.[15] After the mid-1980s, they gradually went far beyond Deng's vision of reform, eventually leading to the removal of Hu Yaobang in 1987 and Zhao Ziyang during the pro-democracy movement in 1989.[16]

Ideological change

Deng made great efforts to restructure the ideology and to transform the radical and revolutionary Party to a reform-oriented and pragmatic one. In the late 1970s, he initiated a campaign called the "First Liberation of Thought" to establish a non-Maoist reform ideology and provide an ideological legitimacy for his own reform agenda. Deng's ideology was pragmatism.

This ideological campaign was a counterattack to the "Two Whatevers." In 1977, Hu Yaobang, then vice president of the Central Party School, encouraged Party cadres to liberalize their thoughts. He started an internal publication, "Theoretical Trend" (*lilun dongtai*), which published articles calling for emancipation of thought. In May 1978, an article titled "Practice Is the Sole Criterion for Testing Truth" was published in the journal and reprinted in other major newspapers such as *Guangming Daily*, *People's Daily*, and *PLA Daily*. The idea that practice is the sole criterion for testing truth received overwhelming support and expanded quickly from Beijing to the rest of the country and from inside the Party to intellectuals. This ideological campaign enabled Deng to promote a pragmatic understanding of Mao Zedong's thought.

The second ideological movement in this period was led by Zhao Ziyang. At the Thirteenth Party Congress in 1987, Zhao proposed the theory of "the primary stage of socialism" in an attempt to provide a new ideological base for economic reform and development.[17] He also made efforts to bring in political reform as an important part of his agenda, but failed. Despite the popularity of his political reform agenda among social groups, especially intellectuals, Zhao was unable to elicit strong political support from entrenched bureaucrats and the seniors.[18]

Elite recruitment

In the post-Mao era, the Party's legitimacy relied increasingly on its ability to deliver economic goods to the people. In order to achieve this goal, the Party needed a new type of elite for effective policy implementation. Elite recruitment is significant for power succession and policy implementation. First, it will increase the sense of loyalty to the Party among newly recruited Party cadres and government officials. As a general rule, when a new leader comes to power, he/she will consolidate his/her power/position by recruiting new elites into the leadership. This is because elite recruitment can lead to the formation of new power networks for the new leader. Second, it can increase the political legitimacy of the Party among people.

Deng made great efforts to change the criteria of cadre recruitment with the aim to replace Maoist revolutionary cadres with technocrats. He argued that the Party could renew itself by recruiting younger cadres into the leadership under a process called *sihua* (literally, "four transformations"), which would bring about cadres who are more "revolutionized, better-educated, more professionally competent, and younger."[19]

During the 1982–87 period, a series of reform was introduced into the cadre recruitment system. After the first round of reform in 1982–84, 62% of officials in the central government and 56% of members in the CC were newly promoted cadres.[20]

The third generation of leaders entered politics during this wave of cadre recruitment reform. This generation completed their college education in the 1950s, and had no revolutionary experience. They were mostly from the sciences and engineering and tended to be more pragmatic and problem-solving than their older ideology-oriented counterparts.[21] This generation of leaders was more competent to carry out Deng's reform policies and to lead China's modernization program.

Political exit for senior leaders

Political exit matters for elite politics. Old leaders have to leave to give way to newcomers. Before Deng, China did not have a system of "exit." Political leaders were able to hold on to their positions until the last day of their life. The "exit" problem had troubled both the top leadership and the country. When leaders become aged, they are not prepared to give up their power/positions, leading to a situation whereby the young leaders "fight" in the front line, and old guards stand behind and watch.

Deng drew lessons from the disastrous effects of life tenure for leading posts in the Mao era. He abolished the life tenure system in the 1980s to facilitate the recruitment of younger cadres. In 1982, the CC released the "Decisions on Establishing Retirement System of Senior Cadres," and set the age limit of cadres at different levels. For instance, candidates for ministers, provincial Party secretaries, and governors have to be below 65 years of age, and those for deputy ministers, deputy provincial Party secretaries, and deputy governors below 60 years of age.

The main problem lay in retiring top senior leaders, namely, those in the Political Bureau, especially in the Standing Committee. Although Deng did not specify the retirement age for these positions, he was able to retire aged senior political leaders. The average age of Political Bureau members was reduced from 71 in 1982 to 62 in 1992.[22] The reform was not thorough, however. While Deng formally established the system of retirement for aged Party cadres and government officials, he also had to reach a compromise with other elders through informal politics. He allowed elders to participate in important decision-making through various informal channels. For example, non-Political Bureau or non-CC elders could make selection decisions behind the scenes or attend enlarged meetings of the Political Bureau and the CC, and could sometimes vote in these meetings in violation of formal Party rules.

Indeed, various formal institutions were established to enable the elders to exercise their informal power. The Central Advisory Commission was established by the 1982 Party Constitution. While it was supposed to be a temporary institution to facilitate the retirement of elderly Party leaders from the Political Bureau and the CC, this institution actually empowered the elders. Of course, the establishment of these formal institutions does not mean that informal power becomes less important. As Zhao Ziyang commented, based on his own experience with Deng, "the political road that Deng was determined to take is that the leadership of the Party must be centralized, and cannot be shared. [For Deng,] this principle cannot be changed and absolutely cannot be shaken."[23] Zhao illustrated this point with reference to an occasion when Chen Yun requested a Standing Committee meeting to make his opinions heard. Deng opposed Chen's initiatives and asked another elder, Bo Yibo, to let Chen know that "there is only one *popo* [decision-maker] in this Party."[24] Of course, although Deng regarded himself as the *popo*, he was not as powerful as Mao and could not make decisions the way Mao did. "Deng did not have the same authority as Mao did, and he himself could not make all decisions as he wished, and he had to consult with other elders," Zhao once remarked.[25]

The influence of the elders in high-level decision-making depends not on their formal positions in the institutions but on their personal stature as revolutionaries.[26] The informal power of the elders played an important role in handling three power successions during the Deng era. The plan to fire Hua Guofeng as Party chairman and to replace him with Hu Yaobang as Party secretary was first made by a series of informal discussions among the elders before a decision was arrived at in a Political Bureau meeting. The CC approved the decision only after it was endorsed by the elders. The decision to oust Hu Yaobang was made first by an enlarged meeting of the Political Bureau that included members of the Central Advisory Commission, two members of the CCDI, and two alternate members of the Political Bureau. Again the decision to oust Zhao was made in a series of enlarged meetings of the Standing Committee and the Political Bureau during the May–June 1989 political crisis.[27]

Grooming younger leaders

Grooming a younger generation of leaders was one of the most important policy legacies of Deng. Since the early 1980s, there has been a consistent process of rejuvenation. The average age of CC members dropped from 62 in the Twelfth Party Congress in 1982 to 57 in the Thirteenth Party Congress in 1987. The average ages in some of the most powerful institutions such as the Standing Committee, Political Bureau, and Secretariat of the Thirteenth Central Committee were much lower than in those of the Twelfth Central Committee.[28]

Jiang Zemin Era, 1989–2002

After the crackdown on the pro-democracy movement in 1989, Deng appointed Jiang as the Secretary General of the CCP in June 1989. In the same year, Deng stepped down from the position of chairman of the CMC, and appointed Jiang as his successor. Thus began Jiang's era, which can be divided into two phases: the first from 1989 to 1997, when Deng still had great influence in decision-making, and the second from 1997 to 2002, when Jiang consolidated his power and made his own reform initiatives.

From conservative to reformist: 1989–92

After the pro-democracy movement in 1989, Jiang, then Party Secretary of Shanghai, was summoned to Beijing and appointed as Deng's successor. Premier Li Peng, who played a key role in the crackdown on the pro-democracy movement, was unhappy with this move and was reluctant to support Jiang. However, Deng was firm in his decision and explained that a core leadership was important for political stability.[29]

According to An Zhiwen, a close associate of Zhao Ziyang in the 1980s, there was a change in Deng's perception of the leadership core before and after the pro-democracy movement. After coming back to power, Deng abolished the Maoist style of dictatorship and was against the idea of a leadership core when Hu and then Zhao were in the frontline. The endorsement of Jiang was triggered by the pro-democracy movement.[30]

However, Jiang lacked the political experience to work in the capital, and needed time to adjust to the new position. The rigorous political, economic, and social situations after 1989 made his adjustment even harder. In the face of such a reality, he adopted a conservative approach.

During his Southern Tour in 1992, Deng openly expressed his disappointment with Jiang. Meanwhile, Jiang's conservative policies were also challenged by other reformist leaders, notably the Yang brothers, Yang Shangkun (the State President) and Yang Baibing (the General). The Yang brothers were long associated with Deng and strong supporters of his reformist policies. They initiated a political attack on Jiang and his conservative policy line prior to the Fourteenth Party Congress in 1992. However, drawing lessons from the cases of Hu and Zhao, Deng did not remove Jiang this time. Instead, he pressured Jiang to reshape the direction and agenda of the Party leadership. The Yang brothers who had expressed their open disloyalty to Jiang were no longer acceptable to Deng and were forced to step down.

After this initial tumultuous period, Jiang began to adhere to Deng's reformist policies. "Deng's theory" was included in the Party Constitution at the Fourteenth Party Congress.

Power consolidation

Jiang began to consolidate his power by building his support base in 1992 when he was formally elected as the Secretary General of the CCP.[31] In the following two years, he made great efforts to promote his loyal supporters into the central leadership. At the Fourth Plenum in 1994, Wu Bangguo, Secretary of the Shanghai Party Committee, was appointed a Political Bureau member and Secretary of the Central Secretariat; and Huang Ju, Mayor of Shanghai, was appointed a member of the Political Bureau.[32] These personnel changes led to the formation of the "Shanghai Gang."

It is important, however, to highlight Jiang's sensitivity in dealing with other political factions. He was successful in winning the support of the PLA and gaining cooperation from Li Peng and formed a Jiang–Li political coalition.[33] In 1995, Jiang greatly reduced the influence of the Beijing faction by removing Chen Xitong, member of the Political Bureau and Mayor of Beijing.[34]

Deng's death in early 1997 marked the beginning of an era in which Jiang could dominate Chinese politics. The Fifteenth Party Congress in the same year reinforced his power base with a major personnel reshuffling. He consolidated the "Shanghai Gang" by bringing Zeng Qinghong into the Political Bureau as an alternate member. The Jiang faction gained in strength as a result of the expansion of the "Shanghai Gang" as well as the support of Jiang's supporters from other regions. Two newly recruited members of the Political Bureau, Li Changchun and Wu Guanzheng, were the respective provincial Party secretaries of Henan and Shandong (Li was transferred to Guangdong later).[35]

Ideological change

At the Fourteenth Party Congress in 1992, Jiang followed Deng's call and placed the theory of "socialist market economy" at the core of the CCP ideology. Prior to the Fifteenth Party Congress in 1997, the CCP initiated a new wave of the "Liberation of Thought" to reaffirm the "theory of the primary stage of socialism." As mentioned earlier, Zhao proposed the primary stage theory at the Thirteenth Party Congress in 1987. With Zhao out of power, the theory was left in the closet at the Fourteenth Party Congress. Jiang had to resurrect the theory as it was apparent that he had encountered serious ideological challenges from the leftists. Rapid economic growth after 1992 had brought about enormous social problems. For leftists, such as Deng Liqun and other old ideologues, these new problems were related to Deng's market-oriented reform strategy. They believed that Deng's reform policy had to be modified to ease the threat it posed to the rule of the Party-state.

These concerns raised by the old and new leftists were not without foundation. By raising many practical issues facing the country, such as income disparities, low morale, money worship, decadent value system, high unemployment, and social chaos, the ideology of the leftists was very appealing to the people. Both the "New Left" and the "Old Left" could pose a serious threat to the leadership. Ignoring these issues would only risk losing the ideological base of political legitimacy. It was against this background that Jiang re-emphasized the theory of the "primary stage of socialism." The theory's attribution of social problems to an inevitable phase in development certainly worked in favor of Jiang.

After the Fourteenth Party Congress, Jiang began to work on his own ideology. In 2000, Jiang raised a new concept of *sange daibiao* (literally, "three represents"), meaning that the CCP represents the most advanced production mode, the most advanced culture, and the interests of the majority of the people. In the following two years, he went all out to establish this as his ideology. At the Sixteenth Party Congress in 2002 when Jiang handed power to Hu Jintao, the "three represents" theory was added to the Party Constitution. This was a significant political move by the Party to transform itself from a proletarian party to a political entity that would represent and coordinate the interests of various social classes.

Elite recruitment

Jiang continued Deng's course of Party transformation by recruiting new types of elite.[36] There were great changes in elite turnover at all levels of Party organization and government during this era. For example, in the Fifteenth CC, 57% of 193 full members (109) were new recruits, compared to 44% of new recruits in the previous CC. Furthermore, most newly recruited elite were technocrats who had their training in engineering and other fields of science and technology. In the same CC, all seven members of the Standing Committee of the Political Bureau and 18 of the 24 Political Bureau members were primarily technocrats.[37]

Political exit

The retirement system for aged cadres was further institutionalized. After the Fifteenth Party Congress, informal rules were developed regarding retiring top leaders. The leadership reached a consensus that no one in the Political Bureau, except for Jiang, could be older than 70.[38] Since then, these practices have been increasingly institutionalized in high politics.

What was more important was to build an exit mechanism for aging senior leaders. During Jiang's period, the age factor became increasingly important to the issue of power succession. Qiao Shi, number two in the Political Bureau of the Fourteenth CC, exited politics at the Fifteenth Party Congress. Qiao was then widely regarded as the political challenger to Jiang.[39] With his departure, Jiang put in place a procedure for old leaders to exit gracefully from their positions when they are of certain age. The retirement of General Liu Huaqing at the same Party Congress also implied that Jiang had full control of the military. It was the first time in the history of the People's Republic that no military representative appeared in the Standing Committee. The weakening of the military's presence at the top leadership tended to provide Chinese leaders with an opportunity to push the country's transition toward a modern pattern of civilian–military relationship.

Grooming younger leaders

Grooming younger generations of leaders was one of the most important policy legacies of Deng, and Jiang and his leadership continued to push this process forward. The leadership recognized from past experiences that power succession was vital both for the Party itself and for the country. In Jiang's time, the Standing Committee of the Political Bureau as a whole played a guardian role to the next generation of leadership. This can be exemplified by the rise of Hu Jintao.

Hu came to the center of political power at the Fourteenth Party Congress in 1992 when he was the youngest member of the Standing Committee. Deng was behind Hu's rise since he believed that it was important to groom successors when they were still young. The political endorsement from Deng granted Hu a unique position within the CCP leadership. In 1999, Hu was elected as the Vice State President.

In the Chinese political context, the most important task is to establish the leadership of the successor(s) over the military. To be an effective successor, Hu had to be provided with an institutional base to develop his relations with the military. This was not an easy process. Jiang tried to install Hu in the CMC on a few occasions, but there was fierce opposition from the generals to the appointment of Hu to the highest PLA decision-making body.

In late 1998, the central government initiated a nationwide campaign to wind up the military's business operations. Hu was appointed director of the Transfer Office (for transferring business operations from the military to the civilian sector) and was put in charge of policy implementation. He also took part in another task force, known as the "Leading Group to Handle the Businesses of Party and Government Units." Chaired by Premier Zhu Rongji, with Hu and General Zhang Wannian as deputies, the main task of the group was to de-link the military from business. The campaign gained some respect for Hu from the military, thus paving the way for him to become vice chairman of the CMC in 1999, three years before he formally took over power from Jiang.

Hu Jintao Era, 2002–12

Elite politics

In 2002, Hu succeeded Jiang as the Party secretary. Technically, this was a successful power transfer. However, though Hu was the top leader in the Standing Committee then, he lacked factional support. Hu could not count on Premier Wen Jiabao, his right-hand man, as Wen appeared very much like a loner in the Standing Committee. In contrast, Jiang could continue to count on six supporters among the nine members of the Standing Committee, including Wu Bangguo, Jia Qinglin, Zeng Qinghong, Huang Ju, Wu Guanzheng, and Li Changchun.

Therefore, Hu had to work hard to consolidate his power. After entering the Standing Committee, Hu was pro-active in building political support from his old network. The *tuanpai* (the Chinese Communist Youth League, CCYL) became the most important base of his power. At the Sixteenth Party Congress (2002), Jiang's faction was dominant in the Standing Committee while Hu's support was strong at the provincial level. Five years later at the Seventeenth Party Congress, Hu's supporters and loyalists entered the Political Bureau and its Standing Committee. At this congress, of the 25 members of the Political Bureau, 10 were new faces. These new appointees were largely from the two most powerful political forces in China today, namely, the *taizidang* ("princelings," or officials who are the offspring of veteran revolutionaries) and the CCYL.

As a mass organization, the CCYL is the most important training ground for the CCP. There are nearly 80 million members in the CCYL, a size similar to the entire CCP membership. Since Hu became Secretary General of the CC, cadres with CCYL background have been speedily promoted to leadership positions at all levels. They have become an important pillar in the Political Bureau and are very powerful at the provincial level. Many Party secretaries and governors in the provinces are from the CCYL.

The *taizidang* were sidelined in the 1980s when Deng was in power. The Chinese people had ill feelings about the *taizidang* at the time for their rent-seeking activities and connections. However, many *taizidang* members such as Xi Jinping, Bo Xilai, and Liu Yandong, were politically ambitious. They gave up business opportunities and accepted low positions in various local Party organizations and governments. Over years, they gained experience in managing Party and government affairs.

The appointment of CCYL and *taizidang* political figures was favorable for Hu. Although his power base is CCYL, he also gains strong support from the *taizidang*, especially old revolutionaries. At the Seventeenth Party Congress, the "Shanghai Gang" was visibly the weaker group in the leadership. Huang Ju died in early 2007, and Chen Liangyu was removed in the same year. Zeng Qinghong, due to his age, had to step down. Jiang's associates Zhang Dejiang and Zhang Gaoli, as members of the Political Bureau, could still wield a certain influence. The *taizidang* and the CCYL, however, do not see eye to eye on certain issues. This is a positive development for Hu as he can manage the relationship between the two political forces.

Removing the disloyal

After Hu took over power, some of Jiang's loyalists seemed to have difficulties shifting their loyalty from Jiang to Hu. In 2004, when the State Council went ahead with new macroeconomic controls to cool the economy, the Shanghai government under Chen Liangyu – one of Jiang's loyalists – declared that no overheating had in fact taken place in his territory.[40] Such open defiance went beyond what Hu could bear. Hu decided to make a case out of the defiant Shanghai Party secretary. In late August 2006, a commentary was published in *People's Daily* linking Chen, anonymously, to an alleged corruption case involving Zhu Junyi, the director of the Shanghai Social Security Bureau.[41] This set the stage for Chen's dismissal, which took place on September 25. Chen's dismissal showed that Hu was not only the *de jure* but also the *de facto* "number one" in China. As in the case of the rivalry between Jiang Zemin and Chen Xitong, the dismissal of Chen Liangyu paved the way for Hu Jintao to take firm control of succession politics.

The latest removal of Bo Xilai is another case in point. Bo was a member of the Political Bureau and the Party secretary of Chongqing. He was one of the most powerful figures in the *taizidang*, due to his father Bo Yibo's deep-rooted connections in the Party. During his tenure in Chongqing, he effectively developed the Chongqing model, a state-led development model that had the wide support of the public. However, Bo's Cultural Revolution style of politics and development was not acceptable to Hu Jintao, Wen Jiabao, and many other reform-minded leaders. The case of Chongqing police chief Wang Lijun and the alleged involvement of Bo's wife in the murder of British businessman Neil Heywood fully justified Hu's eventual dismissal of Bo. Immediately after the National People's Congress in March 2012, Bo was ousted.

Institutionalizing power succession

Hu has also actively searched for institutionalized means to handle power succession. The Seventeenth Party Congress was regarded as vital for power succession since the line-up of the future leadership had to be made. As it turned out, that Party Congress brought Xi Jinping and Li Keqiang into the Standing Committee as candidates for the positions of Secretary General and Premier, respectively, after Hu and Wen. After the Party Congress, the Xinhua News Agency published a lengthy on-the-spot record of the formation of the new leadership:[42]

On June 25, 2007, over 400 people, including members and alternate members of the Sixteenth CCP Central Committee and leading officials of relevant departments participated in picking proposed members of the Political Bureau from a list of almost 200 candidates. Hu Jintao presided over the event and set, on behalf of the CCP Central Committee, the conditions for the new Political Bureau members, with emphasis on political firmness, capacity, and image among the Party members and ordinary people. The candidates must be 63 or younger and were at least on a position of minister, according to the rules. The outcome of the recommendation is in conformity with the reality of the Party cadres as a number of excellent people were recommended.

The democratic recommendation of the new Party leadership is of great importance to the CCP which has over 70 million members and is managing a country with a population of 1.3 billion, Hu was quoted as saying. On September 27, the Standing Committee of the Political Bureau of the Sixteenth CCP Central Committee met and approved the candidates of the new central leadership of the Party. On October 8, the Political Bureau of the Sixteenth CCP Central Committee discussed and approved the list, and it decided to propose the list of candidates to the First Plenary Session of the Seventeenth CCP Central Committee and the First Plenary Session of the Seventeenth CCP Central Commission for Discipline Inspection.

On October 21, the Seventeenth CCP National Congress elected the Seventeenth CCP Central Committee and the Seventeenth CCP Central Commission for Discipline Inspection. And one day later, the Seventeenth CCP Central Committee elected a new central leadership of the Party.

It was the first time that participants of the CC's plenary session could recommend candidates for Political Bureau membership. The report thus regarded this event as a milestone in the history of the Party's efforts to develop intra-Party democracy. The political struggle for power succession had troubled the CCP leadership since its inception. Now that no single leader can dictate the power succession, new institutions and methods, including ones with democratic elements, have to be instituted for the stability of the Party and the state. Indeed, the Bo Xilai affair is an indication of the need to facilitate intra-Party democracy. Without formal rules and norms, ambitious politicians like Bo would challenge the legitimacy of the Party leadership through all possible means.

Ideology change and policy shift

Like Jiang, Hu has also made efforts to formulate his own ideology. In 2004, Hu laid down his ideological cornerstone by raising the concept of "harmonious society." It calls for a drastic reorientation from the development-first strategies implemented by Deng and Jiang, to people-centered policies to address the mounting social problems that China is facing.

In the era of Deng, the government operated under the "get rich first" principle. The state of the poor became secondary to the government's development plans. In the Jiang era, there was an all-out pursuance of Deng's directives. After more than a decade of ruthless, single-minded pursuit of GDP growth, the leadership found it necessary to put a halt to its previous mode of economic development, which has generated enormous undesirable consequences such as income disparities and environmental degradation. Hu began to turn the wheels of China's economic growth around. However, he was aware that the whole idea of a "harmonious society" was contingent on China's continuing push for economic development. The emphasis now is on sustainable development. This is the rationale behind another of Hu's concepts, that of "scientific development." This concept aims to strike a balance between various policies, and raised the importance of social justice to China's long-term development. In 2007, the Seventeenth Party Congress passed a resolution to revise the Party Constitution and incorporated the "scientific development" concept into the core guiding principles of the CCP.[43]

Hu's version of ideology was established. Of course, like the "three represents" theory, the "scientific development" concept is also a political test for Party cadres and government officials to show their loyalty to Hu and his policy. At the Seventeenth Party Congress, Hu won his political rivals over with the promotion of a few of his CCYL colleagues into the Political Bureau and to some other important positions. This was the backdrop to the line-up of the future leadership.

Conclusion

China has made substantial progress in conducting elite politics, particularly in terms of power transfer since the late Deng. One important aspect of Western democracy is to realize peaceful alternation of political elites through periodic elections. China has refused to follow the path of Western democracy and has attempted to find other ways to deal with power succession. The late Deng was successful in establishing several related institutions, including term limits, age limits, and collective leadership. These institutions have greatly facilitated the rapid alternation of political elites.

According to the age limit, a vice minister must retire when he/she reaches 60, and a minister must retire at 65. The limit for superior levels is 72 or 73. The age limit has become very rigid, and no one is exempted from this system. Due to this system, the speed of elite succession at all levels is incomparable to any other system. With the rigid enforcement of age limit, there are thousands of officials leaving their positions every year, with the same number of officials assuming these positions. Although such rapid mobility has its own disadvantages, it undeniably reflects the changed attitude of the times. The term limit also matters. Now in general, leaders including the Secretary General of the CCP, the State President, Premier, and other important positions are allowed to serve at most two terms in office, which is 10 years. This system is not hugely different from many Western presidential systems.

These changes have produced positive effects. First, they avoid the personal dictatorship which prevailed from Mao to Deng. The term limit is an effective institutional constraint on this. When a person or a family has dominated a country for several decades, the system is prone to malpractices and abuses, which are intolerable to the society. Second, they allow rapid rejuvenation of Chinese politics, thus effectively reflecting generational changes and changes of interests. Compared to many other political systems, the Chinese political system facilitates the rapid and massive renewal of public officials. Third, these institutions have also contributed to the development of what China has called "intra-Party democracy" or intra-Party collective leadership. There are serious checks and balances in the highest leadership of the CCP. The Political Bureau Standing Committee, the highest and most powerful decision-making body, is often regarded as the symbol of a highly centralized political system or authoritarianism. However, in the past decades, its members had almost equal power, with each having his decision-making area and the most important say in that area.

The 2012 Eighteenth Party Congress has made another breakthrough. At the Congress, Hu decided to depart from Jiang's path by giving up the post of CMC chairman. The outcome of Hu's choice has a profound impact not only on China's elite politics but also on an array of strategic issues related to its political reform, national security, and civil–military ties. Hu stepped down at the age of 70 and has thereby set an unwritten age rule for Political Bureau members to retire at 70. Even if the rule remains unwritten, this precedent will create a hugely binding effect on his successors. The age limit would nicely match the term limit for all top leaders and will enormously help institutionalization at the apex of power. Hu's retirement also removed discrepancies in the three-in-one formula that has become a symbol of the new leader's mandate. Setting two terms for CMC chair has unified civilian and military leadership. Were Hu to continue to chair the CMC and sign all key military documents, Xi, as the Party and national leader, would have no complete power in running the military, causing profound confusion in the chain of command. More importantly, the fact that Hu gave up all the three positions and passed all his powers to Xi at the same time implies that the power transfer is now becoming more certain.

However, the politics surrounding the Eighteenth Party Congress of 2012 has also revealed a defective system that is incapable of regulating increasingly bitter power struggles among the leaders, after the passing of a strong-man age.

After the death of the late Deng, the elite has become divided in terms of ideological orientation. Over the years, China has witnessed the rise of Maoism and neo-Maoism. The Chongqing model, a state-led development model, was widely regarded as a symbol of the revival of Maoism. Bo Xilai mobilized his political support through Maoist political campaigning, and his political and policy practice in Chongqing was able to attract the support of a large number of intellectuals, particularly the leftists. Among the then nine members of the Standing Committee of the Political Bureau, eight, including Premier Wen Jiabao, had visited Chongqing. Except for Wen, the rest of the seven had evaluated the Chongqing model in a positive way. Wen had been critical about the Chongqing model, while Hu Jintao neither visited Chongqing nor showed his support. Instead, both Hu and Wen visited Guangdong and showed their strong support for the Guangdong model, which was developed by Wang Yang and focuses on the role of market and civil society in leading development. The top leadership was apparently divided over the Chongqing model. Most Party cadres and government officials below the top became anxious and uncertain about the direction China should head. There is too big a gap between the Chongqing model and the Guangdong model, for the former represents Maoism and the latter Dengism. Such a divide means that there was no longer a minimum consensus in the Party's elite circles on reform and development. While the fall of Bo Xilai means that Dengism has prevailed now, political and social forces for Maoism are unlikely to disappear as long as the country is full of social and political diseases such as huge income inequality, injustice, and corruption.

More troubles emerged with power politics, in particular the system of political exit. After senior leaders retire from their formal positions, they can continue to exercise influence through various informal ways behind the scene. This is particularly true of Jiang Zemin who remains politically ambitious even though he formally retired a decade ago. In subsequent years, Jiang would always appear on some unexpected occasions during critical times of power politics. The year 2012 was no exception. Jiang appeared on many occasions. When the Eighteenth Party Congress opened, the Chinese found that all the retired members of the Standing Committee of the Political Bureau were sitting in the Presidium, with Jiang Zemin at the center.

The Chinese leadership today still suffers from the legacy of the gerontocracy or small circle of politics which has continued to trouble China's elite politics. As discussed earlier, under Deng the CCP established the Central Advisory Commission in 1982 which provided elderly Party leaders such as Chen Yun and Li Xiannian with a formal channel to influence decision-making of the Standing Committee of the Political Bureau. This institution was one of major sources behind the power struggles which led to the fall of both Hu Yaobang and Zhao Ziyang in the 1980s. Fortunately, Deng disassembled this organization when he formally retired from politics.

However, to a great degree, the gerontocracy is making a comeback to Chinese elite politics again. China now is with no strong man. The CCP has introduced the so-called "intra-Party democracy" to produce a collective leadership. In terms of power succession, the intra-Party democracy is actually an institutionalized procedure to select future leaders. What has happened is that the retired elderly Party leaders such as Jiang have become a formal part of the selection. For example, the selection of Xi Jinping and Li Keqiang as the next State President and Premier, respectively, was made jointly by the current members and alternate members of the Central Committee and retired elderly Party leaders before the Seventeenth Party Congress five years ago. This practice has been institutionalized and become a legitimate platform for retired elderly Party leaders to extend their political influence and intervene in power succession.

Under the heavy influence of the gerontocracy, the Eighteenth Party Congress has formed a new leadership. The fact that Hu has passed all three positions to Xi has empowered the latter. Power consolidation for Xi is important for his tenure at the top. However, this is only a part, and might be a less important part, for him. In the years ahead, the new leadership under Xi will have to face an immediate and daunting political challenge, that is, how intra-Party democracy can be pushed forward. Intra-Party democracy has so far enabled the CCP to remain open. Certainly, if intra-Party democracy is inevitable, formal rules and norms which can regulate competition would be crucial. To eliminate the possibilities of hidden agendas, competition rules would have to be explicit, fair, and transparent. When hidden rules dominate political competition, democracy will be jeopardized. If democracy is jeopardized, intra-Party competition will not only destroy the unity of the Party but also weaken its overall ability, thus increasing the risk of political instability. The Bo Xilai affair is a good example. This case has seriously undermined the unity of the Party leadership, particularly in the eyes of the people. Apparently, whether or not the CCP will survive depends on how further intra-Party democratization could be introduced.

Notes

1 Harding (1987).
2 For a detailed examination of Chinese politics under Deng Xiaoping, see Baum (1994). Vogel (2011) provided the best and most updated analysis of Deng's life and his role in China's development.
3 For a detailed discussion of the struggle between the Gang of Four and the moderates, see Yang (1998).
4 Ibid., Chapter 3; MacFarquhar and Fairbank (1991); and Xiao (2008).
5 Lieberthal (1995: 123–24).
6 Research Office of the Party History of the Central Committee (1987: 406–7).
7 Saich (2004: 49–50).
8 For a detailed discussion of Deng's attack on the "Two Whatevers," see Yang (2004).
9 Ibid., 124–25.
10 Ibid.
11 Ibid..
12 For detailed discussion of the argument of this camp, please refer to Yang (2004).
13 Xinhua News Agency, *Zhongguo gongchandang dashiji*, 1979.
14 Zheng (2001).
15 Lieberthal (1995: 128).
16 Key documents on the pro-democracy movement include Han (1990); Nathan and Link (2001); and Oksenberg *et al.* (1990). For analysis of the 1989 pro-democracy movement, see Zhao (2001); Calhoun (1994); Saich (1990); and Baum (1993). Zhao Ziyang's memoirs provided an insider's view of the movement, see Zhao (2009).
17 Zhao (1987).
18 Wu (1997a).
19 Xinhua News Agency, *Zhongguo gongchandang dashiji*, 1981.
20 For detailed discussion on the technocratic movement, see Lee (1991).
21 Lee (1993).
22 Bo (2006: 21).
23 Zong (2007: 100).
24 Ibid., 153.
25 Ibid., 43.
26 Shirk (1993: Chapter 4).

27 Ibid.
28 Bo (2006: 21).
29 Deng (2002: 310).
30 Zong (2007: 137).
31 Lam (1993).
32 Ibid.
33 For a discussion of this coalition, see Wu (1997b).
34 You (1996).
35 Baum (2000); Cavey (1997); and Cheng (1998).
36 On the movement of technocracy in the Jiang Zemin era, see Li and White (1998).
37 All figures are based on the author's database.
38 Baum (2000: 24).
39 Ibid.
40 Leslie Foong, "Leadership Dispute Over China Growth." *The Straits Times*, July 10, 2004.
41 Lu Gangfeng, "Exactly How Much Public Funds Were Appropriated? A Revelation by the Shanghai Social Security Scandal." *People's Daily*, August 29, 2006.
42 Liu *et al.* (2007).
43 Xinhua News Agency, October 21, 2007.

References

Baum, R. 1993. "The Road to Tiananmen: Chinese Politics in the 1980s." In Roderick MacFarquhar, ed., *The Politics of China 1949–1989*. Cambridge: Cambridge University Press, pp. 340–472.

Baum, R. 1994. *Burying Mao: Chinese Politics in the Age of Deng Xiaoping*. Princeton, NJ: Princeton University Press.

Baum, R. 2000. "Jiang Takes Command: The Fifteenth National Party Congress and Beyond." In Hung-Mao Tien and Yun-han Chu, eds., *China under Jiang Zemin*. Boulder, CO: Lynne Rienner, pp. 15–32.

Bo, Zhiyue. 2006. *China's Elite Politics: Political Transition and Power Balancing*. Singapore and London: World Scientific.

Calhoun, C. J. 1994. *Neither Gods nor Emperors: Students and the Struggle for Democracy in China*. Berkeley, CA: University of California Press.

Cavey, P. 1997. "Building a Power Base: Jiang Zemin and the Post-Deng Succession." *Issues and Studies* 33, 11 (November): 1–34.

Cheng, J. Y. S. 1998. "Power Consolidation and Further Economic Reforms." In Joseph Y. S. Cheng, ed., *China Review 1998*. Hong Kong: The Chinese University of Hong Kong Press, pp. 25–60.

Deng, Xiaoping. 2002. "Di san dai lingdao jiti de dangwu zhiji" (The Top Priority of the Third Collective Leadership). In *Deng Xiaoping wenxuan (Selected Works of Deng Xiaoping)*, vol. 3. Beijing: Renmin chubanshe.

Han, Minzhu, ed. 1990. *Cries for Democracy: Writings and Speeches from the 1989 Chinese Democracy Movement*. Princeton, NJ: Princeton University Press.

Harding, H. 1987. *China's Second Revolution: Reform after Mao.* Washington, DC: Brookings Institution.

Lam, Willy Wo-lap. 1993. "Leadership Changes at the Fourteenth Party Congress." In Joseph Y. S. Cheng and Maurice Brosseau, eds., *China Review 1993.* Hong Kong: The Chinese University of Hong Kong Press, pp. 17–67.

Lee, Hong Yung. 1991. *From Revolutionary Cadres to Party Technocrats in Socialist China.* Berkeley, CA: University of California Press.

Lee, Hong Yung. 1993. "Political and Administrative Reforms of 1982–1986: The Changing Party Leadership and State Bureaucracy." In Michael Ying-Mao Kau and Susan H. Marsh, eds., *China in the Era of Deng Xiaoping: A Decade of Reform.* New York: M. E. Sharpe, pp. 41–48.

Li, Cheng and Lynn White. 1998. "The Fifteenth Central Committee of the Chinese Communist Party: Full-Fledged Technocratic Leadership with Partial Control by Jiang Zemin." *Asian Survey* 38, 3 (March): 231–64.

Lieberthal, K. 1995. *Governing China: From Revolution through Reform.* New York: W.W. Norton & Company.

Liu, Siyang, Sun Chengbin, and Liu Gang. 2007. "Weile dang he guojia xingwang fada zhangzhi jiuan – dang de xin yijie zhongyang lingdao jigou chansheng jishi" (For the Prosperity and Stability of the Party and State: On the Spot Record of the Birth of the New Party Leadership). Xinhua News Agency, October 23.

MacFarquhar, R. and John K. Fairbank, eds. 1991. *The Cambridge History of China,* vol. 15, *The People's Republic, Part 2: Revolutions within the Chinese Revolution, 1966– 1982.* Cambridge: Cambridge University Press.

Nathan, A. J. and Perry Link, eds. 2001. *The Tiananmen Papers.* New York: Public Affairs.

Oksenberg, M., L. R. Sullivan, and M. Lambert, eds. 1990. *Beijing Spring, 1989: Confrontation and Conflict: The Basic Documents.* Armonk, NY: M. E. Sharpe.

Research Office of the Party History of the Central Committee. 1987. *Zhonggong dangshi dashi nianbiao* (Annual Report of the History of the Chinese Communist Party). Beijing: Renmin chubanshe.

Saich, T., ed. 1990. *The Chinese People's Movement: Perspectives on Spring 1989.* Armonk, NY: M. E. Sharpe.

Saich, T. 2004. *Governance and Politics of China.* New York: Palgrave Macmillan.

Shirk, S. L. 1993. *The Political Logic of Economic Reform in China.* Berkeley, CA: University of California Press.

Vogel, E. 2011. *"Deng Xiaoping and the Transformation of China.* Cambridge, MA: Harvard University Press.

Wu, Guoguang. 1997a. *Zhao Ziyang yu Zhongguo zhengzhi gaige* (Political Reform under Zhao Ziyang). Hong Kong: The Pacific Century Institute.

Wu, Guoguang. 1997b. *Zhulu shiwuda* (Power Competition for the Fifteenth Party Congress). Hong Kong: The Pacific Century Institute.

Xiao, Donglian. 2008. *The History of the People's Republic of China, vol. 10, Turning Point in History: Re-examination of the Cultural Revolution and the Policy of Reform and Opening (1979–1981).* Hong Kong: Research Center for Contemporary Chinese Culture, The Chinese University of Hong Kong.

Yang, Jishen. 1998. *Deng Xiaoping shidai* (The Deng Xiaoping Era). Beijing: Central Compilation and Translation Press.

Yang, Jishen. 2004. *Zhongguo gaige niandai de zhengzhi douzheng* (Political Struggle in China's Reform Era). Hong Kong: Excellent Culture Press.

You, Ji. 1996. "Jiang Zemin: In Quest of Post-Deng Supremacy." In Maurice Brosseau, Suzanne Pepper, and Tsang Shu-ki, eds., *China Review 1996*. Hong Kong: The Chinese University of Hong Kong Press, pp. 1–28.

Zhao, Dingxin. 2001. *The Power of Tiananmen: State–Society Relations and the 1989 Beijing Student Movement*. Chicago, IL: University of Chicago Press.

Zhao, Ziyang. 1987. "Move Forward along the Socialist Road with Chinese Characteristics." In Xinhua News Agency, *Zhongguo gongchandang dashiji*.

Zhao, Ziyang. 2009. *Prisoner of the State: The Secret Journal of Premier Zhao Ziyang*. New York: Simon & Schuster.

Zheng Yongnian. 2001. *Zhengzhi jianjin zhuyi* (Political Gradualism). Taipei: Chinese Eurasian Education Foundation.

Zong, Fengming. 2007. *Zhao Ziyang ruanjin zhong de tanhua* (Zhao Ziyang: Captive Conversations). Hong Kong: The Open Press.

Chapter 3
Economic Reform

China's economic transformation is one of the most significant developments in contemporary world history. Within barely three decades, the country has transformed from a planned economy dominated by the rural sector to a vibrant market economy dominated by modern manufacturing and service sectors. The breathtaking average growth rate of 9.6% in the past 30 years, known as the Chinese economic miracle, bears remarkable testimony to the powerful dynamics unleashed and structured by the economic reform.

The economic reform is a systemic reaction to the economic, political, and social consequences of the Cultural Revolution (CR). During the Mao era, despite remarkable industrial growth rates, living standards remained stagnant for most Chinese. The CR left the second generation leaders under Deng Xiaoping with the urgent task of changing development strategy and seeking new sources of legitimacy.

Deng began China's first phase of reform immediately after his resumption of power. The reform was carried out by a group of relatively young reformers in the central and local leadership. Zhao Ziyang in particular was personally in charge of most of these reforms, first serving as Premier (1982–87) and then as the CCP Secretary General (1987–89). Central to this phase of reform was the contract system and decentralization. Economic development in this phase was sometimes called *reform without losers*, referring to an inclusive growth process that serves to improve the welfare positions across different areas and social classes.[1]

Deng's Southern Tour in 1992 unveiled the second phase of reform (1992–2002). Zhu Rongji presided over the reform process first as Vice Premier (1993–98) and then Premier (1998–2003). From 1994, the "Reform Year," right up to China's entry into the WTO in December 2001, Zhu left strong personal

Contemporary China: A History since 1978, First Edition. Yongnian Zheng.
© 2014 John Wiley & Sons, Ltd. Published 2014 by John Wiley & Sons, Ltd.

marks on the course of China's second phase of reform. This phase of reform, consisting of various programs of recentralization and institutionalization, has shaped the basic institutional structure of the current Chinese economy.

The third phase of reform started when Hu Jintao and Wen Jiabao assumed the positions of Party secretary and Premier in late 2002 and early 2003, respectively. The reform policy under the Hu–Wen administration in the last decade has specifically targeted the distorted structure of the Chinese economy and socioeconomic problems arising from unprecedented economic growth in the previous decade. The limited progress is vivid testimony to the complex obstacles and constraints faced by the reform projects.

Reform under Deng Xiaoping (1978–92)

The rural reforms: Household responsibility systems and township and village enterprises

When Deng assumed leadership in the late 1970s, economic development in China was in many ways on the brink of collapse. The situation was worse in the rural sector; per capita agricultural production had at best stagnated and at worst decreased since the founding of the PRC in 1949. China's economic backwardness, especially vis-à-vis the newly industrialized Asian economies (NIEs), was deeply embarrassing to the alleged superiority of socialism.

The initial urgency to rapidly improve economic performance and the livelihood of the people provided the reformers with much needed grassroots support. The failure of the commune system in rural areas had become more evident in the late 1970s. In many ways, rural reform was started not by the leadership, but by the struggle for basic material needs of the peasants. By the late 1970s, many grassroots brigades had secretly begun redistributing land to the households instead of the collectives. The most exemplary case was in the winter of 1978 when 18 farmers in Xiaogang village, Anhui province, left their fingerprints on a contract that explicitly allocated land to the households.[2] This peasants' secret treaty inadvertently generated a series of chain reactions that would ultimately lead to revolutionary changes in China's rural economic institutions. This was only possible after the adventurous peasants obtained the political support of open-minded provincial leaders like Zhao Ziyang in Sichuan and Wan Li in Anhui, and central leaders under Deng Xiaoping.[3]

In 1983, the household responsibility system (HRS) was enshrined as a socialist economic institution. The People's Commune finally ceased to exist and the HRS became the standard institutional arrangement for rural agricultural households.[4] The HRS established the peasants' claim to the surplus grain after subtracting the fixed contribution to the state and community. The farming households have full rights over the disposal of surplus grain, mostly through state-controlled marketing channels. The state, to encourage agricultural activities, raised the state purchasing price of grain several times between 1979 and 1985.

If HRS was the key to invigorating the rural traditional sector, then rural industry was the key to rural modern sectors. Rural industrialization was already a common phenomenon in the countryside under Mao when radical decentralization took place. Formerly existing as marginal supplementary productive units, commune and bridge enterprises were renamed in 1984 as Township and Village Enterprises (TVEs). The reform policy since 1984 has consistently regarded TVEs as the most important engine of rural economic growth.

The TVEs have enjoyed a massive influx of surplus labor released by the more efficient HRS and unprecedented entrepreneurial freedom enabled by government liberalization policies. Within the year 1984, the number of TVEs more than quadrupled from 1.3 to 6 million. In the following decade, TVEs expanded to 23 million in 1996. During this golden decade (1984–96), the TVEs provided 135 million jobs and contributed almost one-third of the country's industrial products.[5]

The state-owned enterprise reforms in the 1980s

After the initial taste of success from rural reforms, Zhao Ziyang proposed to reform the state-owned enterprise (SOE) sector in 1984.[6] The reforms of the planning system, price system, and economic governance system were identified as the three main areas. The first priority was to transform SOEs into modern corporate enterprises.

The SOE reform began with managerial decentralization. In the socialist system, the economic functions of SOEs were effectively restricted to a workshop under the control of various administrative authorities. After 1985, SOE managers were given more discretion in the making of key economic decisions, such as level of production and matters relating to inputs and outputs, after they completed the planned output. Meanwhile, a new compensation system was implemented to reward economically efficient units and individuals. A contractually based *Production Responsibility System*, similar to the rural HRS, was instituted in 1987, and SOEs had to complete a level of planned production as specified by contract with the bureaucracy in charge.

For surplus produce, SOE managements would have to sell via market channels. To achieve efficient production, market mechanisms were applied to reflect the true economic value of industrial products of SOEs, where SOEs could transact with each other and with other actors, such as collective TVEs and private actors at the market price. This market price was usually higher than the planned price set by planning authorities for transactions between state sectors for produce within the plan. For most SOEs, the planned price continued to dictate the costs of input and all the within-plan outputs. This parallel coexistence of plan and market was commonly known as the dual-track system.

Equally significant changes were made to the corporate revenue system. For decades, SOEs as productive and welfare agents of the state were not subject to any formal corporate tax. Across all sectors and economic domains, implicit taxes and subsidies were substituted by profit remittances and planned prices on the goods and services delivered to the state. The coexistence of underpriced inputs and market price for off-plan sale of outputs enabled most SOEs to operate at a given profit margin. Attempts were made to transform the fiscal roles of SOEs by converting various traditional profit remittances to a multi-year contractual sum, in what came to be known as the "tax for profits" reform from 1986.[7] Under the new scheme, SOEs were to transfer only a fixed portion of their profits to the state and retain the surplus. The amount of tax was determined on a case-by-case and negotiable basis between individual SOEs and their supervising authorities. The tax-for-profit reform became the first step toward new forms of a uniform tax system nationwide.

Fiscal and financial reforms

China's old fiscal system was a highly concentrated one which was designed to serve the planned economy. In 1980, the central leadership initiated a fiscal reform characterized by fiscal decentralization. A key change in the new system was the creation of separate tax bases for local and central revenues, principally based on centrally and locally managed SOEs, which are administratively defined. A few new locally-based tax types were created and allocated to the local coffer, but the tax bases were very insignificant. Within the limited domain of local tax base, the local governments had some freedom of action over their own spending and investment decisions.[8]

In a unitary state like China, fiscal decentralization was the most effective means to inspire and provide local economic initiatives.[9] In 1988, a contractual system of revenue sharing became institutionalized nationwide. Like the responsibility system implemented elsewhere, local governments were only required to send revenue to the central coffer based on multiyear contracts. Local governments became the residue claimants and *de facto* self-financing fiscal units. China entered a five-year period of rapid central fiscal decline, leading to the fiscal reform of 1994.[10]

If fiscal reform was mostly about central–local decentralization, financial reform was better summarized as financial and fiscal separation and decentralization. In the old planned system, the financial system was completely absorbed by the fiscal system. The People's Bank of China (PBC) was merely a department in the Ministry of Finance responsible for monetary mobiliza- tion and cash-flow management. The financial reform set out to create a financial system from this fiscal-financial nexus.

In 1979, the PBC was institutionally separated from the Ministry of Finance to become a state bank with local branches at all administrative levels down to the county. Four years later, three state-owned commercial banks were estab- lished, namely the Agricultural Bank of China, the Bank of China, and the Construction Bank of China, to provide loans and credit services in the domains of agriculture, trade, and infrastructure, followed by the Commercial and Industrial Bank of China in 1984, to provide urban credit services alongside the PBC.[11]

Both fiscal and financial reforms have served to empower and invigorate local governments at the cost of central revenue and control. As a result of fiscal decentralization, local governments became pro-active in expanding their own fiscal bases at the cost of the central share. The local governments also became very interventionist and aggressive in their relations with the local branches of state banks and the PBC through its administrative powers. Until the final recentralization in the mid-1990s, the relentless competition for tax bases and sources of profits had turned local governments against each other through various forms of local protectionism.[12] The resulting economic disor- ders would have an immediate impact on future reforms.

Price reforms, inflation, and the 1989 interludes

Pricing is a key mechanism for any market economy. Reformers had long envisioned a gradual transition to full-fledged application of price mechanisms through a thorough price reform. In the late 1980s, this transition was given new urgency as the dual-track system was plagued by numerous drawbacks. Since the dual-track system stipulated two prices for the same products, rents were generated by simply selling any products at market price obtained via the planned channels. However, the access to products via planned channels was under the tight control of various bureaucratic authorities. This institutional arrangement left those with access to power the opportunity to get rich over- night via rent-seeking, as a prevalent form of corruption. After the adoption of the dual-track system in the mid-1980s, rampant official corruption had caused severe tensions and grievances among the public.

In 1988, the leadership decided to implement a sweeping price and wage reform, in the belief that the economy would be greatly marketized through the rapid but temporary inflation. From April to July 1988, official planned prices for food, fuel, and consumer electronics were adjusted upward by 20–40% to reflect their real market values. In expectation of a sharp rise in prices for daily necessities, waves of speculative buying and hoarding spread across China's major commercial centers, further fueling an inflationary spiral in prices and wages.[13] Within a matter of a few months, the price doubled for most daily necessities.

The rapid unfolding of an inflationary spiral was disturbing. Both the reformers and conservatives were unprepared for such scales of disturbances amidst mounting social grievances. The reformers were initially prepared to force the reforms through, but widespread bank withdrawals and buying in panic gave the conservatives the upper hand. In September 1988, the central leadership decided to end price reform and reimpose fiscal and monetary austerity.[14]

Southern tour

The inflation of 1988, radical socioeconomic changes, and political tensions were push factors for the pro-democracy movement in 1989. After the Tiananmen crackdown, the conservative economic leadership under Li Peng, Yao Yilin, and Song Ping and backed by Chen Yun began to retract the reformist strategy championed by Deng Xiaoping and Zhao Ziyang. The programs included freezing market channels, recentralizing fiscal and financial powers, and imposing harsh credit policies. However, the conservatives' approach proved to be counterproductive. Local governments, the clear gainers from previous reforms, opposed any policy regression to central planning. Also, the market and non-state sectors, once firmly instituted and legalized, could hardly be retrenched.

The fall of Soviet and Eastern European communism between 1989 and 1991 further called into question the credibility of the planned economic system. Deng was deeply concerned with the possible implications for China's development. At this historical juncture, Deng started his month-long Southern Tour in January 1992 in a few economic centers, including Wuhan, Zhuhai, Shenzhen, and Shanghai.

Deng's talks during the tour were initially not well received by the Party leadership in Beijing, but his lasting personal influence in the Party and critical support from a reformist alliance soon turned the tide. In his Southern Tour Talks published in the *People's Daily* on April 13, 1992 Deng reaffirmed reform and opening up as the key to liberating productive forces, elevating people's living standard, and building comprehensive state capacity.[15] In view of these goals, market and plan are the only means to achieve socialist development.

Deng's Southern Tour marked the second phase of China's reform period. The Southern Tour Talks did not simply restate the critical role of market in building socialism, but also outlined China's future economic development as legitimizing the market. Soon after his Southern Tour, the conservatives became more receptive to Deng's urge for further reforms.

Economic Reform under Zhu Rongji (1993–2002)

En route to the reform year

In December 1992, Zhu was promoted to the Standing Committee of the Political Bureau and later to Vice Premier to take charge of economic reform. With a strong personality, technical knowledge and management experiences in economics, and a keen awareness of China's problems, Zhu proved to be a very able and dynamic reformer who eventually shaped what China's contemporary economic institutions are today.

When Zhu first helmed the reform taskforce, the Chinese economy was severely overheated due to the investment fever of local governments and further worsened by a concurrent weakening of central fiscal capacity. The economy was crippled by inflation, currency exchange rate, severe central budget deficit, and malignant competition among local economic actors. Fiscal and financial incentives inherent in the decentralized control and contract system led local governments to compete against each other for the control of vital marketable resources and for greater productive capacity; the resultant disorder however had also facilitated *de facto* marketization and drove the national price level to new heights.[16]

Zhu took these reform challenges on in 1993. When the fiscal and financial disorders came to a head, he personally ordered state bankers to recall short-term high-interest loans and impose a radical hike to interest rates in an all-out effort to avert imminent financial chaos at the cost of the collapse of nascent stock and real estate markets.[17] On some occasions, he applied his administrative power to sack local cadres who openly opposed the reform and to parachute his loyal lieutenants in as replacements.[18]

The reform year of 1994

The year 1994 was one of the most eventful years in the reform era. The Fourteenth Congress of the CCP in 1992 finally reaffirmed Deng's reform agenda. For the first time in the history of the CCP, the market obtained the ultimate legal recognition of the Party. The Congress specified reforms of SOEs, and introduced new foreign exchange systems and modern financial and fiscal systems as key areas of the market economy. These system reforms took place only in 1994, when Zhu took over all responsibilities of economic reform. These reform efforts became the basis of all later reforms. It was no coincidence that 1994 entered the history of reform as the Reform Year.

The exchange rate reform in January 1994 marked the end of dual-track exchange rates. In its place the leadership introduced a managed float system that allowed a narrow margin of fluctuation for the *renminbi* (RMB). From

1997, the *de facto* dollar-pegged exchange rate became the standard until the next major reform in July 2005. With the abolition of retained foreign earnings, the accounting and management of foreign currency reserves were centralized to state banking systems. As a direct consequence, the trade system was unified nationally and put under the control of the State Custom Administration. As the locally fragmented trade system was finally recentralized, the central government was able to start its grand projects of tariff and trade policy readjustment.

The banking system reform marked the most decisive steps toward a modern banking system. In 1994, three policy banks (National Development Bank, China Import-Export Bank, and National Agricultural Development Bank) were set up to take over from major state commercial banks in the provision of policy loan services, thus separating the banking system into two functionally distinctive subsystems. Another parallel project of the financial reform was the central bank. Zhu took it so seriously that he personally oversaw the whole reform process as president of the PBC (June 1993 to June 1995). Toward the end of Zhu's two-year presidency, the PBC was legally affirmed as the central monetary policy authority.

Most important of all, the tax sharing system was implemented in January 1994 to replace the old system of central–local revenue-sharing negotiable contracts. Under the new system, central and local governments base their revenue on specific types of taxes, depending on the nature of the economic activities, and draw from a shared portion of certain national taxes.[19] To avoid local administrative interference, central and local taxes were administered by a separate and independent system of state and local taxation administrations.

The reform year of 1994 was indeed a year of momentous changes. Over the following few years, for the first time in decades, China would gradually have a functioning structure of macroeconomic management, with the central bank, the ministry of finance, and a central policy planning agency. Most of the post-1994 reforms under Zhu were a continuation of the 1994 reforms.

SOE reforms in the 1990s: "Let go of the small"

Enterprise reform remained the most challenging task for the leadership in the 1990s.[20] The principle of enterprise reform in the 1980s was to strengthen the whole state sector. Many SOEs, especially the medium and small ones, were mired in economic inefficiency and posed a perpetual heavy burden on the fiscal and financial systems. Internal governance and management reforms to ensure the sustainability of SOEs seemed to have reached a dead end by the early 1990s.

Zhu's response was not merely continuation of the reform in the 1980s, neither was it a sweeping and indiscriminate shift from planning to the market.

Rather, he opted for selective privatization and restructuring. The reform program was based primarily on the size of the enterprise and the nature of the sectors. Ownership reform applied to small and medium firms in competitive sectors, while restructuring of state ownership applied to large firms in strategic sectors. In both cases, the goal was to enhance the competitiveness of SOEs.

The new company law of 1993 provided the first legal framework of China's modern private enterprises. The conversion was in two stages. From 1994, most small and medium SOEs were corporatized in a variety of ways. In general there has been a shift from the employee-shareholding mode of privatization to Management Buy-Out (MBO).[21] By 2002, most small and medium SOEs had been converted to joint-stock companies or shareholding companies. The total number of SOEs declined from 120,000 in 1995 to a mere 31,750 in 2004.[22]

As the state retreated from competitive sectors of the economy, China experienced a continued rise of the non-state sector and its subsequent growth in economic dynamism throughout the 1990s. The private sector has since taken great leaps in both number and scale. By 1998, the GDP generated by the private sector was already on par with the state sector. Since then the private sector has consistently outstripped the state and collective sectors in its capacity to create job opportunities and in its total value added. At the end of the Zhu reform, the non-public sector (non-state and non-collective) was already the major employer of as much as two-thirds of China's urban labor force.[23]

The SOE reform: "Grip the large"

The reform of large SOEs was to transform these large state firms into powerful enterprise groups in economically and politically strategic sectors. These firms, already dominant national and local monopoly players, including some ministerial-level industrial groups, were transformed into Group Company systems.

From 1994, over 100 centrally managed SOEs and 2,500 locally managed SOEs were created from the regrouping and restructuring of most large SOEs, most in the strategic and monopoly sectors.[24] Due to the political significance of large SOEs, the core SOE reform was implemented very cautiously and gradually and within the time span of more than a decade.

The key procedure was to refinance selective debt-ridden old SOEs. The basic approach under Zhu was restructuring and marketization. By keeping only the most productive businesses and factors of production, most large SOEs became stronger through restructuring. Indeed, most surviving SOEs were allowed to keep some monopoly rights without minimum social welfare responsibilities, except through contributing value-added, resource, and corporate income tax to the government. The much needed source of refinancing was largely obtained through the sale of shares in state-run stock markets dominated by state-linked institutional investors.

The SOE reform has been successful in strengthening the remaining SOE sector dominated by large centrally and provincially owned industrial giants. From 1998 to 2008, the balance sheets of SOEs improved tremendously, recovering from a loss of 100 million *yuan* to achieve a total after-tax profit of nearly 1.3 trillion *yuan* in 2009.[25] An unexpected consequence of this seeming success was the rise of powerful interest groups, in particular those centrally managed SOEs. As the large state-owned banks and financial institutions, they were without exception monopoly or oligopolistic national players on the domestic market, wielding substantial powers on the product, input, and factor markets.

Rural declines and the rise of migrant workers

Just as most small and medium SOEs were on the verge of collapse in the mid-1990s, the TVEs were also reaching the end of their golden decade. In the early 1990s, many TVEs were suffering from poor governance and lack of product competitiveness, but it was not until 1996 that the whole TVE sector declined in terms of share in gross value added and employment. Among the chief reasons were the ill-defined property rights and the poor financial position of grassroots governments, the *de facto* owner of TVEs.[26]

From 1996, the central government launched a series of ownership reforms on TVEs and the collective sector in line with the reform on small and medium SOEs. Most inefficient and poorly managed TVEs were restructured into joint-stock companies and even private enterprises.

The decline and restructuring of TVEs and the related rapid urban economic growth worked to reshape the rural economy. At the most fundamental level, the rural economy, both agricultural and modern sectors, was on a course of inevitable contraction, both in terms of its share in GDP and employment. For the agricultural sector, in the first half of the 1990s, both total grain production and per-acre yield stagnated. The fear of grain shortage even prompted the government to raise purchase prices repeatedly over the years and abolish agricultural tax in 2005. The shift toward overall comprehensive agricultural subsidy, although insufficient to help raise the competitiveness of the agricultural sector in the labor market, has so far been successful in maintaining an adequate level of grain production.

The decline of rural economy and the rise of non-state sectors in the urban economy gave rise to a powerful wave of labor reallocation from rural to urban sectors in the 1990s. In the last two decades, the total number of migrant workers grew from 30 million in 1989 to about 230 million in 2010.[27] Over half of these migrant workers traveled across provincial borders to work in the coastal industrial centers. Migrant workers who make up the urban floating population have established themselves as the mainstream of China's industrial labor force.[28]

The influx of millions of migrant workers in major industrial coastal cities greatly facilitated the structural transformation of China's industry from SOE-dominated import-substituting to export-oriented labor-intensive industries. Migrant workers were behind the phenomenal rise of China's cheaply priced competitive products. Meanwhile, migrant workers have increasingly shaped socioeconomic changes in China's rural hinterland. In pure economic terms, income from waged labor, first beginning as complementary income to farming, later evolved to become the main source of rural income. The return of successful migrant workers to their rural hometowns has fueled development in the rural areas. The returnees brought with them skills, technological know-how, and vision that were much needed in local economic take-offs. Most of China's rural entrepreneurs today have had their stints in the developed economic centers in coastal urban China.

Economic Reform under Wen Jiabao (2003–2013)

Economic reform entering deep waters

The reform in the Hu Jintao–Wen Jiabao era was a response to the problems of the Zhu reform. Among the most salient issues were the rapidly expanding rural–urban income divide and the seriously undersupplied and unequally distributed social welfare. But at the more fundamental level, both the economic structure and the growth pattern were widely regarded as socially, environmentally, and even politically unsustainable.

The new reform measures under Hu–Wen could be placed into two policy categories according to the scope and objective of the reform. In the first category, policy measures such as rural reforms and social policy reform were implemented to address the adverse economic and social implications of the excessive market-oriented approach under Zhu. In the second category, more sweeping reforms were envisioned under the so-called "Scientific Development Outlook" and "Harmonious Society Project," both initiated around 2005/6. The reforms in these categories would require changing the fundamental economic structure, in particular, industrial structures and the income distribution system.

Besides the new measures, market reform continued on different fronts, under different institutional environments. Most of these reforms required only minor adjustments and rearrangements. The second category of reform initiatives was heavily influenced by powerful organized interests. Overall, economic reform under the Hu–Wen administration was far less encompassing and in some sense, less successful. There were several new reform initiatives, but little substantive progress has been made in the structural domain.

Economic reforms continued

Economic reform continued on two fronts. Institutionally, consistent efforts were made to improve central regulatory systems. To further liberalization and marketization efforts, faced with a complex set of institutional constraints and special interests, the central government was very cautious, thus limiting its progress.

Reform measures were introduced to institutionalize a market regulatory system. In 2003, several regulatory functions were recentralized to ministerial-level regulatory authorities under the direct control of the State Council, in particular in the financial sphere, such as the China Banking Regulatory Commission (CBRC), China Insurance Regulatory Commission (CIRC), and China Security Regulatory Commission (CSRC).

In 2005, the reforms of large SOEs found their latest and final institutional embodiment in the new State Asset Supervision and Administration Commission (SASAC). The new agency was created to tackle the very challenging task of overseeing China's powerful SOEs in the interests of the state and the public. More importantly, it was instituted as an agent to further reform the large SOEs. Under the supervision and direction of SASAC, centrally managed and some large locally managed SOE groups were to become globally competitive enterprises. This will require SOEs to undergo complete governance reforms and be ready for competition. While most large SOEs have definitely grown in scale, the reform agenda for competitiveness has so far made little progress.

Indeed, large SOEs have effectively inclined to monopoly positions in the domestic market. In many respects, SOEs have become so powerful that the viability of any further reforms is likely to be conditioned on their compatibility with their prevailing monopoly interests. For instance, the National Grid, Sinopec, and the China National Petrol Cooperation, chief representatives of large SOEs in the energy sectors, have posed powerful resistance against proposed reforms in the energy sector. Their huge profits and political links with the Party-state power apparatus in particular made any meaningful de-monopolization by the SASAC and price and investment control by the National Development and Reform Commission an intractable political task.

SOEs, local governments, and financial deepening

The Hu–Wen administration has arguably gone the furthest in financial deepening. In their first five years, the financial sector expanded much faster than it had in all past decades if measured in numerical scales. However, these developments, in particular the stock market and the market for land and real estate, were closely related to the rise of powerful financial interests of SOEs and the local governments.

The SOE reform project under Hu–Wen was also a continuation of the Zhu reform in the 1990s. Since the Zhu reform, the stock market has already been regarded as one of the several possible channels to refinance the SOE groups. But the share-based reform was still limited in the 1990s. Since 1999, the restructured large SOEs have acquired greater incentives to pursue an expansionary strategy through aggressive market expansion. As the banking sector became more strictly regulated, stock and security markets became one of the chief sources of finance for SOEs. Based on more assertive financial situations and riding on a renewed wave of strong economic growth, some large SOEs, their monopoly edges already strengthened by previous reforms, became even more powerful and expansionist.

In comparison with the growth of the share market, the marketization of land and growth of the real estate market was perhaps even more significant. Local governments, with direct control over land usage and the responsibility to oversee most infrastructure projects as a result of industrialization and urbanization, naturally became key actors.

Since the tax reform assigned the lion's share of major taxes to the central government, local governments were in a perpetual thirst for alternative, off-budget sources of finance. The transfer of land via a land auction system instituted since 1998 and more than a dozen local-based taxes on real estate have provided an ideal source of revenue for local governments. Moreover, since financial centralization set state banks free from local political influence, local governments began to use state-owned urban land as mortgage to secure bank loans. Under the fiscal drives of local government, the acquiescence of the central government, and the influx of foreign capital, the value of land and real estate has soared ahead of GDP growth since 1998.[29]

The deepening of financial reform via stock market, land transfer, and the real estate market was chiefly bottom-up in response to the consequence of economic reform in the 1990s. From the point of view of the central authority, the reform strengthened local governments and SOEs vis-à-vis the center and posed new economic risks and challenges unforeseen in the 1990s. The passive accommodation of powerful interests had some key implications for China's later development.

New vision, new limitations

Since the launch of the "Scientific Development Outlook" campaign in 2004, the Hu–Wen administration has devoted much energy to realizing the new visions.[30] The approach was to increase central government spending in social welfare, poverty alleviation, rural transfer payments, and subsidies for agriculture and new industries. Central government spending since 2004 in these categories has exceeded the rapid rate of increase in government revenue.

The leadership has achieved some measure of success in the reduction of regional income disparity, while rural welfare on average has also improved. The rural agricultural subsidy was particularly helpful in stabilizing China's grain yield, which had suffered a relative decline in the 1990s. New reforms were implemented in social welfare to establish a stronger welfare role for the state, particularly in the health care sector (for social reform, see Chapter 9).

But at a more fundamental level, both structural imbalances and social tensions have increased sharply since the new visions were advanced. Economic imbalance was apparent. The share of household disposable income in GDP continued to decline relative to the share in government and enterprise sectors while the share of consumption likewise fell rapidly. Heavy energy consumption and environmental degradation continued unabated. In addition, the lack of state-subsidized welfare coverage for the majority of poor rural migrants and a large portion of the rising middle class amidst rising living costs might stunt the growth of a strong and independent middle class.

The structural reforms were further stalled by the global financial crisis of 2008. The central government had amassed trillions of *yuan* of investments to ensure economic growth, which again took precedence over industrial upgrading and welfare concerns. Since 2008, domestic and external imbalances have both reached unprecedented proportions, as the investment-fused Chinese economy achieved a globally unparalleled growth rate of 9.1% in 2009.[31] But the overstretched economy was beset with inflationary pressure, credit risks, and a housing price bubble.

Ten years into the Hu–Wen era, the reform now faces a complex situation underlined by powerful organized institutional interests, a disgruntled and stratified society, and a structurally imbalanced economy. The demands for reform from powerful societal voices supported by simple economic rationale clash head-on with powerful interest groups on the commanding heights of the economy. In the aftermath of the investment-driven GDP growth, the Chinese leadership has to grapple with a more daunting task of rebalancing its economy.

Structural Change in the Reform Era

Macroeconomic trend and structural changes

China's economic growth was most rapid in three periods, namely the early Reform (1979–84), the post-Deng's Southern Tour Reform (1992–97), and the first years of the twenty-first century up to 2008. There were two periods of

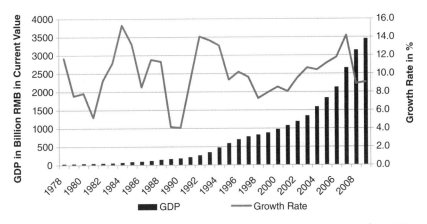

Figure 3.1 China's GDP growth, 1978–2009. Source: National Bureau of Statistics (NBS).

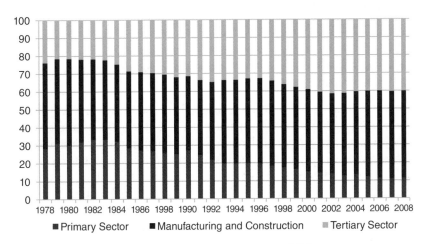

Figure 3.2 Industrial structure by shares in GDP. Source: NBS.

instability and dramatic changes in both growth and inflation, namely the early Reform (1981–84) and the post-Tiananmen period (1989–92). In all the three growth periods, the economy achieved an average growth rate of at least 9% (Figure 3.1). In terms of macroeconomic stability, the last period was marked by high growth and low inflation.

The growth is concurrently a process of rapid industrialization characterized by growth of modern industries and a relative decline of traditional agriculture. As shown in Figure 3.2, the manufacturing and service sectors have grown at a much faster pace than the primary sectors. The manufacturing and construction sectors in particular have become the sectors with the greatest economic weight. The strengthening of the manufacturing industry since the mid-1990s has been in accordance with the fundamental changes in the principal growth dynamics from consumption to investment.

The changes in industrial structure are equally sweeping in terms of employment structure. From 1978 to 2008, and especially since the mid-1990s, there had been a consistent and significant shift from primary to modern sectors, in particular the tertiary sector. The share of modern sector employment has more than doubled as the Chinese economy modernizes and industrializes. The most drastic changes observable were the 40% fall in the share of agriculture and the 150% increase in the labor force in the service sector. Changes in employment structure also took place in terms of the ownership of modern enterprises. The SOE employment contracted most rapidly in the late 1990s, when the conversion of small and medium enterprises shed 40% of SOE employment under the Zhu reform. The rise of the private sector since the mid-1990s has made it the major employer of urban labor (86 million, 40% of the mid-1990s urban labor force), a defining feature of the Chinese economy as a mixed economy.

Structural changes in growth dynamics and national income distribution

A very important aspect of China's economic transformation is the distribution of national income. This dynamic process of distribution is primarily the product and driving force of the process of economic growth. Until the Zhu reform, as shown in Figure 3.3, China's economic growth in the reform era had been driven by domestic consumption. Since then, especially when the new macroeconomic architecture was installed, state-driven investment and net export became more important. This is especially true under the Hu–Wen leadership, when investment consistently outstripped consumption as the key contributing factor to overall economic growth.

The different dynamics of economic growth correspond with shifts in national income distribution patterns. In general, the structural distribution of national income in the reform era is characterized by the initial fall and subsequent rise of the share of government (Figure 3.4). The first stage of the reform (1978–92) resulted in quite drastic structural shifts that favor the household and enterprise sectors at the cost of government revenue, while the later stages marked a gradual but decisive reversal of the trend, as the share of government expanded steadily at the cost of others, in particular the household sector.

The expansion of government sector share in total GDP has key implications for the contemporary Chinese economy. For one thing, the economic oppor-

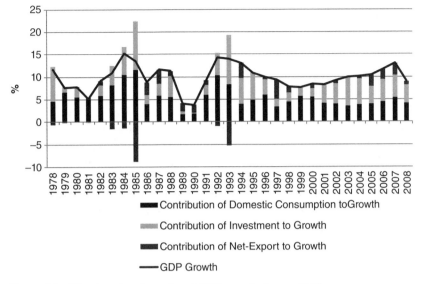

Figure 3.3   The changing dynamics of GDP growth. Source: NBS.

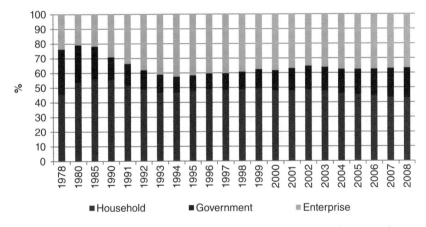

Figure 3.4   Structural distribution of national income. Source: Based on NBS data.

tunities and fruits of growth are redistributed from entrepreneurs and hard-working middle and lower-class wage-earners to various state agents. In other terms, economic benefits tend to accrue to the political and economic elites who already enjoy various commanding positions. Meanwhile, rapid expansion of income gaps has become the norm since the early 1990s. Measured in terms of the Gini Index, China started the reform with a relatively low Gini

Index of 0.28, but in merely 30 years it had reached 0.47 in 2009, with the top 10% of households earning 22 times more than the lowest 10%, making China among the most economically unequal societies in the world.[32]

Chinese Economic Reform at the Crossroads

The three periods of reform each have their unique characteristics. The first wave of reform was essentially the work of millions of passionate entrepreneurs from the grassroots, including reform-minded CCP cadres backed by charismatic leadership, with a shared belief that private wealth and national development were somehow neatly connected goals. There were strong wills to reform at the top and equally strong entrepreneurial drives from below. The second wave of reform had gradually nurtured the organizational structure and economic institutions, while maintaining the strong will from the top, but the dynamics from the bottom was increasingly replaced by a systemic drive from the state. With the onset of the third wave, the organizational structure and economic institutions seemed to have closed much of their access to the grassroots and were open only for the organized political and economic elites; the reformers and the reform itself were somewhat stunted by the giant organizational creations and by the chief beneficiaries of reforms, especially the new political and economic elites who are enjoying exclusive access to opportunities.

The Chinese economy is now characterized by huge economic imbalance and income inequality. The growth pattern based on simple extensive mobilization of cheap labor, land, natural resources, and capital from the state credit system will certainly meet its end once the demographic structure approaches its inevitable shift in the next decade, not to mention the resource depletion and the threat of inflation.

In the next period of time, the Chinese economic reform will likely face harsher political and economic tests, the outcome of which will determine China's future course of development. If organized interests could be legally constrained and the closed access order could gradually be opened, there is still hope that China could disentangle itself from the conundrum and start new rounds of reform. In the event of the contrary, reform may give way to some other more drastic changes and rapid social movements.

Notes

1   Lawrence *et al.* (2001).
2   Wu (2001: 15–17).
3   Naughton (1994: 141). For analysis of rural changes in the post-Mao era, see Unger (2002); Zweig (1997); and Zhou (1996).

4 Naughton (2008: 240).
5 Naughton (1994: 141).
6 Ibid., 200–02.
7 Ibid., 103–04.
8 Yang and Yang (2007: 78–81).
9 Zheng (2007: 141).
10 Wong and Bird (2008).
11 Lardy (1998: 62–64).
12 Wedeman (2007: 53–55).
13 Naughton (1994: 280–81).
14 Fewsmith (1994: 226–28).
15 Zhao (1993).
16 Wedeman (2007: Chapter 7).
17 For a detailed account of Zhu's measures in 1993, see Brahm (2002: Chapter 1).
18 Zheng (2000).
19 For a detailed account of the tax-sharing system, see Wong and Bird (2008).
20 On China's SOE reforms, see Steinfeld (1998).
21 Garnet et al. (2006).
22 Naughton (2008: 313).
23 Wu (2005: 198–99).
24 Naughton (2008: 313).
25 Ministry of Finance Circular, Xinhua News Agency, January 20, 2010.
26 Yueh (2010: 51–53).
27 China National Bureau of Statistics Circular, Xinhua News Agency, March 24, 2010.
28 On China's migrant workers, see Murphy (2002) and Solinger (1999).
29 Sun and Zhang (2007).
30 On the impact of the "Scientific Development Outlook" policy on poverty reduction, see Donaldson (2011).
31 "China 2009 GDP Growth Up to 9.1%." China Daily, July 2, 2010.
32 Chen Jia, "Country's Wealth Divide Past Warning Level," China Daily, May 10, 2010.

References

Brahm, L. J. 2002. *Zhu Rongji and the Transformation of Modern China*. Singapore: John Wiley & Sons.

Donaldson, J. A. 2011. *Small Works: Poverty and Economic Development in Southwestern China*. Ithaca, NY: Cornell University Press.

Fewsmith, J. 1994. *Dilemma of Reform in China*. New York: M. E. Sharpe.

Garnet, R., Ligang Song, and Yang Yao. 2006. "Impact and Significance of State-owned Enterprise Reform." In Belton M. Fleischer et al., eds., *China, Policy Reform and Chinese Markets: Progress and Challenges*. Cheltenham, UK: Edward Elgar, pp. 40–42.

Lardy, N. 1998. *China's Unfinished Economic Revolution*. Washington, DC: The Brookings Institution.

Lawrence, J. Lau, Yingyi Qian, and Gerard Roland. 2001. "Reform Without Losers: An Interpretation for China's Dual-Track Approach to Transition." *Journal of Political Economy* 108, 1: 120–43.

Murphy, R. 2002. *How Migrant Labor is Changing Rural China*. Cambridge: Cambridge University Press.

Naughton, B. 1994. *Growing Out of the Plan: Chinese Economic Reform 1978–1993*. Cambridge: Cambridge University Press.

Naughton, B. 2008. *The Chinese Economy: Transition and Growth*. Cambridge, MA: MIT Press.

Solinger, D. J. 1999. *Contesting Citizenship in Urban China: Peasant Migrants, the State, and the Logic of the Market*. Berkeley, CA: University of California Press.

Steinfeld, E. S. 1998. *Forging Reform in China: The Fate of State-Owned Industry*. Cambridge: Cambridge University Press.

Sun, Lijian and Shengxing Zhang. 2007. "An Externally Dependent Economy and Real Estate Bubbles." In Ross Garnaut and Ligang Song, eds., *China: Linking Markets for Growth*. Canberra: National University of Australia Press, pp. 360–61.

Unger, J. 2002. *The Transformation of Rural China*. New York: M. E. Sharpe.

Wedeman, A. 2007. *From Mao to Market*. Cambridge: Cambridge University Press.

Wong, C. and R. Bird. 2008. "China's Fiscal System: A Work in Progress." In Loren Brandt and Thomas G. Rawski, eds., *China's Great Economic Transformation*. Cambridge: Cambridge University Press, pp. 431–35.

Wu, Jinglian. 2005. *Understanding and Interpreting China's Economic Reform*. Mason, OH: Thomson South-Western.

Wu, Xiang. 2001. *Zhongguo nongcun gaige shilu* (Veritable Records of China's Rural Reform). Hangzhou: Zhejiang People's Publishing House.

Yang, Yongzhi and Yang Zhigang. 2007. *Zhongguo caizheng zhidu gaige 30 nian* (Thirty Years of China's Fiscal Reform). Shanghai: Shanghai People's Publishing House.

Yueh, L. 2010. *Economy of China*. Cheltenham, UK: Edward Edgar.

Zhao, Suisheng. 1993. "Deng Xiaoping's Southern Tour: Elite Politics in Post-Tiananmen China." *Asian Survey* 33, 8: 739–56.

Zheng, Yongnian. 2000. *Zhu Rongji xinzheng* (The New Deal of Zhu Rongji). Singapore and London: World Scientific.

Zheng, Yongnian. 2007. *De Facto Federalism: Reform and Dynamics of Central–Local Relations*. Singapore and London: World Scientific.

Zhou, K. 1996. *How the Farmers Changed China: Power of the People*. Boulder, CO: Westview Press.

Zweig, D. 1997. *Freeing China's Farmers: Rural Restructuring in the Reform Era*. Armonk, NY: M. E. Sharpe.

Chapter 4

Globalization

The critical accounts of the economic transformation of contemporary China should emphasize not only the reform from a command economy to a market-oriented one, but also the process of opening up. After three decades of opening to the outside world, China is now an integral part of the world economy.

China's openness in the post-Mao era can be divided into three phases. The first was the 1978 economic reform initiated by Deng Xiaoping. In the pre-reform era, the Chinese economy was isolated from the world. The economic stagnation forced the post-Mao leadership to rethink its development strategy and search for a new base of political legitimacy.[1] The government launched its program of economic opening, not only to bring in critical industrial materials and modern technologies, but to yield tremendous benefits in trading on the basis of comparative advantages.

The second phase started in 1992 after Deng's Southern Tour. The crackdown on the pro-democracy movement in 1989 resulted in unfavorable domestic and international repercussions for China's integration into the world economy. The conservatives within the leadership openly questioned the ideological legitimacy of economic reform and opening up when most Western governments imposed economic sanctions on China. Deng rejustified the opening policy during his Southern Tour by pointing to the benefits the country had gained from the initial stage of opening up. The new concept of "socialist market economy," which Deng coined during his trip, removed the ideological obstacle standing in China's way to joining the World Trade Organization (WTO). To join the WTO, China agreed to undertake a series of important commitments to better integrate into the world economy and to create a more predictable environment for trade and foreign investment in accordance with WTO rules. China managed to achieve a greater degree of

Contemporary China: A History since 1978, First Edition. Yongnian Zheng.
© 2014 John Wiley & Sons, Ltd. Published 2014 by John Wiley & Sons, Ltd.

openness in foreign trade before its WTO accession than was generally acknowledged.[2]

China's accession to the WTO on December 11, 2001 marked the third phase of its opening. Since then, the country has fulfilled a set of sweeping WTO accession commitments that required it to expand market access, protect intellectual property rights, and improve transparency. In the international market, "Made in China" products have shown a strong competitive edge, while "Outflows from China" have been greatly encouraged by the country's "go global" policy introduced in the early 2000s. As time went by, however, a huge gap between the Chinese perception and the Western expectation of trade integration has emerged. The West perceived that China has complied with international rules selectively to benefit its economy and at the expense of other countries. Many countries have filed an increasingly large number of cases against China with the WTO's trade tribunals.[3] With the rise of overseas acquisitions by Chinese companies, China is also regarded as a huge "vacuum cleaner," sucking enormous amounts of assets, businesses, and natural resources. In particular, given China's growing role as an investor in Africa, concerns over China's investment behavior are rising and Chinese companies are under increasing pressure to become more responsible global players.[4]

This chapter focuses on two major forces that have contributed significantly to China's integration into the world economy, namely, the liberalization of foreign trade and investment. In each section, we first measure China's integration and sketch the pattern of the integration, and then review the history of China's trade and investment policies over the aforementioned three phases. Each section concludes with a discussion about the impact of globalization on the Chinese and world economies, and the challenges both China and the world are facing in the process of globalization.

Foreign Trade

Over the past decades, China has made substantial efforts to reduce trade barriers and to make its economy more open to foreign competition. The fact that China's foreign trade exploded from US$21 billion in 1978 to US$2,563 billion in 2008 attested to its success. During the same period, China's share in world merchandise exports grew from 1 to 9%, while its import share increased from 1 to 7% (Figure 4.1).

Trade integration

The most frequently used indicator of trade integration is the share of exports and imports in GDP, or the trade openness ratio. It indicates not only the

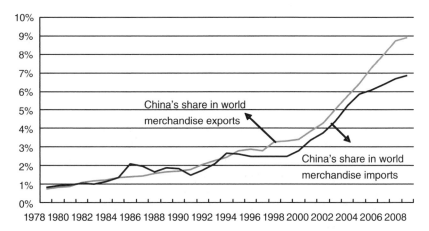

Figure 4.1   China's share in world merchandise exports and imports, 1978–2008. Source: International Trade Statistics, WTO.

intensity of a country's trade but also the degree of dependence on foreign markets of domestic producers and the degree of reliance of domestic demand on foreign supply.[5]

Before 1978, China was essentially insulated from the international system and its total merchandise trade amounted to no more than 10% of GDP, much lower than the world's average share of 30%. In 1978 when the reform began, China's foreign trade gained momentum, and by the end of 1992 its trade openness ratio reached a point of 34%, much higher than the 18% of India, 16% of the United States, and 15% of Brazil. The total trade share increased modestly in the following decade, partly due to the real appreciation of the *renminbi* between 1994 and 1997, and partly due to the 1997 Asian financial crisis. It was not until 2002 after China's accession to the WTO that its trade integration regained impetus. China's entry to the WTO noticeably affected the growth of international trade and the expansion of world output. In 2006, China's trade openness ratio reached a record level of 65%, compared with the 32% of India, 23% of the United States, and 21% of Brazil. Although the trade share regressed to 57% in 2008 due to the global recession, China remains a global trade power and plays a leading role in reshaping the post-crisis global economy.

The Evolution of China's Trade Polices

Centrally planned system before 1978

Prior to the trade liberalization in the late 1970s, China's share of world trade was less than 1%, and its exports and imports together amounted to only 10%

of its GDP in 1978. As a typical Soviet-style command economy, China's merchandise trade was determined almost entirely by central economic planning, and conducted by 12 state-owned foreign trade companies (FTCs). The state formulated a plan to bring in consumer goods and raw materials that were insufficient in the domestic market, as well as modern technologies that were essential for the country to achieve industrialization. Exports, on the other hand, were regarded simply as a source of foreign exchange to finance imports, rather than as a potential driving force for economic growth.

Under the planned trade system, prices were insulated from the influence of the world market, and played little or no role in the allocation of resources. In effect, export producers quoted the same price for goods sold in the international market as well as domestic market from the FTCs, and did not have any claim to foreign exchange income from those exports. Therefore, producers of export goods had no incentive to expand their international sales, and were insensitive to the demands of the international market and to the fluctuation in exchange rates. Without price mechanism, the composition of China's export was not based on its comparative advantage in labor-intensive products. Indeed, the economy relied heavily on the revenue from the export of petroleum products. Import prices were also distorted by economic planning and currency policy. Most imports were priced at a level that was similar to those of comparable domestic goods to protect domestic companies against foreign competition. For imports that had no domestic equivalents, domestic pricing was determined by the cost of imports converted to domestic currency at the official exchange rate. Since the currency was fixed at an overvalued level during that period, it subsidized the high-priority imports of machinery, equipment, and raw materials which could not be produced domestically.

Decentralization, 1978–92

During this period, the government dismantled the centrally planned trade regime by expanding trading rights, reforming pricing mechanisms and modifying the foreign exchange system. While policy instruments such as substantial tariff and non-tariff barriers were widely adopted to protect the domestic market, they were still conducive to China's opening up as they were less restrictive than the centrally planned regime.[6] As a result, China's foreign trade soared from US$21 billion in 1978 to US$166 billion in 1992, and its share of world trade grew steadily from 0.9% in 1978 to 2.2% in 1992.

Export-processing (EP) played a central role in this stage of transition. It first appeared in 1978 when Hong Kong businesses signed EP contracts with companies in the Guangdong province. Legalized and promoted by the government in 1979, this form of trade swiftly expanded to special economic zones (SEZs) first and then to the entire coastal region, creating huge export-processing zones (EPZs). Domestic enterprises engaged in EP were eligible for tariff exemptions. Foreign investors were also allowed to establish joint ventures and foreign-owned companies in SEZs and other coastal provinces, and foreign invested enterprises (FIEs) are entitled to sidestep China's complex import controls.

The development of EP had two consequences for the economy. One was a dualistic trade regime.[7] EP trade integrated rapidly into the world economy, accounting consistently for more than 40% of the total trade since 1992. FIEs also became crucial players in foreign trade, as exports increased from 1% in 1985 to 20% in 1992 and imports from 5% to 33% during the same period. The traditional trade system, however, remained much more insulated from the international economy. Tariff and non-tariff barriers suppressed the involvement of domestic companies in foreign trade. The other consequence was the shift of China's export to labor-intensive products. Manufactured goods replaced petroleum products as the main contributor to export growth. For instance, China's textile exports escalated from US$2.54 billion in 1980 to US$8.58 billion in 1992, and its world share increased from 4.6% in 1980 to 7.3% in 1992.

With the decentralization of foreign trade, trading rights, one of the most important non-tariff barriers adopted by the government, were no longer limited to the 12 state-owned foreign trade companies. By 1988, over 5,000 domestic companies had been authorized to conduct foreign trade. Like FIEs, some large state-owned manufacturing enterprises were also granted direct trading rights. Even for companies without trading rights, imports and exports could be conducted through transactions with specialized trading companies. Moreover, the number of commodities with limited trading rights was drastically reduced.

In addition to the expansion of trading rights, the reform of the exchange rate system made trade behavior more sensitive to market signals. The government introduced a foreign exchange retention system in 1979, which allowed EP companies, provincial governments, and industrial ministries to retain a share of their foreign exchange earnings. In order to stimulate export growth, retention rates were set up at various levels.[8] Preferential rates were given to exports conducted by companies under local management in 1979; new forms of trade such as processing and compensation trade enjoyed higher rates in 1982, and specified regions and sectors also received preferential retention rates by 1986. Hence, exporters were highly motivated to expand international trade since they could finance imports with retained foreign exchange.

Moreover, the government steadily and substantially devalued the Chinese currency (*renminbi* or *yuan*) over this period. Before opening up, China maintained an overvalued currency that simply made losses on export products. These losses were usually offset by the profits on imported goods within individual FTCs; if an FTC kept incurring net losses, the Ministry of Foreign Trade would subsidize the company with the proceeds from other profitable FTCs. The need to revise exchange rate policy became urgent for the government in 1980 as aggregate import profits failed to cover aggregate export losses. To solve the problem, the central government set up an internal settlement rate of 2.8 *yuan* to the US dollar in 1981 (abolished in 1984), and gradually adjusted the official exchange rate to 3.5 *yuan* in 1986. Although the official exchange rate remained stable in the following three years, the depreciation of the *renminbi* actually continued when a formal swap market for foreign exchange was introduced in late 1986. The swap market traded foreign exchange through public auction. Since foreign exchange was scarce at that time, its price was continuously driven high by market force. As a result, a market swap rate and an official rate existed side by side. For a country which was in transition from the command economy to the market system, the dual exchange rate regime not only ensured the price stability of import goods but indirectly subsidized export enterprises by increasing their earnings in domestic currency.

When China moved into a market-oriented trading system, some conventional trade policies in the market economy such as tariffs and non-tariff barriers were also developed. Beginning in the early 1980s, as the government gradually dismantled the centrally planned trade system, it relied heavily on import tariffs to protect the domestic market. China's average statutory tariff rate stood as high as 56% in 1982 and stayed at that level for the next decade. Due to tariff exemptions on goods imported via EP, China's tariff revenues as a percentage of the total import value were much lower than the average statutory tariffs. As more EP imports were eligible for tariff exemption, the ratio dropped dramatically in the mid-1980s, from 16% in 1985 to 5% in 1992. The tariffs played a positive role in China's transformation, since they were less restrictive than a centrally planned system. To some extent, it was inevitable for a country to adopt these policies if it was determined to open up gradually, so that the transformation would be achieved with minimum economic disruption and relative social stability. The same can be said of non-tariff barriers such as licenses and quotas.

Harmonization with international standards, 1993–2001

Tariff reduction was one of the most important efforts made by the Chinese government in the years before the WTO accession. After the government introduced high tariff walls to control and regulate imports in the 1980s, by 1991 the unweighted average tariff rate of China stood at 44% while the average tariff rate of the world was 13%. A transition occurred in 1992 when China standardized the naming and coding of commodities in accordance with international practice and then lowered the tariff rate to 40%. The tariff reduction on a wide range of items has continued ever since. China's tariff rate was reduced at an annual 10% from 1991 to 2001, and by the eve of WTO accession it had declined to 15%, close to the 10% of the world average.

Meanwhile, China eliminated numerous non-tariff barriers. In terms of trading rights, joint venture trading companies were set up for the first time in 1997, followed by the establishment of private trading companies in 1998. In early 1999, large industrial enterprises were allowed to conduct foreign trade as long as they registered with the Ministry of Foreign Trade. By 2001, the trading rights were expanded to almost 35,000 domestic companies of all types. The number of tariff lines subject to import licenses and quotas was also reduced from 1,247 in 1992 to 257 in 2001.

China also made significant strides in its foreign exchange reform by unifying the official and swap rates. After the introduction of the swap market in 1986 the gap between the market swap rate and official exchange rate kept widening. In 1993, the official rate was set at 5.72 *yuan*, while foreign exchange was traded at 8.72 *yuan* in the swap market. More than 80% of foreign exchange trade was conducted in the swap market, while less than 20% of foreign exchange was sold to designated banks at the official exchange rate. Consequently, China's official foreign reserves shrank dramatically in the early 1990s. It incurred a huge trade deficit of US$12 billion in 1993.

To remedy the problem, the government abolished the dual exchange rate regime in 1994 and fixed the official exchange rate at the market clearing rate of 8.72 *yuan*. Since Chinese goods suddenly became cheap in the world market, China's exports almost tripled from 1994 to 2001. Its trade balance was in surplus and has remained positive ever since. Although the government deprived domestic enterprises of the right to retain their foreign exchange earnings in 1994, the enterprises could purchase foreign currency as long as they provided proof of commercial contracts. Besides, the government allowed FIEs to keep their foreign exchange earnings, and permitted limited purchase of foreign exchange by households. With a series of measures to relax restrictions on foreign exchange trading under other current account items, China officially achieved the full convertibility of the *renminbi* under current accounts at the end of 1996.

The currency appreciated steadily during the period 1994–96 until the outbreak of the 1997 Asian financial crisis. The decision to keep the *renminbi* stable during the crisis earned China high praise from its Asian neighbors, but it contained seeds of trouble as the currency stability was achieved by pegging the *renminbi* against the US dollar (USD). The appreciation of the *renminbi* did not resume after the crisis; instead, between the beginning of 1998 and mid-2005, the *renminbi* remained at between 8.27 and 8.28, depreciating by 15% in real effective terms. When China's exports started to grow swiftly after 2002, the strategy of pegging the *renminbi* against the USD has become China's key policy issue that is subject to international criticism.

Membership in the WTO, 2002–

China's membership in the WTO has substantial implications for its trade integration into the world economy. While China has seen its global trade figures increase drastically since joining the WTO in December 2001, it is also becoming increasingly more involved in WTO disputes, both as a respondent and as a complainant.

China has made significant progress in many aspects of trade liberalization since its accession. In terms of tariff reduction, China has implemented its tariff commitments timely each year. For example, China started to reduce and eliminate tariffs on information technology products in accordance with the Information Technology Agreement (ITA) in 2002, and succeeded in eliminating all ITA tariffs in 2005 from a pre-WTO accession average of 13.3%.[9] China's average statutory tariff rate dropped to 8.6% in 2008, close to the world average rate of 7.1%. Also, the country has removed various non-tariff barriers by applying international norms to its testing and standards administration, revising regulations requiring local content, and improving overall regulatory transparency. Moreover, the country revised its Foreign Trade Law in 2004, making trading rights automatically available for all FIEs through a registration process.[10] In 2005, China took a critical step in the reform of its foreign exchange regime: it abolished the previous USD peg and introduced a managed float system in which the *renminbi* was allowed to trade in a narrow band against a basket of other currencies. The *renminbi* immediately appreciated against the USD by 2.1%, and the real effective exchange rate of *renminbi* rose by almost 20% between mid-2005 and mid-2008. This appreciation was disrupted by the 2008 financial crisis, similar to what happened after the 1998 Asian financial crisis.

While China appears to be in compliance with WTO rules in most areas, recent years have seen more and more disputes brought against China. In the first few years after its accession to the WTO in 2001, China had been involved in only one dispute. However, between 2006 and 2009, 16 cases involving a variety of industries were initiated against China. Meanwhile China has also filed more cases against other countries within the tribunal of the WTO. China filed only three cases in the first seven years of its membership, but it filed three cases of the total 14 cases in 2009. As the exporting country facing most antidumping (AD) charges, China has also become a leading user of the AD measures. China had initiated 178 antidumping measures by the end of 2009, 148 of which were submitted after its accession to the WTO in 2001. These measures affected imports from 26 countries or regions, and thus raised concerns about the transparency and procedural fairness of China's AD practice.

What draws most criticism from the international community has been China's currency policy since the 2008 financial crisis. To maintain financial stability and to stimulate exports, China decided to halt the gradual appreciation of the *renminbi* and pegged it against the USD once again in the wake of the crisis. Consequently, the *renminbi* depreciated by about 5% in real effective terms between August 2008 and June 2009, and China's foreign reserves rose by US$590 billion from mid-2008 to the end of 2009.

Impacts of Foreign Trade

China's export structure has changed over the past three decades. In the early 1980s, petroleum dominated China's exports, and primary goods accounted for more than 50% of total merchandise exports. In the 1990s, China's exports dramatically shifted from natural resource-based commodities to labor-intensive products.

While the enormous population gives China a comparative advantage over developed countries in labor-intensive industries, some industrial countries are beginning to feel the pressure in the capital-intensive arena as China expands its share even in high-tech industries. The value of China's high-tech exports surged from US$10 billion (6.8% of total exports) in 1995 to US$416 billion (29% of total exports) in 2008.[11] China had overtaken the US, the EU, and Japan as the largest high-tech exporter in the world in 2006.[12]

The rapidly changing export structure, however, does not make the traditional notion of comparative advantage implausible. Neither does it constitute evidence that Chinese industries have moved up to the high end of the global value chain. In fact, processing of exports accounted for 82% of total high-tech exports in 2008. China's exports of high-tech products thus rely heavily on prior imports of high-tech inputs. The country has emerged as a major producer and exporter of integrated circuits and electronic components in recent years. Its exports of these products were about US$43 billion in 2008, accounting for 11% of the world's total. At the same time, the country is the world's largest importer of integrated circuits and electronic components. Its imports of these products were worth US$148 billion in 2008, accounting for 30% of the world's total. This phenomenon implies that the contribution of Chinese enterprises to high-tech exports under processing of exports is not advanced technology, but cheap labor, the country's comparative advantage.

China's rise as a global trade power has also posed momentous opportunities and challenges for the world economy. The growth in trade between China and the US has been robust. Bilateral trade, including both exports and imports, grew from US$1 billion in 1978 to US$366 billion in 2009. Particularly, US exports to China increased by nearly 270% after China's accession to the WTO, from US$19 billion in 2001 to US$72 billion in 2009. China's exports to the US also grew dramatically, rising from US$102 billion in 2001 to US$296 billion in 2009.

As the economic relation between China and the US became closer, China's trade surplus with the US had exploded from US$83 billion in 2001 to US$267 billion in 2008. With China accounting for more than 40% of total US trade deficit, and with Chinese foreign exchange reserves approaching US$2 trillion, trade disputes between the two countries have continued to rise, turning their economic relation into a political issue. Overshadowing all trade disputes is the *renminbi* exchange rate. While the US claims that an undervalued *renminbi* helps Chinese exporters gain unfair advantage in the international market, China considers its currency policy as merely a protective shield for a fledging economy, which is acceptable under IMF rules. Criticism of China's currency policy also spread to developing countries like India, Indonesia, and South Africa. These countries are fearful of a loss of competitiveness relative to China if they let their currency rise against USD and of hot money inflows if they do not appreciate their currencies when USD weakens. Under international pressure, China announced in June 2010 that it would stop pegging its currency against USD and allow the gradual rise of the *renminbi*. However, there has been minimal rise in the currency's value since then. China's currency regime continues to take center stage on the international scene as its trade surpluses uphold its escalating trend.

While China's trade surplus with the US and the EU continues to rise, its trade deficit with Asia ballooned from US$6 billion in 2001 to US$35 billion in 2009. Since China's accession to the WTO, Taiwan, Japan, and South Korea have all run a trade surplus with China. It is important to note that China is playing a role as the last stage assembler in the unique production system of East Asia: it imports intermediate products from other Asian economies, assembles them with its cheap labor, and then exports the final products to the third markets, mainly the US and the EU. The system is largely due to the rising labor cost in other Asian economies and China's liberalization of its foreign investment environment. Therefore, the widening US trade deficit with China equates to US trade deficit with all the trading partners involved in this production system.

Foreign Investment

China has launched several waves of opening up of its economy to attract foreign direct investment (FDI) since the early 1980s. It was not until 1992 that FDI flows started to flood China. FDI is particularly sensitive to political risk. Deng's Southern Tour in early 1992 greatly relieved the anxiety of foreign investors. As a result, FDI flows to China in that year dramatically grew by 152% over the previous year, and inward FDI amounted to a record level of 17% of the Chinese Gross Fixed Capital Formation (GFCF). Even in the wake of the Asian financial crisis in 1997, FDI flows to China remained relatively stable, dropping marginally by 11% in 1999. After its accession to the WTO, China's inward FDI has trended steadily upward, and in 2009 it attracted US$95 billion, accounting for 17% of total FDI flows to developing countries.

Although FDI outflows from China so far account for only a trivial portion of total world outward FDI, China has become an increasingly important FDI exporting country. China's outward FDI was minimal prior to 1978, but it began to take off in the early 1980s after the government released the country's first outward FDI policy to regulate overseas operations and investments. Within a year, the outward FDI increased from US$134 million in 1984 to US$629 million in 1985.[13] The second wave of FDI outflows was in 1991 when the government issued a policy to strengthen the management of overseas investment projects. Chinese outward FDI reached US$4 billion in 1992, more than four times that of the previous year. Recent years have seen a strong growth of FDI outflows from China as the central government introduced the "go global" policy in the early 2000s. According to the UNCTAD, outflows from China amounted to US$52 billion in 2008, accounting for 35% of the cumulative stock of Chinese outward FDI by the end of that one year. In 2009, China was the world's sixth largest outward investor.[14]

Pattern of Foreign Investment

Capital inflows

The distinctive feature of China's foreign investment has been the dominance of FDI in capital inflows. The country is an attractive destination for FDI. For those who seek market growth potential, China has a large untapped market in almost all kinds of industries; for those who seek efficiency, China has the competitive edge on labor-intensive industries; and for those who seek favorable policies, China provides preferential tax treatment for FIEs relative to domestic companies. For China, FDI constitutes a preferred form of capital inflow since it promotes the economic growth of the host country by bringing in technology, managerial expertise, and marketing channels along with capital.

The source of China's FDI inflows is mainly from the Asian economies such as Hong Kong and Taiwan. Table 4.1 shows the number of projects and value of actually utilized FDI by various sources during the period 1979–2008. Hong Kong is by far the biggest investor in China, accounting for 45% of total projects and 63% of the cumulative value of actual investment. Because of its specific advantages in export-oriented FDI and its unique links with China, Hong Kong was the first economy that seized investment opportunities when

Table 4.1   Cumulative FDI in China by source, 1979–2008. Source: Ministry of Commerce, China. Compiled by the author.

Country/Region	No. of Projects	%	Investment Actually Utilized (USD 100 m)	%
Total	659,885	100.0	8,991	100.0
Asia	508,012	77.0	5,631	62.6
Hong Kong	298,620	45.3	3,496	38.9
Taiwan	77,506	11.7	477	5.3
Republic of Korea	48,808	7.4	419	4.7
Japan	41,126	6.2	654	7.3
Singapore	17,372	2.6	378	4.2
Macao	11,988	1.8	82	0.9
Others	12,592	1.9	125	1.4
EU	28,274	4.3	616	6.8
North America	67,501	10.2	660	7.3
Canada	10,891	1.7	64	0.7
US	56,610	8.6	597	6.6
Free Islands	29,634	4.5	1,290	14.3
Others	26,464	4.0	794	8.8

China opened its door in the late 1970s, thus gaining the lion's share of foreign investment in China. It played a "transit" role for foreign companies with regional headquarters in the city.[15]

Other East Asian economies like Taiwan, Korea, and Singapore accounted for a crucial amount of FDI in China as well. In addition to geographic proximity, different stages of economic development could explain their substantial FDI in China. The capital flows to China helped these NIEs transfer their mature industries to China to exploit the latter's cheap labor force.

While China succeeded in attracting huge amounts of FDI from its neighbors in Asia, it failed to be an appealing destination for major industrial countries. The United States, together with Canada, the EU, and Japan only contributed 21% of the cumulative FDI in China over the 1979–2008 period, whereas developed countries contributed 87% of FDI worldwide in the same period. One possible reason for the unbalanced origin of FDI in China is that the investment from these industrialized countries was mainly motivated by market-seeking, and that from other Asian countries was for exports.[16]

In terms of sectoral distribution of FDI, manufacturing has attracted the largest part of FDI inflows. It accounted for 65% of the cumulative investment in the 1979–2008 period, while the services sector accounted for only 34%. In contrast, 35% of FDI went to the manufacturing sector worldwide in the 1987–2008 period while the services sector had a weight of 58% in the same period. This phenomenon could largely be attributed to China's comparative advantage in labor cost and the restrictions it has imposed on foreign entry into the critical services sector. However, it is observed that the concentration has shifted from secondary industries to tertiary industries since China's accession to the WTO. The services sector generated higher investments than manufacturing in 2008, accounting for almost 50% of total FDI utilized. For example, the value of FDI utilized in the financial sector rose to 15% in 2008, despite the sector's small share in the number of total projects.

Capital outflows

Three features have marked China's outward FDI. First, most of Chinese outward FDI has been directed to Asian economies, with which China has close cultural links. It is especially true for Hong Kong, which accounted for 67% of China's outward FDI stock by the end of 2009. As a bridge between mainland China and the rest of the world, Hong Kong provides well-rounded financial services and international business networks. Thus, it has been widely considered as the safest and most efficient place for firms from the Mainland to build their affiliates. Latin America, Africa, and Oceania together also accounted for 19% of China's outward FDI stock by the end of 2009. The large-scale investment there is considered resource-oriented as China needs enormous amounts of natural resources to sustain its economic growth. China's FDI in developed areas such as Europe and North America was less than 6% of the outward FDI stock, since market-seeking has been the main force behind Chinese investment there. Second, the bulk of Chinese outward FDI was carried out by stated-owned enterprises (SOEs). By the end of 2009, more than 69% of Chinese outward FDI had been made by SOEs, and all the ten largest multinational Chinese enterprises by outward FDI stock are SOEs. Third, sectoral distribution of China's outward FDI has been diversified. By the end of 2009, the business services sector had accounted for the largest share of Chinese outward FDI (30%), followed by finance (19%), mining and petroleum (17%), wholesale and retail (15%), transportation and storage (7%), and manufacturing (6%).

The Evolution of Foreign Investment Policies

Special economic zones, 1979–92

China's inward FDI and foreign loans were extremely small prior to 1979. The "joint-venture" law passed by the National People's Congress in July 1979 provided the legal framework for FDI by allowing foreign investors to establish equity joint ventures with Chinese partners. A series of related laws were also passed in the subsequent years to regulate taxation and management of these FIEs.

Moreover, the importance of the establishment of the first four SEZs cannot be overstated as they attracted inflows of foreign investment, technology, know-how, and managerial expertise. Since the SEZs were established to encourage export processing and foreign investment, their location was of great significance. Of the four SEZs, three (Shenzhen, Zhuhai, and Shantou) are located in Guangdong province and one (Xiamen) in Fujian. The two coastal provinces are adjacent to Hong Kong, Macao, Taiwan, and Southeast Asian countries, which facilitated not only the imports of raw materials and intermediate products essential for export processing but also access to the SEZs for foreign investors. Since both Guangdong and Fujian are the home provinces of many overseas Chinese in Hong Kong, Macao, and Southeast Asian countries, they were attractive investment destinations for these overseas Chinese.

To encourage foreign investment inflows to the SEZs, the government offered not only preferential treatment in taxes, but also a variety of conveniences to facilitate operations. For example, corporate income tax was generally lower in the SEZs than in other parts of China, and the FIEs in the SEZs also enjoyed more tax holidays than those offered under the national tax legislation. In the SEZs, raw materials and production facilities were imported duty-free and taxes on some exports such as mineral oil, tobacco, and liquor were reduced greatly. In addition to the tax incentives, the administrative and customs procedures in the SEZs were simplified and streamlined, which greatly reduced the operation costs of the FIEs.

Every major wave of liberalization in China was marked by the creation of more SEZs.[17] In 1984, the central government decided to launch a new wave of liberalization by opening another 14 coastal cities.[18] In 1985, the government established three Open Economic Zones (OEZs) in the Yangtze River Delta, Pearl River Delta, and the South Fujian triangle area. In 1986, the government turned the Shandong Peninsula and the East Liaoning Peninsula into OEZs. Hainan Island was granted a full SEZ status in 1987. In 1989, Shanghai's Pudong Development Zone was established.

Transition period, 1993–2001

After the brief interlude of the Tiananmen crackdown, FDI inflows resumed and grew rapidly. Between 1992 and 1993, there was a surge in China's inward FDI. Twenty-eight cities and eight regions in the Yangtze River Delta were opened to the outside world. Foreign investment was also welcomed in some previously forbidden sectors such as domestic retail, finance, real estate, and shipping. As a result, FDI flows to China in 1992 dramatically reached US$11 billion, and inward FDI amounted to a record level of 17% of the Chinese GFCF.

The investment boom in China started to cool down from 1994 and the decline lasted for the rest of the decade. Several reasons can be identified. First, macroeconomic conditions were unfavorable for foreign investment. In 1994, the central government adopted monetary and fiscal policies to curb inflation, which suppressed aggregate demand and economic growth. When the economy began to recover, the Asian financial crisis broke out in 1997. The crisis reduced both domestic and foreign demands, which rendered many FIEs unprofitable. Second, there was increasing competition for inward FDI. At that time, other transitional economies in Asia, South America, and Central and Eastern Europe went on an all-out push to encourage foreign investment. Third, China's State Council announced in 1995 that it would reimpose duties for machinery, equipment, and materials imported by FIEs. Although the policy was amended in 1997 to exempt FIEs in some industries from import duties, it discouraged new FDI projects and reinvestment from the existing ones.[19]

During this period, the Chinese government began to pay attention to the structure of FDI and its impact on the upgrading of domestic industries. The State Council released its first guidelines for industries on foreign investment in 1995. All industries were divided into three categories based on whether FDI was encouraged, restricted, or forbidden. Over the years, the guidelines have been updated several times. By adjusting industries' foreign investment, the government aims to promote resource conservation and environmental protection, bring in cutting-edge technology, and even balance regional economic development.

Going global, 2002–

After China's WTO accession, its inward FDI regained momentum. Since 2003, the country has been ranked one of the top destinations worldwide for foreign investment. It has also become a critical source of outward FDI. According to UNCTAD, rapid economic growth at home, high commodity prices, and outward FDI liberalization have been feeding a boom in outward FDI from China.[20] Among these factors, China's "go global" policy at the beginning of this century has played a decisive role.

The "go global" policy has been stressed for a number of reasons. First, as the world's leading exporting economy, China has been facing rising trade protectionism that hinders its access to existing export markets. The cheap "Made in China" goods have allegedly impacted negatively on some sunset industries in developed countries and thus have encountered strong resistance from local enterprises. Outward FDI, however, establishes affiliate enterprises and factories in destination markets, which not only creates local employment but also serve the markets better by customizing products to accommodate the preference of local customers. Second, merger and acquisition of overseas companies has helped Chinese enterprises obtain brand assets of local companies. Third, outward FDI in resource-abundant countries has been driven by China's large and increasing domestic demand for natural resources to fuel its economic growth.

To promote outward FDI, the government has streamlined approval procedures and relaxed the restrictions on the use of foreign exchange for outward investment. Two policy banks (China Development Bank and China Export and Import Bank) and state-owned commercial banks have also made available below-market rate loans to Chinese enterprises on the priority list for overseas investments. To protect the legal rights and interests of Chinese enterprises investing abroad, China has ratified double taxation treaties with 88 countries and bilateral investment treaties with 121 countries.[21] Chinese enterprises, especially large SOEs operating in priority sectors, have benefited tremendously from the country's "go global" strategy.

While China has actively promoted its business overseas, it has also made attempts to protect its own industries against foreign investment in recent years. In 2006, the Chinese government introduced the "indigenous innovation" strategy to bolster national technological capabilities, and to transform China into an "innovation-oriented" nation by 2010 and a global leader in science and technology by 2050. To boost indigenous innovation, the government decided to make a strategic shift from the resource intensive or input-driven type of development to a technology-intensive one. It has been actively developing technology policies to facilitate the transition, including the promotion of its own technology standards and the requirement of domestic innovation in government procurement. These indigenous innovation policies soon created deep concerns among foreign businesses and governments in the post-2008 financial crisis era. The technology standards strategy was seen as a new form of protectionism in violation of WTO terms. As a result, the Chinese government decided to drop the controversial policies and delink indigenous innovation from government procurement. However, doubt still remains as to how China's techno-nationalism will affect its environment for foreign investment.[22]

Impacts of Foreign Investment

FDI constitutes a major factor in the expansion of China's foreign trade. Over the past three decades, the country's exports have greatly benefited from foreign investment. In 1981, China's exports of FIEs were a negligible US$30 million, or less than 1% of China's total exports. In 2008, these exports soared to a remarkable US$791 billion, or more than 55% of total exports. Even in the wake of the Asian financial crisis, the exports of FIEs increased by 8%, while those of domestic companies decreased by 5%. Without foreign investment, China's export-led economic growth strategy would not have been so successful. Moreover, most of the FIE exports were under the export processing (EP) regime; it is proved that FDI plays a greater role in economic growth in EP countries than in import substitution economies.[23] The imports of FIEs also grew drastically to US$619 billion in 2008, or 55% of China's total imports. The imports of FIEs have a great impact not only on the quantity and value of China's imports but also on import prices.

Besides, FDI has contributed to structural changes of the Chinese economy through technology transfers and spillovers. Superior technology and know-how are the most important factors that distinguish FIEs from domestic firms. For example, the invention patents granted to FIEs in China were 16,391 in 2008, accounting for almost 30% of total invention patents. Considering FDI constitutes less than 10% of GFCF in China in recent years, foreign invention patents must have played a disproportionately significant role in propelling China's technological advancement and knowledge creation. Indeed, as China's high-tech exports rose from US$20 billion to US$354 billion, the share of FIEs in high-tech exports also grew steadily from 74% in 1998 to 88% in 2008. Although China still focuses on the final assembly stage of high-tech production, it was estimated that up to 30% of total technological progress in China could have been due to the effect of FDI.[24]

China's success in attracting FDI has raised concerns that this has been at the expense of other countries. In particular, China's FDI surge is a matter of concern to its Southeast Asian neighbors, since they have similar comparative advantage and also depend heavily on transnational corporations to drive their industrial, services, and export growth. Nonetheless, empirical studies show that China did not crowd-out FDI inflows into other Asian countries. A study based on the period 1986–2001 found that China did not deprive Southeast Asian economies of FDI. On the contrary, it helped them attract more FDI as part of the integrated production networks that handle most of their technology-based exports.[25]

However, FDI flows to China seem to have a negative impact on other regions. The OECD countries appear to be vulnerable to FDI diversion to China, particularly Japanese FDI diversion from OECD countries in favor of China as Japanese manufacturing companies seek to produce close to markets with great potential.[26] It was also found that although there was no substantial Chinese effect on FDI into Latin America as a whole, FDI flows to China did have a negative impact on those to Mexico until 2001 and those to Colombia after that year.[27]

As China's outward FDI has rapidly increased since the introduction of the "go global" policy, the country's impact on other economies has been rising. In particular, China's direct investment in Africa has drawn wide attention. As resource-seeking is the main consideration of China's outward FDI, major African recipient countries of FDI are all rich in natural resources, including Sudan, Zambia, Algeria, Nigeria, and South Africa. In recent years, China has also signed the Agreement on Bilateral Facilitation and Protection of Investment with 28 African countries. By the end of 2009, the country's outward FDI stock in Africa had amounted to US$9.3 billion. Though China accounts for less than 2% of total FDI stock in Africa, the country tends to invest in African countries plagued by human rights abuses, corruption, and repressive regimes. This leads the international community to urge China to be a more responsible investor in Africa. Moreover, it is alleged that China intends to use aid to achieve its political and economic goals in Africa. According to the OECD, China's official development aid has helped African countries build infrastructure and politically important public buildings so that its SOEs can receive political support for enormous natural resources FDI deals.[28] There are growing concerns that China's presence in Africa is new colonialism or presents this opportunity.

In sum, China has taken impressive steps over the past three decades to open its economy. Like its domestic economic reform, China's openness did not follow a rigid and comprehensive blueprint; instead, it was characterized by pragmatism and gradualism. While China's economic power has profoundly changed the world economy, the world has been also holding the country fully accountable to international rules and its responsibility to maintain the stability of the world economy. Given the changing characteristics of current globalization trends and the emerging spread of global value chains, both opportunities and challenges lie ahead for China and the rest of the world.

Notes

1   Zheng (2004).
2   Lardy (2002).
3   "China Exploiting Trade Loopholes," *International Herald Tribune*, February 16, 2010.
4   OECD (2008: 9).
5   OECD (2005: 177).
6   Lardy (2002: 39).
7   Naughton (2007: 386).
8   Lardy (1992: 53).
9   US Trade Representative (2009).

10 China still reserves the trading rights of goods subject to tariff-rate quotas such as grains, cotton, and tobacco, which is allowed under the terms of China's Protocol of Accession to the WTO.
11 Xing (2010).
12 Meri (2009).
13 Ministry of Foreign Economic Relations and Trade (1985).
14 Hong Kong (China) ranked the fifth outward investor in 2009, with outward flows amounting to US$52 billion.
15 According to Naughton, about 1,000 foreign companies have their regional headquarters in Hong Kong, of which 256 are from the United States, 198 from Japan, and 106 from China.
16 Zhang (2000).
17 Naughton (2007: 409).
18 The 14 coastal cities include Dalian, Qinhuangdao, Tianjin, Yantai, Qingdao, Lianyungang, Nantong, Shanghai, Ningbo, Wenzhou, Fuzhou, Guangdong, Zhanjiang, and Beihai.
19 Wei and Liu (2001).
20 UNCTAD (2010).
21 OECD (2008).
22 On China's indigenous innovation policy and its techno-nationalism, see Pan and Zheng (2011a, b) and Zheng and Pan (2012).
23 Balasubramanyam et al. (1996).
24 Yao and Wei (2007).
25 Zhou and Lall (2005).
26 Eichengreen and Tong (2006).
27 Garcia-Herrero and Santabarbara (2005).
28 OECD (2008).

References

Balasubramanyam, V. N., S. Mohammed, and D. Sapsford. 1996. "Foreign Direct Investment and Growth in EP and IS countries." *Economic Journal* 106: 92–105.
Eichengreen, B. and H. Tong. 2006. "Fear of China." *Journal of Asian Economics* 17, 2: 226–40.
Garcia-Herrero, A. and D. Santabarbara. 2005. "Does China Have an Impact on Foreign Direct Investment to Latin America?" *China Economic Review* 18, 3: 266–86.
Lardy, N. R. 1992. *Foreign Trade and Economic Reform in China, 1978–1990.* Cambridge and New York: Cambridge University Press.
Lardy, N. R. 2002. *Integrating China into the Global Economy.* Washington, DC: The Brookings Institution.
Meri, T. 2009. *China Passes the EU in High-tech Exports.* Luxembourg: Eurostat, Science and Technology.
Ministry of Foreign Economic Relations and Trade. 1985. *Provisions Governing Control and Approval Procedures for Opening Non-Trade Enterprises Overseas.* Beijing.

Naughton, B. 2007. *The Chinese Economy: Transitions and Growth*. Cambridge, MA: MIT Press.

OECD. 2005. *Measuring Globalization. OECD Handbook on Economic Globalization Indicators*. Paris: OECD.

OECD. 2008. *OECD Investment Policy Review. China, Encouraging Responsible Business Conduct*. Paris: OECD.

Pan, Rongfang and Yongnian Zheng. 2011a. "Is China's Environment for Foreign Investors Deteriorating?" *EAI Background Brief 601*, East Asian Institute, National University of Singapore.

Pan, Rongfang and Yongnian Zheng. 2011b. "China's Indigenous Innovation Strategy." *EAI Background Brief 649*, East Asian Institute, National University of Singapore.

UNCTAD. 2010. *World Investment Report: Investing in a Low-Carbon Economy*. Geneva: UNCTAD.

US Trade Representative. 2009. *2009 Report to Congress on China's WTO Compliance*. Washington, DC: US Trade Representative.

Wei, Y. Q. and X. M. Liu. 2001. *Foreign Direct Investment in China*. Cheltenham, UK and Northampton, MA: Edward Elgar Publishing.

Xing, Y. Q. 2010. "China's High-tech Exports: Myth and Reality." *EAI Background Brief 506*, East Asian Institute, National University of Singapore.

Yao, S. and K. Wei. 2007. "Economic Growth in the Presence of FDI: The Perspective of Newly Industrializing Economics." *Journal of Comparative Economics* 35: 211–34.

Zhang, K. H. 2000. "Why Is U.S. Direct Investment in China so Small?" *Contemporary Economy Policy* 18, 1: 82–94.

Zheng, Yongnian. 2004. *Globalization and State Transformation in China*. Cambridge: Cambridge University Press.

Zheng, Yongnian and Rongfang Pan. 2012. "From Defensive to Aggressive Strategies: The Evolution of Economic Nationalism in China." In Anthony P. D'Costa, ed., *Globalization and Economic Nationalism in Asia*. Oxford: Oxford University Press, pp. 84–108.

Zhou, Y. P. and S. Lall. 2005. "The Impact of China's FDI Surge on FDI in South-East Asia: Panel Data Analysis for 1986–2001." *Transnational Corporations* 14, 1: 41–65.

Chapter 5

Civil Society

China's economic reform and the consequent economic transformation discussed in the last two chapters have also brought about radical social changes. The rise of civil society is a product of the legitimation of market economy by the Chinese state as a way of pursuing China's wealth and power. The development of a market-oriented economy has fundamentally changed the foundation of Chinese society from a Maoist ideology-based social order to an interest-based social order. While the market economy has created material conditions and economic infrastructure for the rise of civil society, it has also rendered a pluralistic and divided Chinese society. Different segments of society are demanding that their voices be heard. This chapter first examines how Chinese society has been transformed and then explores how the market-oriented reform has given rise to civil society by focusing on the emergence of the private sector, middle classes, non-governmental organizations (NGOs), and netizens.

The rise of civil society has implications for political changes in general and state–society relations in particular. In the next chapter, we will explore how civil society has staged resistance and protests on the one hand, and political and social participation on the other. In the chapters thereafter, we will discuss how the Chinese Communist Party (CCP) has attempted to restructure its political processes to expand its social basis by accommodating newly rising social forces, and thus explore different new sources of its political legitimacy.

Contemporary China: A History since 1978, First Edition. Yongnian Zheng.
© 2014 John Wiley & Sons, Ltd. Published 2014 by John Wiley & Sons, Ltd.

Market Economy and Political Interests

In the pre-reform era, the CCP organized Chinese society according to the Maoist ideology. After Deng came to power in the late 1970s, the leadership began to shift its emphasis to economics as a way of reorganizing society. During the 1980s, China achieved high rates of economic growth by expanding its market space. However, it was only after Deng's Southern Tour in 1992 that the Chinese leadership legitimized market economy as a way of promoting economic expansion and organizing society.

Market economy could have been legitimized in the 1980s. After the bitter and uncertain 30 years of experimentation following 1949, many leaders, especially Deng himself, realized that capitalism is a stage that cannot be easily skipped on the way to socialism. Although the CCP had an idea of capitalism drawing on Marx's nineteenth-century experience, the reform and open-door policy enabled Party cadres and government officials to see how capitalism had developed from the experiences of China's neighboring economies, especially the "four little dragons," namely, Hong Kong, Taiwan, Singapore, and South Korea, besides Japan and the United States. From all these societies, the leadership saw how capitalism had helped raise the standard of living of the vast majority of the people there, and enhanced their status in international arenas, goals that the CCP had fought for since its establishment. The impact of the experiences of the "four little dragons" on China's leaders has been substantial since they have shown that Chinese culture is not a barrier but a catalyst to economic growth.[1] The leaders realized that what was important was not cultural but institutional, and rapid economic growth could only come with an overhaul of the Chinese economic system. This was the motivation behind the decision of the leadership to implement economic reforms. Many social groups, especially young intellectuals, advocated publicly for capitalism in the belief that capitalism could pave the way for China to grow into a strong and affluent nation. Spurring the country on was the capitalist West, which was quite friendly to China in the 1980s. It took the view that China's market-oriented economic reform and open-door policy would eventually lead to two transformations of China: from a planned economy to a free market system, and from political authoritarianism to democracy.

The Chinese revolutionary leaders had quite different perceptions of the market economy at the time though.[2] At the practical level, they did not oppose the different forms of capitalistic experiment; ideologically, however, they remained wary of the effects of capitalism.[3] Capitalism only gained its foothold when the socialist system these leaders had fought so hard for proved increasingly incapable of providing for China's population on its own. It is a gradual process that is reflected in the changes in the official definition of China's economic system. At the CCP's Twelfth Party Congress in 1982, the leadership defined the country's economic system as one in which the "planned economy is the main pillar and market economy a supplementary element," implying that the market economy did not possess ideological legitimacy. Five years later in 1987, at the Thirteenth Party Congress, the market economy was finally placed on par with the planned economy when the leadership redefined the economic system as one "combining planned and market economies." However, during the 1989 pro-democracy movement and its aftermath, capitalism had come under serious attack. Conservative leaders regarded the pro-democracy movement as a result of the spread of capitalism as an idea and as a practice.[4]

Indeed, the legitimization of a market economy had not been an easy political task. In this process, Deng himself played a key role. He was known for his pragmatism throughout his entire political career and was not particularly against capitalism as a way to promote economic growth. While Mao emphasized "morality" or "virtue" as a way of motivating people's behavior, Deng seemed to favor "interests" and material incentives. Unlike other Chinese leaders, Deng did not believe that there was a contradiction between socialism and a market economy. In effect, Deng's idea of market economy had been consistent ever since he initiated the reform and open-door policy. After Deng's Southern Tour in early 1992, the Fourteenth Party Congress in the same year formulated a new ideology of "socialist market economy," thus incorporating market economy into the core of the CCP ideology.

To a degree, what happened after the Southern Tour was actually a continuation of the trend started by Deng in the 1980s. This, however, does not explain why Deng made such great efforts to push the leadership to legitimize capitalism and why the CCP accepted capitalism when it strongly opposed it in the previous decades. In the early 1990s, a serious crisis of political legitimacy hit the CCP following the crackdown on the pro-democracy movement in 1989, the imposition of economic sanctions against China by the West, and the collapse of communism in the Soviet Union and Eastern European countries. Regime survival became the highest priority, leading the leadership to tighten its control by engaging in both political and economic rectifications. Nevertheless, Deng also realized that the fall of the Soviet Union and the collapse of Eastern European communism were mainly due to the failure of economic development. Therefore, the ruling Party needed to achieve rapid economic growth if it were to avoid such a misfortune and restrengthen its political legitimacy. Thus, what Deng chose to do was to continue to tighten political control while radically liberalizing the economic system.[5]

There was also political rationale behind the legitimization of market economy. Although the government tightened its political control in the aftermath of the 1989 movement, social demands for political reform were still prevalent. In order to divert popular passion for political interests to those for economic interests, the government had to provide social members with an economic exit. While the crackdown on the 1989 movement had demonstrated to the social groups the high cost of pursuing political interests, the opening of an economic exit was a carrot for the shift from political interests to economic interests. The political significance of such an economic exit motivated the leadership to put aside capitalism as an ideology and to utilize it a means of economic expansion. This strategy resulted in rapid development and socio-political stability in the following decades.

The Expansion of the Private Sector and Private Space

An interest-based social order is not the natural result of market expansion, but a conscious pursuit of the CCP leadership. What the leadership pursued was not only market expansion itself, but also its beneficial political consequences. Market expansion has generated enormous political benefits because it not only increased the regime's political legitimacy, but also, more importantly, changed the space structure in the country. The conscious pursuit of economic expansion has led to the emergence of an interest-based social order,[6] which in turn has resulted in the creation and expansion of a private arena.[7]

The rapid expansion of the private space is reflected in the decline of the state sector and the development of the non-state sector. In China, enterprises are usually classified as state-owned enterprises (SOEs) and non-state enterprises (NSEs) in terms of ownership. The distinction between SOEs and NSEs is that the former are heavily operated by the government while the latter operate according to market principles. In the 1980s, collective enterprises, especially township and village enterprises (TVEs), constituted the majority of NSEs. Thereafter, foreign-invested enterprises (FIEs) and Hong Kong, Taiwan, and Macau-funded enterprises became other major components of NSEs. Many FIEs are joint ventures with SOEs so they retain a significant element of state ownership. However, given that they are market-oriented, the joint ventures are also regarded as part of the non-state sector.

The domestic private sector has expanded quickly in pace and scale. Within 20 years from 1990 to 2009, the number of domestic private enterprises increased from less than 1 million to 7.2 million, or 70% of total registered enterprises.[8] The total registered capital of domestic private enterprises increased from around 10 billion *yuan* in the early 1990s to around 1.3 trillion *yuan* in 2000, and further achieved a ten-fold increase in the following decade.[9]

In 1978, the state sector accounted for 78% of the gross industrial output, while the non-state sector contributed merely 22%.[10] By the end of 2008, NSEs produced about 72% of the gross industrial output, and the remaining 28%

came from the SOE sector. In 2000, the domestic private sector accounted for about 43% of the country's total GDP, compared with about 13% by FIEs and Hong Kong, Macau, and Taiwan enterprises. The total share of NSEs was about 56%. Since 2005, the proportion of the domestic private sector has been around 50% of the total GDP, while the total share of the NSEs has reached 65%.[11]

The employment data is an indication of the scale of the non-state sector in the Chinese economy. From 1978 to 2008, there was a substantial increase in the share of employment from 40% to 84% in NSEs. Correspondingly, the share of employment of the state sector experienced a contraction from 60% to 16% in the same period.[12]

The rapid expansion of private space has undermined the old ideologically constructed social order in various ways. The household registration system was already eroded with an emerging market economy in the 1980s. With basic daily necessities available through the market, the state was no longer able to effectively control population movement from rural to urban areas, from interior to coastal areas, and from small to large cities. The system was further undermined by intensive economic competition among regions. To attract talented people, many cities have substantially relaxed the original registration required for the employment of non-local residents.[13]

In Russia and some other Eastern European communist states, the collapse of the ideologically constructed social order had resulted in socioeconomic disorder. But this is not the case in China. The creation and expansion of a private arena explains the difference in the outcome. Although the rising private space is confined to the non-political arena, it is politically significant as it provides social groups with an exit from the public arena. Without a private exit, social members would have to struggle for what they want in a highly politicized public arena, with the risk of gaining nothing or even losing everything. This undoubtedly intensified political conflicts among social members. Therefore, the expansion of a private arena reduces greatly the intensity of political conflicts, and thus the political burden of the CCP and its government.

Furthermore, the existence of a private arena makes it possible for citizens to remain apolitical. In an ideologically constructed society, political indifference is possible, but politically risky. Since all economic benefits are distributed through political means, social members had to pay attention to politics. In contrast, an interest-based social order not only allows people to pay less attention to politics, but also encourages them to devote themselves to economic activities. In other words, political indifference is no longer risky, and politically indifferent citizens can obtain their basic necessities through the market.

With an interest-based social order, China's economic development has gained a spontaneous and natural momentum. In an ideologically constructed social order, any political change would inevitably affect economic activities.

But in an interest-based social order, economic activities are less affected by political changes. An interest-based social order has an inherent capability to resist the impact of political changes. Government intervention in economic activities is reduced, but economic development continues. This in turn increases the legitimacy of the government, though it is now less responsible for economic development.

The Rise of the Middle Class

The development of the market economy and the expansion of the private sector have created material conditions for the rise of the middle classes. Even today, China is still far from being a middle-class society like those in the developed West. But compared to the Mao era where the class structure remained as simple as the "alliance" of workers, peasants, and intellectuals, middle classes have emerged and gained in number, complexity, cultural influence, and sociopolitical prominence. From 1949 to 2006, agricultural labor decreased from 88.1% of the population (0.54 billion) to 50.4% of 1.31 billion, and the occupational groups expanded between 2.6 times (self-employed) and 22.4 times (sales and service workers).[14]

China's middle classes were different in different time periods. The first generation of middle class consisted of the self-employed, small merchants, and manufacturers, grown out of China's early market liberalization in the late 1970s and early 1980s. In the mid-1990s, a new middle class of mainly salaried professionals, technicians, and administrative employees working in large corporations began its initial expansion and soon overshadowed the old generation in terms of status and prestige. The privatization program of Premier Zhu Rongji in the mid-1990s facilitated the growth of the new generation of the middle class. The burgeoning capitalist class – mostly the owners of small and medium enterprises – is usually regarded as part of the rising Chinese new middle class. Overall, China's middle class comprises not only the majority of white-collar workers and well-educated professionals, but also those at the top of the social hierarchy in terms of wealth.

Scholars from the Chinese Academy of Social Sciences (CASS) have proposed three criteria to identify the middle classes in China: middle-level income (at local standard), white-collar occupation, and credentials from high educational institutions. They found that about 25% of the total population meet at least one of the three conditions. However, the proportion would drop dramatically to 3% when all the three conditions have to be met.[15] Realizing how heterogeneous this group is, the CASS scholars divided the middle class into three echelons based on their occupation and employment relationship at work, including "new middle class," "old middle class," and "marginal middle

Table 5.1   Components of China's middle class by occupation. Based on CASS, China
General Social Survey, 2006.

	By Occupation	% Nationwide
New middle class	Leading cadres and government	12.5
	Managerial personnel	
	Private entrepreneurs	
	Professionals	
	Clerical workers (senior level)	
Old middle class	Self-employed	9.5
Marginal middle class	Clerical workers (middle/lower level)*	
	Sales and service workers	17.1

Note: * The different levels of clerical worker cannot be distinguished in the China General Social
Survey, 2006. Since the financial situation of the majority of clerical workers was similar to the
marginal middle class, they were included here. Therefore, the actual proportion of new middle
class should be a bit higher and correspondingly, the marginal middle class should be a few per-
centages lower.

class." New and old middle classes are two groups that are comparable to the
middle classes in the West: new middle class includes CCP and government
officials, enterprise managers, private entrepreneurs, professionals, and senior-
level clerical workers; old middle class is traditional self-employed personnel;
and marginal middle class is a large group of people working as lower-level
routine non-manual workers and/or employees in the sales and service sectors.
It is also not surprising to see more new middle classes obtaining quality education and higher income compared with the other two groups.

From whatever perspective, the growth of middle classes is evident. The
whole middle class increased from 7.9% in 1949 to 39.1% in 2006, made up
of 12.5% of new middle class, 9.5% of old middle class, and 17.1% of marginal
middle class (see Table 5.1).[16] Since 1995, the proportion of middle classes has
been steadily increased by 1% each year for over 15 years.

Non-Governmental Organizations (NGOs)

With growing economic and social freedom since the late 1970s, NGOs have
come to play an increasingly important role in the rise of civil society in China.
There has been a revival of traditional institutions (lineage, markets, and
temples) and a rise of new forms of social organization.

China's official definitions of NGOs are mainly based on their registration
typologies. All NGOs are registered as one of the following three categories: 1)
social organization (*shehui tuanti*); 2) private non-enterprise unit (*minban*

feiqiye danwei); and 3) foundation (*jijinhui*), which includes branches of the overseas foundations (*jinwai ji jinhui daibiao jigou*).[17] In the official documents of the government, the terms "civil organizations" (*minjian zuzhi*) as well as "social associations" (*shehui zuzhi*) are sometimes used to refer to the above three categories of NGOs as a whole.[18]

China's official statistics of "civil organizations" are only available from 1988. The number of registered NGOs has since been increasing steadily except for the years 1998–2000 (see Table 5.2). The decline in NGOs during that period was attributed to the stricter regulation of social organizations in 1998.

In addition to the registered NGOs, there are millions of unregistered NGOs. As these unregistered NGOs have more autonomy than registered NGOs, they are ironically the most promising and functional ones in China. It is estimated that the number of unregistered NGOs is about 10 times that of registered ones.[19] With the inclusion of these non-registered NGOs, the total number of civil organizations would have reached 8.8 million by 2003.[20] Despite their rapid development, NGOs in China are still underdeveloped. For example, by the mid-2000s, the number of civil organizations per 10,000 people was 1.45 in China, but 110.45 in France, 51.79 in the United States, 12.66 in Brazil, 10.21 in India, and 2.44 in Egypt.[21]

At the central level, NGOs come under the jurisdiction of the Ministry of Civil Affairs and the State Administration for Religious Affairs. The former is responsible for developing, drafting, enforcing regulations regarding the registration of social organizations, foundations, and private non-enterprise units.[22] The latter is responsible for investigating the status of religion, drafting, supervising, and propagandizing regulations and policies on religion, and preventing illegal religious activities.[23]

There are three official regulations issued by the State Council and enforced by the Ministry of Civil Affairs, including: 1) *Regulations on the Registration and Administration of Social Organizations*; 2) *Regulations on the Registration and Administration of Private Non-enterprise Units*; and 3) *Regulations on the Registration and Administration of Foundations*. According to these regulations, social organizations or private non-enterprise units must be approved by and registered with the Ministry of Civil Affairs at the county level or above, and the foundations must be approved at the provincial or central government level. Furthermore, before applying for registration, every social organization, private non-enterprise unit, and foundation is required to find a "professional management unit" (*yewu zhuguan danwei*), a state organ above the county level that is relevant to the activities proposed by the NGO, as its sponsor.

Special attention has been given to the governance of religious organizations. As religious activities are regulated stringently, registered religious organizations are less autonomous than other NGOs (i.e., academic associations or voluntary service organizations), and unregistered religious organizations are more likely to be banned based on various regulations. Religious NGOs

Table 5.2 Registered civil organizations in China, 1988–2009.* Compiled by the author based on the data on social organizations in China provided by the Ministry of Civil Affairs of the People's Republic of China.

Year	Total	Social Organizations	Private Non-enterprise Units	Foundations
1988	4,446	4,446	–	–
1989	4,544	4,544	–	–
1990	10,855	10,855	–	–
1991	82,814	82,814	–	–
1992	154,502	154,502	–	–
1993	167,506	167,506	–	–
1994	174,060	174,060	–	–
1995	180,583	180,583	–	–
1996	184,821	184,821	–	–
1997	181,318	181,318	–	–
1998	165,600	165,600	–	–
1999	142,665	136,764	5,901	–
2000	153,322	130,668	22,654	–
2001	210,939	128,805	82,134	–
2002	244,509	133,297	111,212	–
2003	266,612	141,167	124,491	954
2004	289,432	153,359	135,181	892
2005	319,762	171,150	147,637	975
2006	354,393	191,946	161,303	1,144
2007	386,916	211,661	173,915	1,340
2008	399,390	220,000	178,000	1,390
2009, Q1	414,614	230,000	183,000	1,614

Note: * "Foundations" are included in the "Social Organizations" column before year 2002 for data tabulated here.

Sources: 1988–2004: Statistics of Civil Organizations (1988–2004); 2005: Statistics of Civil Organizations in 2005; 2006: Statistics of Civil Organizations in 2006; 2007: Statistics of Civil Organizations in 2007 – all available at *Social Organizations in China* (Zhongguo shehui zuzhi), <http://www.chinanpo.gov.cn>; 2008: Statistics of Civil Organizations in 2008, available at *Social Organizations in China* (Zhonghua renmin gongheguo minzhengbu), http://cws.mca.gov.cn/accessory/200902/1233554233793.htm; 2009: Statistics of Civil Affairs Quarterly (1st Quarter, 2009) (minzheng shiyetongji jibao), available at the Ministry of Civil Affairs of the People's Republic of China, <http://cws.mca.gov.cn>

and their activities are regulated by the State Council's *Regulations on Religious Affairs*. The State Administration for Religious Affairs, a vice-ministerial level department under the State Council, is designed specially to supervise religious affairs, including the religious NGOs' activities. Although Article 6 of the *Regulations on Religious Affairs* stipulates that "religious organizations' formation, change and cancellation should be in accordance with the *Regulations on the Registration and Administration of Social Organizations,*"[24] there are 48 specific articles in the *Regulations on Religious Affairs* which regulate the formulation, change, cancellation as well as activities of the religious organizations.

According to the *Regulations on the Registration and Administration of Foundations,* branches of international NGOs (INGOs) or overseas foundations may register in China; however, there is still a lack of clear regulations regarding the registration of non-foundation international NGOs and their activities. According to the *Regulations of Branches of Social Organizations, Representative Agencies' Registration,* the registration of social organizations from Taiwan, Hong Kong, Macao, and foreign countries should be "in accordance with another specific regulation," which has not been issued yet.[25] Lacking in regulations, the government often adopts a "case by case" approach to the INGOs. This implies that INGOs will have to gain the government's trust before they could operate in China. For example, while the application of INGO Greenpeace for registration in China had been rejected, the China Council of Lions Club was approved by the State Council on June 14, 2005 as a special case. China Council of Lions Club comes under the supervision of the China Disabled Persons' Federation.[26]

Activities of NGOs have largely been restricted and marginalized. The legislation process remains problematic and few NGOs are consulted when regulations on NGOs are being formulated. As a result, laws and policies enacted are not conducive to building a well-functioning NGO sector and forming productive partnerships between government and NGOs. NGOs' finances are fragile. Most of the grassroots NGOs receive little financial support from the government and are struggling to survive. Government provides funds to NGOs according to their political ties. Only those well connected to the government are likely to get some funding from the "professional management unit."[27] On the other hand, grassroots NGOs rarely get donations from local communities because new NGOs do not have a good track record in winning the trust of the local people.

Under the current regulations, if the same type of NGO has already been registered in the same administrative area, the area is considered off limits to other NGOs. For example, if there is already an association of environment protection in existence at the city level of Beijing, no new associations on environment protection will be approved in Beijing. The regulations therefore restrict the number, type, and range of registered associations.[28] Without competition from other NGOs, the registered NGOs have more incentives to work and comply with the government than to develop themselves into independent NGOs with extensive support from society. Some NGOs went so far as to offer themselves as tools of the state.

The finding of a state organ as a "professional management unit" is another deterrent to NGOs. Not many government agencies are willing to act as the professional management unit as they have to play a supervisory role to these NGOs, thus adding to their workload. As a result, some grassroots NGOs are not qualified to register and remain illegal for years, while some registered themselves as businesses with the Industry and Commerce Bureaus instead.

Strict registration requirements therefore push the majority of NGOs into the unofficial world, which poses a great challenge to the regulation of the NGO sector. There are a large number of unregistered NGOs which are not necessarily banned by the government. The government tends to apply the principle of "no contact, no recognition, and no ban" to associations that engage in social services, and refrain from intervening in their activities. Under this circumstance, some unregistered NGOs are very active. For example, one famous NGO, which has successfully conducted environment protection work all over China, is an unregistered NGO.[29]

The INGOs can also hardly be registered in China. However, interactions between Chinese NGOs and INGOs are becoming increasingly frequent.[30] Some Chinese citizens participate in unregistered INGOs in China and are thus involved in the international cultural and social exchange activities. The membership density of China's INGO per million of population increased from 1.2 in 1993 to 1.9 in 2003, a 60% increase in a decade.[31]

In recognition of the strengths of NGOs, the Chinese government has been promoting the "socialization of social welfare" by encouraging NGOs to play a larger role in philanthropy and social welfare. However, the government and NGOs are still devoid of trust, and the development of NGOs in different areas has been uneven. Religious NGOs, INGOs, and NGOs advocating human rights are often viewed with skepticism and subject to much stricter control. For example, the control of NGOs was stepped up in 2009 because of the government's anxiety about politically sensitive anniversaries, including the sixtieth anniversary of the founding of the PRC.[32] On 17 July, 2009 Chinese officials shut down *Gongmeng* (Open Constitution Initiative), a legal aid and research centre founded by pioneering Chinese lawyers. The authority has also revoked the licenses of more than 50 lawyers, many known for tackling human rights issues.[33]

While government control remains, NGOs continue to expand, particularly in developed coastal areas, pushing the government to liberalize its NGO policy. For instance, the Guangdong government greatly liberalized NGO regulations in 2012. The new regulations simplify the registration requirements and do away with the requirement of a "professional management unit."[34] The Minister of Civil Affairs has indicated that the Guangdong experiment is likely to be expanded to the rest of the country in the near future since it reduces tension between government and society.[35]

Social Media and Netizens

Since China plugged into the Internet in 1994, the number of Internet users has grown tremendously. The total number of Internet users reached 2 million in 1998, surpassed 100 million in 2005, rose to 298 million by the end of 2008, and replaced the United States as having the largest Internet usage in the world in the same year. The most recent survey, published in January 2012, showed that Internet users had reached a new high of 513 million by December 2011 (38.3% of China's total population) with 356 million users browsing the web on their cell phones.

The combination of wired Internet with wireless cell phones has qualitatively changed the scope of Internet coverage. People can now communicate via the Internet while on the go. First-hand information delivery (both in text and in video) is much faster and more efficient with mobile phones than with a terminal.

The age of Internet users ranges from 10 years old (or even under) to 80 years old, with the bulk from 10 to 30 years old. Most of the Internet users have middle school and high school qualifications.

Based on professions, the two largest groups of Internet users are students and professional white-collar workers, each taking 28% or so of the share. Self-employed and unemployed groups are a distant third and fourth in ranking.

While Internet users are concentrated in cities, Internet penetration in rural areas has increased dramatically. For example, rural Internet users increased at an annual growth rate of 127% from 2000 to 2007, much higher than the annual growth rate of 38.2% over the same period in the urban areas.[36] By the end of 2009, rural Internet users had surpassed 100 million.[37]

The top 10 applications of Internet users at present are music, news, instant message, video, search engine, email, games, blogs/personals, forums/ bulletin board services (BBS), and shopping.[38] From various Internet surveys, the bulk of Internet users go online for entertainment purposes.

The development of the Internet in China can be divided into three recognizable periods. In the first period, from 1994 to 1999, the Chinese government built a basic legal and administrative framework for regulating computer network and information security. In 1994, for example, the State Council issued "Safety and Protection Regulations for Computer Information Systems." In 1997, the Ministry of Public Security issued "Computer Information Network and Internet Security, Protection and Management Regulations," which outlines the duties and responsibilities of China's Internet service providers. In the second stage, from 2000 to 2003, the state introduced a set of policies to control content through the regulation and registration of ISPs, ICPs, and ordinary users. For example, regulations specifically targeting BBS were announced in November 2000, stipulating that bulletin board services should follow a licensing procedure.[39] The third phase, from 2004 onward, marks the expansion of Internet regulation and control from government to governance and governmentality.[40] Examples are official initiatives to promote self-discipline and a professional code of conduct targeting both IT businesses and consumers.[41]

The Chinese government worries about the undesirable political consequences of the free flow of information facilitated by the new Information and
Communication Technology (ICT). For decades, the government has ruth-
lessly suppressed any organized dissent inside China through information
control and other coercive measures. The freedom of information associated
with the Internet is a reflection of contradictions between market and politics.
On one hand, due to various market factors, multinational firms and domestic
firms alike have to cooperate with the Chinese government. On the other hand,
exactly also for market reasons, firms have to liberalize the regulations and
requirements set up by the government in order to be competitive in the
market. Competition between market and politics becomes intensive. The
government can make frequent attempts to limit the functioning of the market,
but the market tends to prevail over politics eventually.

While the government does control the new ICT, it also uses the technology
to mobilize social support for its own cause. Once the government uses the
technology for social mobilization, opportunities are created for other social
forces to do likewise, which are not necessarily in line with the government's
policies. This can be exemplified by the rise of Internet nationalism. Since
nationalism has become an increasingly important source for the political
legitimacy of the Chinese state, nationalist diatribes have a better chance of
getting past the censors than other forms of political comment. But nationalism has also provided a convenient cover for experimenting with new forms
of activism on the part of social forces. The power of instant messaging, for
instance, became evident in April 2005 when it was used to organize anti-
Japanese protests in several Chinese cities, including Beijing, Shanghai,
Guangzhou, and Shenzhen. In the build-up to the protests, Sina organized an
online campaign to demonstrate public opposition to Japan's bid for permanent membership of the UN Security Council. Some 20 million people submitted their names. In competing with Sina, Sohu also gathered more than 15
million names. These Internet-based nationalistic campaigns certainly provided strong support for the government's Japan policy. Nevertheless, the government soon found that it had to contain such nationalistic mobilizations
since the social forces began to exert strong pressure on the government when
mobilized.[42]

There are also many other cases in which the new technology was used
by the government to mobilize social support. The desire to expose various
forms of malfeasance, such as corruption and mine disasters, and the more
"people-centered" approach to governance as promulgated by Hu and Wen,
has legitimized certain forms of exposure, thus allowing citizens to push those
limits. The boundary between what is legitimate to expose and illegitimate to
expose is always shifting. This opens up possibilities for Chinese activists
to bring about political change. Due to its fast growing influence, even the Party

leadership now has to pay attention to the deluge of public comment. Eager to acquire some legitimacy, but anxious to avoid democracy, it is trying to appeal to populism via the new technology. Premier Wen Jiabao said during the National People's Congress in March 2006 that the government should listen extensively to views expressed on the Internet. In February 2009, Wen participated in his first online chat jointly hosted by the websites of the Chinese government and the official Xinhua News Agency. A few months earlier, in June 2008, President Hu Jintao also fielded questions from Chinese netizens through the Strong China Forum (*Qiangguo luntan*), an online bulletin board of the *People's Daily*. Both the Party and government have given their imprimatur to capitalize on the Internet's potential.

The Internet is not only a tool that can be used both by the state and society in their interaction. More importantly, it is a new and unexplored political realm for both the state and society to expand its own political space. In doing so, the game between the two actors is not always a zero-sum one. Internet development could be a win-win game between the state and society, and when some conditions are present, it is mutually empowering for the two actors.[43]

Conclusion

In the post-Mao era, the Chinese government has successfully justified market economy as the way to rapid economic growth. However, market-oriented economic growth has generated a significant social consequence – the rise of civil society. This chapter has demonstrated how economic development has given rise to middle classes, NGOs and netizens, and laid down the material base for civil society to emerge.

What civil society means for China indeed has become an increasingly hot topic in academic and policy circles, especially in the West. Central to all the debates are the potential political consequences that civil society could bring to China. It is widely believed that the rise of civil society is likely to have a great sociopolitical impact on China's authoritarian system. Many have hoped that civil society would facilitate political change and transform China into not only an open society, but also an open and democratic regime.

The rise of civil society does generate greater dynamics for political changes. China's newly rising civil society has become an increasingly active actor in politics. Civil activities ranging from Internet-based individual protests to large-scale collective actions have introduced changes to the state and society. In the next chapter, we will discuss how social groups have engaged in different forms of collective action in various fields of society and politics.

Notes

1 Wang (1995).
2 For a discussion of different perceptions of socialism and capitalism, see Sun (1995).
3 Wang (1995: Part One) discussed why the leadership used the term "socialist market economy" rather than capitalism.
4 Sun (1995).
5 Deng (1993: 379).
6 This is not the place for a full discussion of this rising interest-based social order. But it is worth noting that terms associated with economic interests such as "interest" (or "interests") and "class" have been increasingly used by scholars in China to analyze Chinese society since Deng's *Nanxun*. See Zhu *et al.* (1998); Liang (1998); Lu and Tiankuai (1994); Qin and Ting (1993).
7 For the development of the private sector, see Guthrie (1999). For discussions of increasing autonomy of social groups, see Wang *et al.* (1993); Davis *et al.* (1995); Brook and Frolic (1997); White *et al.* (1996).
8 Dou Hongmei, "State Administration of Industry and Commerce: Non-state Sector Absorbed 90% New Employees." *Beijing Daily*, June 12, 2010.
9 Ibid.
10 Lai (2004: 4).
11 Zheng and Yang (2009). No reliable figures on the shares of NSE and the private sector of total GDP since 2005 were found; only the vague words of "over 2/3 of total GDP" were constantly mentioned in the relevant reports released by the government.
12 *China Statistical Yearbook* (2009).
13 Mallee (1993).
14 Lu (2010).
15 Li and Yi (2008).
16 Ibid.
17 Related documents available at <www.mca.gov.cn> (accessed May 20, 2009).
18 Many examples could be found at the website of the social associations (*shehui zuzhiwang*), which is hosted by the Bureau of Civil Organizations (*minjian zuzhi guanli ju*). See also <www.chinanpo.gov.cn> (accessed May 20, 2009), and the statistical report of the website.
19 Wang and Jia (2003).
20 Cited in He (2008: 162).
21 Ibid., 163.
22 "The Main Duties" (*zhuyao zhize*), available at the Ministry of Civil Affairs, <http://www.mca.gov.cn/article/zwgk/jggl/> (accessed May 6, 2009).
23 "Introduction to the State Administration for Religious Affairs," available at the State Administration for Religious Affairs <www.sara.gov.cn> (accessed May 6, 2009).
24 "Regulations on Religious Affairs," available at the State Administration for Religious Affairs <www.sara.gov.cn> (accessed May 6, 2009).

25 "Regulations of Branches of Social Organizations, Representative Agencies'
     Registration," available at <www.bh.gov.cn> (accessed July 20, 2009).
26 "Zhongguo shizihui chengli: shifou wei guoji NGO denglu dakai menfeng" (The Setup
     of China Council of Lions Club: Does the international NGO open its door in China?),
     Global Link Initiative, available at <www.glinet.org> (accessed July 20, 2009).
27 He (2006).
28 Cooper (2006).
29 Qi (2004).
30 Kaldor *et al.* (2003).
31 Anheier *et al.* (2005: 304).
32 "Asia: Open Constitution Closed; China, the Law and NGOs." *The Economist*, July
     25, 2009, 38.
33 Tania Branigan, "China Officials Shut Legal Aid Centre," *The Guardian*, July 18,
     2009, available at <http://www.guardian.co.uk/world/2009/jul/18/china-shuts-legal-
     aid-centre> (accessed May 20, 2009).
34 "What Should Belong to Society Should Go to Society," *The New Century Magazine*,
     March 26, 2012, available at <http://china.caixin.com/2012-03-26/100372889.html>
     (accessed May 25, 2012).
35 "Civil Affairs Minister Talks about 'Social Association'," *The New Century Magazine*,
     March 26, 2012, available at <http://china.caixin.com/2012-03-26/100372888.html>
     (accessed May 25, 2012).
36 CNNIC's report on Internet Development in Rural Areas dated March 2008, at
     <www.cnnic.net.cn> (accessed May 20, 2009).
37 <www.cnnic.cn> (accessed April 26, 2010).
38 CNNIC Statistical Survey Report on the Internet Development in China dated
     January 2009, at <www.cnnic.cn> (accessed May 20, 2009).
39 For a complete list of Internet regulations in China, see CNNIC's official website,
     <www.cnnic.net.cn> (accessed May 20, 2009).
40 If government refers to the formal institutions, rules, and practices of the state,
     then governance refers to the formal and informal institutions, rules, and practices
     of both the state and non-state actors, while governmentality denotes "the cultural
     and social context out of which modes of governance arise and by which they are
     sustained." See Braman (2004: 13).
41 Yang (2009: 21).
42 For some latest works on Internet nationalism in China, see Yang and Lim (2010);
     Wu (2007); and Shen (2007).
43 Zheng (2008: Chapter 1).

References

Anheier, H., M. Glasius, and M. Kaldor, eds. 2005. *Global Civil Society 2004/5*. London:
     Sage Publications.
Braman, S. 2004. "The Emergent Global Information Policy Regime." In Sandra Braman,
     ed., *The Emergent Global Information Policy Regime*. Basingstoke, UK: Palgrave
     Macmillan pp. 12–18.

Brook, T. and B. M. Frolic, eds. 1997. *Civil Society in China*. Armonk, NY: M. E. Sharpe.

China Statistical Yearbook. 2009. Beijing: China Statistical Press.

Cooper, C. M. 2006. "This Is Our Way In: The Civil Society of Environmental NGOs in South-West China." *Government and Opposition* 41, 1 (Winter): 133.

Davis, Deborah S., Richard Kraus, Barry Naughton, and Elizabeth J. Perry, eds. 1995. *Urban Spaces in Contemporary China: The Potential for Autonomy and Community in post-Mao China*. Washington, DC / Cambridge: Woodrow Wilson Center Press / Cambridge University Press.

Deng, Xiaoping. 1993. "Zai Wuchang, Shenzhen, Zhuhai, Shanghai dengdi de tanhua yaodian." In *Deng Xiaoping wenxuan* (Selected Works of Deng Xiaoping), vol. 3, *1982–1992*. Beijing: Renmin chubanshe.

Guthrie, D. 1999. *Dragon in a Three-Piece Suit: The Emergence of Capitalism in China*. Princeton, NJ: Princeton University Press.

He, Zengke. 2006. "Zhongguo gongmin shehui zuzhi fazhan de zhiduxing zhangan fenxi" (Analysis of the Institutional Obstacles of the Development of Civil Society Organizations in China). *Journal of the Party School of CPC Ningbo Municipal Committee* 6: 23–30.

He, Zengke. 2008. "Institutional Barriers to the Development of Civil Society in China." In Yongnian Zheng and Joseph Fewsmith, eds., *China's Opening Society: The Non-State Sector and Governance*. London and New York: Routledge. pp. 161–73

Kaldor, M., H. Anheier, and M. Glasius, eds. 2003. *Global Civil Society 2003*. Oxford: Oxford University Press.

Lai, Hongyi. 2004. "Surge of China's Private and Non-state Economy (I)." *EAI Background Brief 187*, East Asian Institute, National University of Singapore.

Li, Peilin and Zhang Yi. 2008. "Zhongguo zhongchan jieji de guimo, rentong he shehui taidu" (Size, Identity and Attitudes of the Middle Class in China). *Shehui* (Society) 2. Available at <http://www.sachina.edu.cn/Htmldata/article/2008/12/1699.html> (accessed November 17, 2010).

Liang, Xiaosheng. 1998. *Zhongguo shehui ge jieceng fenxi* (An Analysis of Social Strata in China). Beijing: Jingji ribao chubanshe.

Lu, Xueyi, ed. 2010. *Report on Social Class Study in Contemporary China, Social Structure of Contemporary China*. Beijing: Institute of Sociology, Chinese Academy of Social Sciences.

Lu, Xueyi and Jing Tiankuai, eds. 1994. *Zhuanxing zhong de Zhongguo shehui* (Chinese Society in Transition). Harbin: Helongjiang renmin chubanshe.

Mallee, Hein. 1993. "China's Household Registration System under Reform." In Alan Hunter and Kim-kwong Chan, *Protestantism in Contemporary China*. Cambridge: Cambridge University Press, pp. 10–16.

Qi, H. 2004. "Jieshe ziyou yu fei faren shetuan zhidu" (The Freedom of Association and the System of Non-corporate Associations). *Cass Journal of Foreign Law* 3: 303.

Qin, Shaoxiang and Jia Ting. 1993. *Shehui xin qunti tanmi: Zhongguo siqing qiyezhu jieceng* (A Study of a New Social Group: China's Private Enterprise Class). Beijing: Zhongguo fazhan chubanshe.

Shen, Simon. 2007. *Redefining Nationalism in Modern China: Sino-American Relations and the Emergence of Chinese Public Opinion in the 21st Century*. New York: Palgrave Macmillan.

Sun, Yan. 1995. *The Chinese Reassessment of Socialism, 1976–1992.* Princeton, NJ: Princeton University Press.

Wang, Gungwu. 1995. *The Chinese Way: China's Position in International Relations.* Oslo: Scandinavian University Press.

Wang, M. and X. J. Jia. 2003. "Zhongguo NGO fa lü zheng ce de ruo gan wen ti" (Problems about Legislation for China's NGOs). *Journal of Tsinghua University* (Philosophy and Social Sciences) 18, S1: 100–06.

Wang, Ying *et al.* 1993. *Shehui zhongjian ceng: gaige yu Zhongguo de shetuan zuzhi* (Intermediate Social Strata: The Reform and Social Groups in China). Beijing: Zhongguo fazhan chubanshe.

White, Gordon, Jude Howell, and Shang Xiaoyuan. 1996. *In Search of Civil Society: Market Reform and Social Change in Contemporary China.* Oxford: Oxford University Press.

Wu, Xu. 2007. *Chinese Cyber Nationalism: Evolution, Characteristics, and Implications.* Lanham, MD: Lexington Books.

Yang, Guobin. 2009. "Historical Imagination in the Study of Chinese Digital Civil Society." In Xiaoling Zhang and Yongnian Zheng, eds., *China's Information and Communication Technology Revolution: Social Changes and State Responses.* London and New York: Routledge.

Yang, Lijun and Chee Kia Lim. 2010. "Three Waves of Nationalism in Contemporary China: Sources, Themes, Presentations and Consequences." *International Journal of China Studies* 1, 2: 461–85.

Zheng, Hongliang and Yang Yang. 2009. "Chinese Private Sector Development in the Past 30 Years: Retrospect and Prospect." University of Nottingham, China Policy Institute.

Zheng, Yongnian. 2008. *Technological Empowerment: The Internet, State, and Society in China.* Stanford, CA: Stanford University Press.

Zhu, Guanglei *et al.* 1998. *Dangdai Zhongguo shehui ge jieceng fenxi* (An Analysis of Social Strata in Contemporary China). Tianjin: Tianjin renmin chubanshe.

Chapter 6

Social Discontent

China's market-oriented reform and globalization have promoted economic development and changed the social landscape. Economic development in turn has benefited many Chinese, but also brought social injustice to many others. Some groups and regions benefit more than others, with some becoming winners and others becoming losers. In other words, social groups and regions have unevenly benefited from an increasingly market-oriented economy and globalization. Those who are able to participate in the process have gained, and those who have not have become disadvantaged. In minority areas, social injustice has become an even more serious concern as ethnic factors are involved.

Since the early 1990s, there has been a steady upsurge of what in China is called "mass incident" (*quntixing shijian*) or social unrest. In both the scholarly community and policy circles, a mass incident generally refers to any of the following activities that involve more than 10 participants: 1) submitting collective petitions to upper-level government offices and conducting sit-ins; 2) organizing illegal assemblies, parades, and demonstrations; 3) staging strikes; 4) blocking traffic; 5) initiating social disturbances; 6) besieging Party and government buildings; 7) smashing, looting, and burning; and 8) obstructing the performance of government administration. According to various sources and calculations, mass incidents had increased from 8,700 in 1994, to 90,000 in 2006, and to 127,000 in 2008.[1]

More serious is the frequent occurrence of "large-scale mass incident," mass incidents with more than 500 participants. A study indicates that there were 248 large-scale mass incidents between 2003 and 2009. It also shows that there was a huge upsurge of large-scale mass incidents in the years 2007 and 2008, jumping from 25 cases in 2006 to 63 in 2007 and 76 in 2008. In terms of geographical distribution, Guangdong had the most incidents with 54, three times

Contemporary China: A History since 1978, First Edition. Yongnian Zheng.
© 2014 John Wiley & Sons, Ltd. Published 2014 by John Wiley & Sons, Ltd.

that of the next province, Hubei, which had 17 cases. In contrast, Jiangsu, which is at a comparable level of socioeconomic development, had only eight incidents during the period.[2]

This chapter examines some of the general conditions leading to social discontent and then documents the different types of social resistance and protests. These conditions will be analyzed against the different forms of social injustice, and the chapter will further demonstrate how the rise of civil society has been a facilitating factor behind social resistance and protests.

Income Disparities and Social Grievance

Social grievance has been closely related to widening income disparities throughout the reform era.[3] Three decades ago China was one of the most egalitarian societies in the world, but it is now among the most unequal countries in the world. China's Gini coefficient, a standard measure of inequality, has exceeded that of the US and approaches those of highly unequal countries like Brazil, Mexico, and Chile. Conceptually, overall income inequality can be broken down into three components, namely, inequality between urban and rural areas, within urban areas, and among regions. Since the reform, China's rising income inequality has been propelled by the urban–rural income gap and by the growing disparity between highly educated urban professionals and the working class.

Urban–rural disparities

When China began its economic reform, urban per capita income was 2.6 times greater than the rural equivalent.[4] In the early years of reform, urban–rural disparities were reduced as reform was first implemented in the countryside. However, since urban reform began in 1984, the gap has widened gradually. China's rural–urban gap is now large by international standards. In most countries, rural incomes are on average 66% or more of urban incomes. In China, rural incomes were merely 40% of urban incomes in 1995, down from a peak of 59% in 1983.[5] In 2007, average per capita disposable income in rural areas was 4,140 *yuan*, 30% of 13,785 *yuan* in the urban area. Put differently, urban income was 3.3 times the rural counterpart, following a trend since 1997 that has been increasing, albeit at a diminishing rate.

Inequality in urban areas

Inequality within China's cities has heightened over time, especially after 1991. According to a National Bureau of Statistics report, in 1996 nearly two-thirds of the bottom 20% of households found that their income had fallen, and almost half of the next 20% of households found their income had declined. In contrast, the top 20% of urban households enjoyed an increase in their income.[6] In 1990, their average income was only 4.2 times higher than that of the bottom 20%, but by 1998 it had jumped to 9.6 times. The share of total income enjoyed by the richest 10% of households increased from 23.6% in 1990 to 38.4% in 1998. During the same period, the share of the bottom 20% declined from 9% to 5.5%.[7] Urban residents used to come under the "haves," as opposed to the hundreds of millions of "have-nots" in the vast countryside. However, by 2000 about 30 million urban residents were living in poverty and their incomes were no more than one-third the national average.[8] After the turn of the century, urban inequality deteriorated with the Gini coefficient reaching 32.9 in 2003.

Regional disparity

China's overall income inequality has its roots in the regional disparity across provinces and regions. In terms of per capita GDP, the income of the richest province in China was 9.8 times that of the poorest province in 1994. This ratio peaked at 10.8 in 2003 before falling back to 9.0 in 2007. Grouping the provinces into coastal and interior provinces, it is clear that the coastal provinces have consistently enjoyed a higher GDP per capita than the inland provinces, and that the discrepancy between them had increased in 2007, compared to its 1997 level.

Political Distrust

The market-oriented reform has led to an increasingly divided society, which is becoming more difficult for the Chinese state to govern. More importantly, this same process has also resulted in a fall in people's confidence in the government. When there is a decline in the state's capacity to maintain and deliver public goods to its people, popular worries increase, along with their motivation for protest.

While the Chinese state has played an extremely important role in the country's economic transformation, the state has become increasingly corrupt during the process. The close linkages between the government and businesses have led to widespread corruption among Party cadres and government officials. Corruption has become increasingly serious since the early 1990s.

Three main trends of corruption can be identified: increasing involvement of high-ranking government officials, increasing group or collective corruption cases involving many officials in a department or local government since the 1990s, and increasing incidents of bribes and embezzlement of funds.[9] The causes of corruption are many and deeply rooted in China's system of political economy. In the 1980s and early 1990s, radical administrative decentralization changed central–local fiscal relations, giving local governments more power over funds and resources, thus triggering more local corruption cases. The 1994 tax-sharing system reform recentralized China's economic power by expanding the central government's role in fiscal redistribution among provinces; it also gave local governments jurisdiction over urban land-use tax, business tax, house property tax, land value-added tax, and some other taxes relating to local development, as local revenues. The new tax system incentivized local governments to put much emphasis on developing urban construction and real estate, acquiring land from farmers at low cost and selling at high prices and sharing the profit made with developers. As the GDP index is the most important criterion for the promotion of local officials, developing real estate and infrastructure in the process of urbanization is one of the most effective ways for local governments to boost the economy. Local land transaction and credit markets have become hotbeds for corruption. The government maintains tight control over most investment projects through the issuing of long-term bank credit and granting of land-use rights.

Economic liberalization does not mean the significant withdrawal of the state from the economy. The state remains deeply entrenched in the partially marketized economy. China's rapid marketization process after 1992 has opened up more opportunities for rent-seeking activities. Large SOEs and local governments have the highest incidence of corruption. Sectors such as energy, financial services, transportation, telecommunications, tobacco, iron and steel, and non-ferrous metal, where SOEs are either monopolists or dominant players, are breeding grounds for bribery, embezzlement, squandering, and other rent-seeking activities. The government-granted monopoly or oligopoly has helped SOEs reap soaring after-tax profits, which remain mostly in the coffers of SOEs rather than flow to the public purse in the form of dividends. Owning monopolistic power and vast assets, large-scale SOEs act just like independent kingdoms, with their leaders usually nominated by CCP organization departments and enjoying higher (or equal) administrative ranks than local judicial and Party disciplinary officials. The fact that almost all top political leaders have family members who have substantial stakes in the corporate world has complicated the issue further.

Beside government officials' monopolistic and discretionary powers over budgets, resources, and investment decisions, Party officials also retain authority over the judicial system through the political-legal committees and the selection of personnel through the *nomenklatura* system. Judicial corruption cases and sale-of-official-post scandals have been exposed from time to time.

Corruption has undermined public confidence in the ability of the CCP to ensure fairness and cast doubts on its legitimacy to rule the country. It has further led to a collapse in social morale. Ordinary citizens witness the wealth and greed of Party cadres and government officials, and find it difficult to understand why they should be holding back. Gradually, they no longer regard the system in which they live as being fair to them. Government officials have also found that it is increasingly difficult to maintain a morally and socially upright community.[10]

Rural Protests

Farmers' protests in rural China are common. In the 1980s and 1990s, farmers protested against the heavy burdens imposed upon them by the different levels of government.[11] This is officially called "peasant burdens" (*nongmin fudan*), which refers to various types of taxes, fees, and charges imposed by the government at different levels and by other administrative organs.[12] Social protests against excessive taxation in rural areas were frequent in the 1990s. The most outstanding case was the mass protest in Renshou county of Sichuan province in 1993. Protests however declined in the following years. There were only two such instances of protests against excessive taxation in 2004. The protests, however, spread to multiple counties and attracted more than 100,000 participants. For example, in Henan province, in Anyang, Puyang, Hebi, and Kaifeng counties nearly 200,000 peasants demonstrated, gathered, and occasionally occupied the office buildings of several township governments. In Jiangxi province, Yichun, Xinyu, and Jian counties also had large-scale peasant protests. With the abolition of the agricultural tax on January 1, 2006, protests against excessive taxation have largely disappeared as the structural cause of such rural protests has been eliminated.

Since the turn of the new century, rural protests against land and relocation have increased. Due to high economic growth, land requisition for industrial or commercial uses has become common. The disputed issue was mostly on the compensation for the requisitioned land, which was often considered unfair by the affected population.[13]

A well-known case of land dispute occurred in Hanyuan county of Sichuan province in 2004. Local villagers were forced to surrender their land and relocate to make way for the building of a hydroelectric plant. Many relocated farmers did not receive proper compensation and had to settle on allocated land that was of a poorer quality. A mass incident involving tens of thousands of people eventually broke out in October when angry peasants attacked the electricity plant and government buildings and also detained the governor of Sichuan province, who was at the scene trying to settle the dispute for more than 10 hours. The conflict resulted in several deaths and many injuries. The incident shocked the central government and an investigation group was dispatched. The investigation group announced that the electricity plant would be temporarily closed until the relocation disputes had been settled.

Another case is the large-scale mass incident in Dongzhou village, Shanwei county, Guangdong province in 2006. The electricity plant built in 2002 occupied a large land area in the village. The villagers believed that they were not properly compensated and protested. They built sheds outside the factory and attempted to stop the construction. The arrest of three villagers during the effort to demolish the sheds escalated the situation and protestor numbers soared to several thousands. The government dispatched an armed police force and used tear gas to dispel the crowd. The riot became violent in December 2006. Major parts of the plant were destroyed in the riot. The protest ended with the armed police opening fire, causing several deaths and injuries. The protests of Wukan, Guangdong, also known as the Siege of Wukan, which continued from September 2011 to February 2012, were also the result of a land grab by local officials.

Labor Protests

Labor protests are not new in China. The Hundred Flowers Campaign and the Cultural Revolution were labor movements mobilized from above and the well-documented 1989 pro-democracy movement[14] involved labor protests from below. Nevertheless, the market reform has contributed to the rise of new labor insurgencies, especially since Deng's Southern Tour in 1992.

After the Chinese Labor Law came into effect nationwide in 1995, the labor dispute cases had increased from 33,030 in 1995 to 447,000 in 2006 and the number of dispute cases per million workers had soared from about 48 to 585 in the same period.[15] The majority of these cases were collective disputes which involved more than three workers. These labor disputes went through the institutional channel, the Labor Dispute Arbitrational Committees (LDAC), for resolution. Workers also expressed their dissatisfaction through a variety of non-institutional channels such as protests and lodging collective complaints to the government.

From 1993 through 2003, the number of social protests increased from 10,000 to 60,000 and the number of participants increased from 730,000 to 3.07 million. In 2003, workers were the largest participatory group in social protests (1.44 million) and accounted for about 47% of total participants.[16] Migrant workers are also resorting to suicides to call for government help on their arrears of payment. For instance, the fire department in Wuhan city reported in 2006 that about 80% of public suicides were committed by migrant workers waiting to get their due payment from their employers.[17]

The global financial crisis in 2008 worsened labor relations and led to significantly rising numbers of labor disputes. For instance, in Guangdong province, there were 669 and 786 cases of absconding employers who failed to compensate their workers in 2006 and 2007, respectively. In 2008, the number of such cases shot up to 1,985, which involved about 206,000 workers and arrears of 600 million *yuan*.[18] Nationwide in 2008, there were more than 280,000 legal cases of labor disputes, a 94% increase from 2007.

In the Mao era, workers worked for state-owned enterprises (SOEs). In general, the working class as a whole was a politically and economically privileged class.[19] The situation began to change after the post-Mao reform. Although the working class as "the nation's leading class" has been kept intact in frequently revised Constitutions of 1982, 1988, 1993, 1999, and 2004, previous political and economic advantages associated with this political status have become less and less. The majority of the working class has been trapped in a very disadvantaged position after the full marketization of the economy.

The workers in SOEs have lost their job security since 1990s. Layoffs surged in the early 1990s. In 1992, the Fourteenth Party Congress established market economy as the goal of the country's economic reform. Various market-oriented reform measures were introduced to SOEs.[20] These reforms led to the massive layoff of workers. In the mid-1990s, the labor contract system replaced the permanent job system nationwide,[21] implying that even workers in SOEs could lose their jobs. There were only about 6.0 million unemployed (in Chinese usage "off-post") workers in 1995, but in 1997, the figure rose to about 7.4 million when a partial privatization program was implemented.[22] The situation deteriorated after 1997 when further privatization measures such as the shareholding system were implemented. By the end of 1997, layoffs affected 9.4 million workers.[23] Although the government initiated various employment programs to cope with the problem, they failed to improve the situation.[24] According to official statistics, there were only 5.8 million unemployed urban residents in 1999,[25] but the figure of off-post workers reached about 10 million.[26] According to an estimate, total unemployment amounted to 15–16 million in 1998 and 18–19 million in 1999.[27] Unemployment was especially critical in the traditional heavy industries of the northeast provinces, namely, Liaoning, Jilin, and Heilongjiang, where the real unemployment rate ranged from 12.8% to 15.5% in 1998. Unemployment was also a serious problem in interior provinces such as Hunan, Sichuan, and Shaanxi, as their unemployment rate stood above 10% in the same period. In contrast, the coastal provinces including Guangdong, Shandong, Zhejiang, Jiangsu, Hebei, Shanghai, and Beijing, saw low rates of unemployment.[28]

In the late 1990s, SOEs launched a series of massive layoffs to cut production costs and improve business efficiency. By 2005, over 85% of small and medium-sized SOEs were restructured and privatized,[29] which resulted in about 30 million laid-off workers, almost half of SOE workers.[30] For those who were fortunate enough to keep their jobs in SOEs, most previously guaranteed benefits have been completely withdrawn or offered at a much lower level. Almost all SOEs have stopped providing free housing for their employees. Employees have to share their insurance costs with employers after major benefits such as medical care and pensions were outsourced to government sponsored social insurance agents. On the other hand, SOE workers enjoy a relatively free labor market, because their job mobility is much freer than before the reform.

The market reform has significantly increased and institutionalized the wage gaps between different subgroups of the working class. According to a study, there are four subgroups: 1) Party, state, and society administration cadres (including supervisors and administrative staff; 2) enterprise management; 3) professional and technical staff; and 4) ordinary staff and workers (including migrant workers). These groups represent a respective 14%, 6%, 10%, and 70% of the total.[31]

The wage gap between large SOEs' higher management and ordinary workers has also widened greatly. In some cases, the annual wages of the heads of SOEs were 100 times more than ordinary workers' wages.[32] Even among ordinary workers, wages vary greatly by region, industry, and enterprise ownership. Workers in more developed regions such as the east coast and the industries monopolized by large SOEs, such as finance, energy, telecom, tobacco, and power industries, earn much more than those in other regions and industries.

Violations of labor rights in enterprises in the non-state sector, which accounts for the bulk of employment, are rampant.[33] In 2009, over 70% of workers worked in non-state sector enterprises including private, foreign funded, joint-venture, other share-holding enterprises, and so on.[34] According to an investigation conducted by All China Federation of Trade Unions (ACFTU) in late 2007 in 10 cities including Shanghai, Wuxi, and Lanzhou, private enterprises had the lowest level of implementation of the labor contract system.[35] National investigations into the implementation of the Labor Law and Labor Union Law conducted by the National People's Congress (NPC) in 2005 and 2009 also showed that labor rights violations, such as extremely low wages, overtime without payment, arrears of payment, lack of major insurances and safety protection, abuse of probation, and short-term contracts, were especially common in non-state sector enterprises.[36]

Migrant workers were the worst hit. They were not officially recognized as part of the working class until 2003.[37] In 2008, there were 287 million urban workers and migrant workers made up 140 million. Migrant workers account for more than half of the industrial and service workers in China,[38] and yet they are subject to the most frequent and severe violations of labor rights: half of them work without labor contracts and are thus not employed officially. Many of them had no unemployment insurance (89%), no pension (83%), no medical insurance (70%), and no work accident insurance (65%).[39]

Wages constitute less than 10% of the total cost of Chinese enterprises, while the wage cost of enterprises in developed countries is about 50%.[40] In the Pearl River Delta, the productivity is about 17% that of the US, but workers' wages are only about 6.7% those of the US. From 1990 through 2005, the share of labor remuneration in GDP declined from 53.4% to 41.4% in China. From 1993 through 2004, while Chinese GDP increased by 3.5 times, total wages increased by only 2.4 times.[41] Most workers' income has not only remained low, but is also increasing at an extremely slow rate.

Meanwhile, the representation of ordinary workers in the NPC has declined significantly since 1978. Specifically, the share of ordinary workers in the NPC had decreased from 26.7% in 1978 to 10.8% in 2003. Peasant representation has also witnessed a declining trend since the reform. Similarly, the share of ordinary workers in the CCP has also declined from 18.7% in 1978[42] to only 9.7% in 2008.[43] Furthermore, only 7.5% of new CCP members in 2008 were ordinary workers.[44]

Workers were defenseless in the face of the heavy-handed enforcement of a capitalistic logic and an increasingly despotic factory regime.[45] They do not have the rights to strike, rights which were originally granted to workers but were removed by the 1982 Constitution. The 1992 Trade Union Law also did not bestow workers with such rights. ACFTU, which should be a mouthpiece of the workers, had failed to represent the interests of workers. Even after the introduction of considerable changes, it is clear that the allegiance of ACFTU is to the state and not the workers.[46]

Since the turn of the new century, improvement of labor conditions has topped the agenda of the Chinese government. The central government has taken various measures to address this issue. For example, in the Eleventh NPC in 2008, the share of ordinary worker and peasant members increased by over 100% and over 70%, respectively. In addition, for the first time three migrant workers were selected to represent China's 140 million migrant workers in the NPC.[47] The ACFTU has also endeavored to protect workers' interests more effectively in recent years. It contributed greatly to the drafting and promulgating of the Labor Contract Law of 2007, which is strongly pro-labor. Furthermore, in the Fifteenth National Congress of Chinese Trade Unions in 2008, for the first time 47 migrant workers were selected to represent the 65 million migrant workers in trade unions.[48]

Middle-Class Protests

With the growth of China's middle class, there has been growing interest in the sociopolitical attitudes of this rising group. Early predictions of the emergence of middle classes depicted them as the most active pursuers of democracy. However, Chinese scholars found that the middle classes were supportive of government policies and economic reform, and were politically conservative. They are thus unlikely to develop into a strong and stabilizing societal force.[49]

Most recent research shows that China's middle classes were a mix of liberalists and conservatives due to their divergent backgrounds and life experiences. They tend to have more positive feelings about democracy and high expectation of social justice, and show more confidence in understanding and participating in the politics. Most of them hope to benefit from economic growth and maintain their current lifestyles; they thus value sociopolitical stability and look to the authoritarian government for economic security. In general, the middle classes appear to be more open-minded regarding the pursuit of democracy, and have better understanding of politics than the working class and agricultural labor class. They acknowledge the income gap problem and agree on taxing the rich to help the poor, but they are equally ready to accept the pursuit of profit as a means to sustain economic growth. As the majority of the middle classes are business professionals, government officials, and intellectuals, their career and professional life are placed a rung higher than their social life.[50]

However, middle classes do engage in social protests. They were the main force behind the pro-democracy movement in 1989.[51] Since the mid-2000s, there have been quite a number of large-scale social protests initiated by the new middle class in the cities. In all these protests, urban citizens have demonstrated their increasingly strong concerns for the environment and other social issues.[52] Two protests in Xiamen and Shanghai were related to environmental protection and the other was the anti-dog killing gathering in Beijing. The protest in Xiamen was against the building of a paraxylene chemical plant near Xiamen city. A chemistry professor at Xiamen University warned that the chemical might cause cancer among residents nearby. On June 1, 2007 citizens of Xiamen launched a "walking" protest against the project, eventually forcing the government to relocate the project. The protest in Shanghai was against the building of a magnetically levitated (maglev) train between Shanghai and Hangzhou. The reason for the protest was the anticipated radiation effect from the magnet. On January 12, 2008 protesters in Shanghai took the form of strolling to voice their concerns. As the maglev is a huge developmental project and the Shanghai government was already committed to it, the protest did not achieve its goal. But the incident delivered a message to the authority that more scientific research and public hearing are needed for projects of such a scale. The protest in Beijing was against the killing of dogs that were homeless or exceeded the officially prescribed height and weight. Thousands of participants gathered in front of Beijing Zoo on November 11, 2006 with the "Protect the animals" slogan. The anti-dog killing protest successfully put a halt to the dog killing campaign in Beijing.

These protests reflect certain postmodern values of citizens. Environmental awareness will prevail when a society has reached a high stage of economic development. The new middle classes are the beneficiaries of China's economic boom. Therefore their concerns are primarily about the quality of life. Unlike protests against pollutions that directly threatened the survival of the affected population, the protests in Shanghai and Xiamen are against a potential future threat, reflecting the educational and knowledge level of the urban middle class. These types of protests are rare, but have demonstrated the different features of mass incidents in China. All three mass incidents were peaceful in style. Thousands of people had been mobilized mainly by cell phones or Internet messages.

Ethnic Conflicts

The market-oriented development has also given rise to different forms of ethnic conflict and resistance.[53] During the early years of the reform after 1978, moderate and tolerant policies had been implemented to gain the confidence of the minority groups. To some extent, economic growth can constrain or alleviate ethnic nationalism by delivering more economic benefits to the minority groups. In reality the reverse may be true. Economic development may result in the rise of ethnic nationalism. Economic changes are often accompanied by cultural changes. In China, reform policies have intensified ethnic consciousness and led to the emergence of ethnic nationalism as exemplified in the case of Tibet.

In 1980 two top leaders, Hu Yaobang and Wan Li, made a highly publicized visit to Tibet and outlined a six-point program for Tibetans. This program increased the number of Tibetan cadres in local government in replacement of a number of Chinese officials withdrawn, dissolved collectives, exempted Tibetans from state taxes and requisitions for a period of time, permitted commerce along the borders, and promoted the native economy. Hu also encouraged a moderate cultural policy that permitted a renaissance of Tibetan religious tradition to spark greater tolerance for Chinese rule and greater political stability. Nevertheless, instead of producing positive results, these policies led to rebellions and riots.[54]

The central government's moderate policies also resulted in strong reactions from other major minority areas, especially in Xinjiang where minority groups claimed that the Chinese were exploiting them and taking away their resources for redistribution to the rest of the country. Various riots and rebellions occurred throughout the reform. As these minority groups inhabit China's border areas, ethnic nationalism is frequently influenced by forces outside China. With the collapse of the Soviet Union, the newly independent status of the Central Asian states has allowed separatist groups in Xinjiang to locate some sources of support, leading to over 30 reported bombing incidents claimed by groups militating for an "Independent East Turkestan" in the Xinjiang region in 1994.[55]

The economic reforms have generated many problems which have significant consequences for ethnic groups. The central government's uneven development policy has deepened "uneven development" between the Han majority and minority nationalities. Many local officials argued that a typical colonial economy has been developed in terms of minority–majority relations. Minority groups usually sell their raw materials at a cheap price and have to pay a high price for their consumer goods.[56] Ethnic groups are said to feel "relatively deprived" and politically restless in certain circumstances. In some areas, ethnic groups have demanded favorable policies from the central government in order to improve their economic situation. In others, they have expressed their dissatisfaction through rebellions and riots. The rise of ethnic nationalism has posed a serious threat to China as a multinational state.

At the turn of the new century, ethnic conflicts have become even more violent. There were six major reported ethnic conflicts between 2003 and 2009. Ethnic conflicts characterized by violence attract huge crowds quickly. Some of these conflicts are often ignited by a minor incident but they have the tendency to become large-scale disturbances. The rigidity of ethnic identities has generated the "us" vs. "them" sentiment among different ethnic groups.

Today, ethnic conflicts have become organized and involve political agendas. The incidents in Lhasa in March 2008 and in Urumqi in July 2009 came under this category.[57] In the Urumqi case, a random Uyghur–Han conflict that occurred on June 26, 2009 in Shaoguan county of Guangdong was rumored to be the trigger of the July 5 Urumqi incident. A girl of Han ethnicity was reportedly raped by one of the Uyghur workers in a toy factory. The rape led to massive fighting between Han and Uyghur workers and the death of two Uyghur workers with 120 (Uyghur 81, Han 39) injured. The authorities were blamed by Uyghur workers for failing to handle the Shaoguan incident in a fair manner. A large-scale protest was subsequently launched in the same month by Uyghurs in Urumqi, the capital city of the Xinjiang Uyghurs Autonomous Region. According to the official report, the riot began as a protest, but later escalated into violent attacks, leaving 197 people dead. Among them, 156 were innocent citizens (Han 134, Hui 11, Uyghur 10, and Man 1).

Ethnic differences are the most persistent cause of social frictions and the most effective means of political mobilization. To achieve ethnic harmony, much is dependent on the creation of a common national identity and the nurturing of shared attitudes toward the existing sociopolitical system. But the reality is that such common identity does not exist. According to a survey, the minority people are less likely than the Han to identify themselves as "Chinese." Economically, minority citizens perceive fewer gains partaking in China's rapid economic development than the Han group. They are less satisfied with their lives, and feel less happy than their Han neighbors. They are not only indifferent to Chinese political issues, but also psychologically alienated from the political system. While the minorities generally feel capable of participating in public affairs, this sense of capacity is lowest with ethnic groups in the western provinces. Minorities are also less likely to believe that the government is responsive to their needs, and trust the government less than the Han.[58]

National integration remains a central task for China. Substantial measures need to be taken to close the gaps between the Han and minority groups in terms of political and social orientations. Without effective policies and measures on all fronts including reducing income inequalities across ethnicities, increasing life satisfaction of minorities, improving minorities' participation capability, and enhancing governmental responsiveness, ethnic conflicts will likely remain as a thorny issue for the Chinese leadership.

Conclusion

With the exception of ethnic conflicts and nationalistic demonstrations, social protests in today's China revolve around economic issues or social grievances. These grievances were generated by rapid socioeconomic transformation on the one hand, and poor governance on the other. So far, most social protests are localized and isolated incidents, except for a number of protests that occurred simultaneously in multiple adjacent counties, such as the teachers' strikes in Sichuan province, and the taxation protests in Henan and Anhui. Local governments are often the target of protests as they are directly or indirectly responsible for the grievances. Social protests are a part of normal social life in China and in other parts of the world. The rise of social protests does not necessarily mean an unstable ruling regime. In many cases, social protests did not involve politically strategic populations nor did they mount serious challenges to the regime.[59]

Many social protests are developmental and a result of China's socioeconomic transformation, and could be negated by further development. The more dangerous trend is in the increasing number of social disturbances and riots triggered by minor incidents. While it seems that the participants had no particular purpose or interest, these incidents reflect profound and broad social grievances that are not easy to address. Ethnic conflict is probably the most difficult to handle as simmering ethnic tensions could erupt into violent riots and on an uncontrollable scale.

Since social protests will continue to exist and develop, what matters is how they can be effectively managed. The government needs to launch an extensive effort to improve the quality of governance, from major leaders to the lower echelon of members of the government. The rise of civil society is generating new dynamics for reorganizing China's social order. What kind of new social order would be best suited to the world's second largest economy? Are alternatives available? These are issues the following chapters will address.

Notes

1   The figure for 2008 was an "estimate" as reported by Andrew Jacobs, "Dragons, Dancing Ones, Set-off a Riot in China." *New York Times*, February 10, 2009.

2   Tong and Shaohua (2010).

3   There is a growing body of literature on China's income inequality and its consequences, see Oi *et al.* (2010); Whyte (2010a, b); and Davis and Wang (2009). For China's changing poverty alleviation strategy, see World Bank (2009).

4   Wang (2000).

5   World Bank (1997).

6   National Bureau of Statistics (1998: 9).

7   Xu and Li (1999: 34).

8   Wang (2000: 385).

9   Li Ming, "City Beefs up Anti-Graft Drive." *China Daily*, April 22, 2000.

10   Bakken (2000).

11   Zhao and Zhou (2000).

12   Bernstein and Lu (2000).

13   Yew (2011).

14   Walder (1991).

15   Wang (2008).

16   Qiao (2007).

17   <http://www.cnhubei.com/200703/ca1286244.htm> (accessed December 29, 2009).

18   <http://www.npc.gov.cn/npc/zfjc/ghfzfjc/2009-10/30/content_1524883.htm> (accessed December 29, 2009).

19   For an analysis of the dependency of workers on the state, see Walder (1986). For an analysis of changes in the urban workplace in the post-Mao era, see Bian (2005).

20   For a discussion of some immediate reactions to these policies, see Yang and Lu (1992).

21   Zhang (2009).

22   China Labor Statistical Yearbook (1996: 409).

23   *China Daily*, February 28, 1998.

24   Gu (1999).

25   Yang (2000: 151).

26   Ibid., 150.

27   Hu (2000b).

28   Hu (2000a).
29   <http://www.caogen.com/blog/infor_detail.aspx?ID=152&articleId=16924>
     (accessed January 31, 2010).
30   Qiao (2007).
31   Shao (2006).
32   For example, see <www.jxcn.cn> (accessed January 28, 2010).
33   See, for example, the recent investigation report on the implementation of Labor
     Union Law by the National People's Congress at <http://www.npc.gov.cn/npc/zfjc/
     ghfzfjc/2009-10/30/content_1524883.htm> (accessed December 29, 2009).
34   <http://theory.people.com.cn/GB/10155027.html> (accessed December 29, 2009).
35   Bing (2008).
36   <http://jpkc.njau.edu.cn/hr/Article_Show.asp?ArticleID=486>   (accessed June 6,
     2010), and <http://www.npc.gov.cn/npc/zfjc/ghfzfjc/2009-10/30/content_1524883.
     htm> (accessed December 29, 2009).
37   <http://www.china.com.cn/news/txt/2009-09/11/content_18507165.htm>   (accessed
     January 28, 2010).
38   <http://theory.people.com.cn/GB/10155027.html> and <http://www.china.com.
     cn/news/txt/2009-09/11/content_18507165.htm> (accessed December 29, 2009).
39   Recalculated   from   data   in   <http://www.china.com.cn/news/txt/2009-09/11/
     content_18507165.htm>.
40   Qi (2010: 13).
41   Ibid.
42   Wang (2003).
43   <http://renshi.people.com.cn/GB/139620/9578659.html> (accessed January 29,
     2010).
44   Ibid.
45   Lee (1999).
46   Hishida *et al.* (2010); Perry (1995); and Jiang (1996).
47   <http://renshi.people.com.cn/GB/139620/9578659.html> (accessed January 29,
     2010).
48   <http://cpc.people.com.cn/GB/64093/64099/8194680.html> (accessed January 29,
     2010).
49   For example, Li and Yi (2008). There is also a growing body of literature on the
     political role of the middle classes, particularly private entrepreneurs in China, see
     Li (2010); Chen and Dickson (2010); Dickson (2008); and Tsai (2007).
50   Zhou (2006: 111–35).
51   On urban political participation, see Shi (1977). On changing urban life, see Tang
     and Parich (2000).
52   On China's environmental issues, see Edmonds (1998) and Economy (2004). On
     China's environmental activism, see Mertha (2008) and Xie (2009).
53   For the question of China's ethnic minorities, see Gladney (1991); Dillon (1999);
     Heberer (1989); Bulag (2000); and Rossabi (2004).
54   Karmel (1995–96).
55   Gladney (1995: 6); for a discussion of "Independent East Turkestan," see Wang
     (1998).
56   Hu (1994).

57   Bo and Chen (2008); Huang (2008); Shan and Chen (2009).
58   Shan (2010).
59   Walder and Zhao (2007).

References

Bakken, B. 2000. "State Control and Social Control in China." In Kjeld Erik Brodsgaard and Susan Young, eds., *State Capacity in Japan, Taiwan, China and Vietnam*. Oxford: Oxford University Press, pp. 185–202.

Bernstein, T. and Xiaobo Lu. 2000. "Taxation without Representation: Peasants, the Central and the Local States in Reform China." *The China Quarterly* 163 (September): 742–63.

Bian, M. 2005. *The Making of the State Enterprise System in Modern China: The Dynamics of Institutional Change*. Cambridge, MA: Harvard University Press.

Bing, Han. 2008. "Difficulty and Countermeasures of Safeguarding Rights by Trade Unions in Enterprises" (Dangqian qiye gonghui weiquan de kunjing ji falu duice). *Administration and Law* (Xingzheng Yu Fa) 8 (August): 31–34.

Bo, Zhiyue and Gang Chen. 2008. "Beijing's Tibet Problem: Policies and Dilemmas." *EAI Background Brief 384*, East Asian Institute, National University of Singapore.

Bulag, Uradyn E. 2000. "Ethnic Resistance with Socialist Characteristics." In Elizabeth J. Perry and Mark Selden, eds., *Chinese Society: Change, Conflict and Resistance*. London and New York: Routledge, pp. 178–97.

Chen, Jie and Bruce Dickson. 2010. *Allies of The State: China's Private Entrepreneurs and Democratic Change*. Cambridge, MA: Harvard University Press.

China Labor Statistical Yearbook. 1996. *Zhongguo laodong nianjian* (China Labor Statistical Yearbook). Beijing: Zhongguo nianjian chubanshe.

Davis, D. and F. Wang, eds. 2009. *Creating Wealth and Poverty in Post-Socialist China*. Stanford, CA: Stanford University Press.

Dickson, Bruce. 2008. *Wealth Into Power: The Communist Party's Embrace of China's Private Sector*. Cambridge: Cambridge University of Press.

Dillon, M. 1999. *China's Muslim Hui Community: Migration, Settlement and Sects*. Richmond, UK: Curzon Press.

Economy, E. 2004. *The River Runs Black: The Environmental Challenges to China's Future*. Ithaca, NY: Cornell University Press.

Edmonds, R. L. 1998. "China's Environment." Special Issue of *The China Quarterly* 156 (December).

Gladney, Dru C. 1991. *Muslim Chinese: Ethnic Nationalism in the People's Republic*. Cambridge, MA: Harvard University Press.

Gladney, Dru C. 1995. *China's Ethnic Reawakening*. AsiaPacific issues 18. Honolulu: East-West Center.

Gu, Edward X. 1999. "From Permanent Employment to Massive Lay-Offs: The Political Economy of 'Transitional Unemployment' in Urban China (1993–8)." *Economy and Society* 28, 2 (May): 281–99.

Heberer, T. 1989. *China and Its National Minorities: Autonomy or Assimilation?* Armonk, NY: M. E. Sharpe.

Hishida, Masaharu, Kazuko Kojima, Tomoaki Ishiii, and Jian Qiao. 2010. *China's Trade Unions: How Autonomous Are They? A Survey of 1,811 Enterprise Union Chairpersons.* London and New York: Routledge.

Hu, Angang. 1994. "Shengdiji ganbu yanzhong de dongxibu chayu" (Income Disparities between Eastern and Western China in the Eye of Leading Cadres of the Provincial and Prefectoral Levels). *Zhanlue yu guanli* (Strategy and Management) 5: 88–90.

Hu, Angang. 2000a. "High Unemployment in China: Estimates and Policies." Paper presented at the International Conference on "Center–Periphery Relations in China: Integration, Disintegration or Reshaping of an Empire?" The French Center for Contemporary China and the Chinese University of Hong Kong, Hong Kong, March 25, 2000.

Hu, Angang. 2000b. "Kuaru xin shiji de zuida tiaozhan: woguo jinru gaoshiye jieduan." In Hu Angang, ed., *Zhongguo zouxiang* (Prospects of China). Hangzhou: Zhejiang renmin chubanshe, pp. 49–77.

Huang, Jing. 2008. "China's Tibet Problem: Still No Way Out?" *EAI Background Brief 383*, East Asian Institute, National University of Singapore.

Jiang, Kevin. 1996. "Gonghui yu dang-guojia de chongtu: bashi niandai yilai de Zhongguo gonghui gaige" (The Conflicts Between Trade Unions and the Party-State: The Reform of Chinese Trade Unions since the 1980s). *Hong Kong Journal of Social Science* 8 (Autumn): 120–58.

Karmel, S. M. 1995–96. "Ethnic Tension and the Struggle for Order: China's Policies in Tibet." *Pacific Affairs* 68, 4 (Winter): 485–508.

Lee, Ching Kwan. 1999. "From Organized Dependence to Disorganized Despotism: Changing Labor Regimes in Chinese Factories." *The China Quarterly* 157 (March): 44–71.

Li, Cheng, ed. 2010. *China's Emerging Middle Class: Beyond Economic Transformation.* Washington, DC: The Brookings Institution.

Li, Peilin and Zhang Yi. 2008. "Zhongguo zhongchan jieji de guimo, rentong he shehui taidu" (Size, Identity and Social Attitudes of Chinese Middle Classes). *Society* 28, 6: 1–19.

Mertha, Andrew C. 2008. *China's Water Warriors: Citizen Action and Policy Change.* Ithaca, NY: Cornell University Press.

National Bureau of Statistics. 1998. *Annual Prices and Family Incomes and Expenditures in Chinese Cities, 1998.* Beijing: Zhongguo tongji chubanshe.

Oi, J. C., S. Rozelle, and X. Zhou, eds. 2010. *Growing Pains: Tensions and Opportunity in China's Transformation.* Stanford, CA: Stanford University Press.

Perry, E. 1995. "Labor's Battle for Political Space: The Role of Worker Associations in Contemporary China." In Deborah S. Davis *et al.*, eds., *Urban Spaces in Contemporary China: The Potential for Autonomy and Community in Post-Mao China.* Washington, DC and Cambridge: Woodrow Wilson Center Press and Cambridge University Press, pp. 302–25.

Qi, Dongtao. 2010. "Chinese Working Class in Predicament." *EAI Background Brief 528.* East Asian Institute, National University of Singapore.

Qiao, Jian. 2007. "Zai guojia, qiye he laogong zhijian: Zhongguo gonghui xiang shich-angjingji zhuanxing zhong de duo chong juese" (Among State, Enterprises and Labor: Chinese Trade Unions' Multiple Roles in the Transition to Market Economy). *Bulletin of Labor Research* 22 (July): 67–101.

Rossabi, M., ed. 2004. *Governing China's Multiethnic Frontiers*. Seattle and London: University of Washington Press.

Shan, Wei. 2010. "Grievances of China's Ethnic Minorities: Analysing Their Political Attitudes." *EAI Background Brief 515*, East Asian Institute, National University of Singapore.

Shan, Wei and Gang Chen. 2009. "China's Flawed Policy in Xinjiang and Its Dilemmas." *EAI Background Brief 463*, East Asian Institute, National University of Singapore.

Shao, Huiping. 2006. "Dangdai gongren jieji neibu fenceng" (Stratification within Current Chinese Working Class). *Jingji yu shehui fazhan* (Economic and Social Development) 4, 7: 186.

Shi, Tianjian. 1977. *Political Participation in Beijing*. Cambridge, MA: Harvard University Press.

Tang, Wenfang and W. L. Parich. 2000. *Chinese Urban Life under Reform: The Changing Social Contract*. Cambridge: Cambridge University Press.

Tong, Yanqi and Lei Shaohua. 2010. "Large-Scale Mass Incidents in China." *EAI Background Brief 520*, East Asian Institute, National University of Singapore.

Tsai, K. S. 2007. *Capitalism without Democracy: The Private Sector in Contemporary China*. Ithaca, NY: Cornell University Press.

Walder, A. 1986. *Communist Neo-Traditionalism: Work and Authority in Chinese Industry*. Berkeley, CA: University of California Press.

Walder, A. 1991. "Workers, Managers and the State: The Reform Era and the Political Crisis of 1989." *The China Quarterly* 127 (September): 467–92.

Walder, A. and Litao Zhao. 2007. "China's Social Protests: Political Threat or Growing Pains?" *EAI Background Brief 357*, East Asian Institute, National University of Singapore.

Wang, David. 1998. "The East Turkestan Movement in Xinjiang: A Chinese Potential Source of Instability?" *EAI Background Brief 7*, East Asian Institute, National University of Singapore.

Wang, Kan. 2008. "A Changing Arena of Industrial Relations in China: What Is Happening after 1978." *Employee Relations* 30, 2: 190–216.

Wang, Shaoguang. 2000. "The Social and Political Implications of China's WTO Membership." *Journal of Contemporary China* 9, 25: 386.

Wang, Xian. 2003. "Wodang lishishang dangyuan shehui chengfen biandong qing-kuang" (Social Composition of CCP Members in History). *Dang De Jianshe* (CCP's Construction) 8: 39.

Whyte, M. K. 2010a. *Myth of the Social Volcano: Popular Responses to Rising Inequality in China*. Stanford, CA: Stanford University Press.

Whyte, M. K., ed. 2010b. *Rural–Urban Inequality in Contemporary China*. Cambridge, MA: Harvard University Press.

World Bank. 1997. *Sharing Rising Incomes*. Washington, DC: World Bank.

World Bank. 2009. *From Poor Areas to Poor People: China's Evolving Poverty Reduction Agenda: An Assessment of Poverty and Inequality in China*. Washington, DC: Poverty Reduction and Economic Management Department, World Bank.

Xie, Lei. 2009. *Environmental Activism in China*. London: Routledge.

Xu, Xinxin and Peilin Li. 1999. "1998–1999 nian Zhongguo jiuye shouru he xinxi chanye de fenxi he yuce" (Employment, Income, and IT Industry: Analysis and Forecasts, 1998–1999). In Ru Xin, Lu Xueyi, and Shan Tianlun, eds., *1999 nian Zhongguo shehui xingshi fenxi yu yuce* (Analyses and Forecasts of China's Social Situation in 1999). Beijing: Shehui kexue wenxian chubanshe.

Yang, Aihua and Sishan Lu. 1992. *Zapo "santie" hou de Zhongguo ren* (Chinese After the Smashing of the "Three Irons"). Beijing: Beijing ligong daxue chubanshe.

Yang, Yiyong. 2000. "2000nian Zhongguo jiuye xinshi jiqi zhengce xuanze" (Employment in 2000 and Policy Options). In Liu Guoguang *et al.*, eds., *Jinji lanpishu 2000* (Economic Bluebook 2000). Beijing: Shehui wenxian chubanshe.

Yew, Chiew Ping. 2011. "How Property Boom Generates Social Tension in China." *EAI Background Brief 651*, East Asian Institute, National University of Singapore.

Zhang, Xiaodan. 2009. "Trade Unions under the Modernization of Paternalist Rule in China." *Working USA: The Journal of Labor and Society* 12: 193–218.

Zhao, Yang and Feizhou Zhou. 2000. "Nongmin fudan he caishui tizhi" (Peasants' Burdens and Fiscal System). *Hong Kong Journal of Social Sciences* 17 (Autumn): 67–85.

Zhou, Xiaohong, ed. 2006. *Zhongguo zhongchan jieceng diaocha* (Survey on Chinese Middle Class). Beijing: Zhongguo shehui kexue chubanshe.

Chapter 7

Cultural Changes

While the market-oriented reform has led to rapid economic development and social transformation, it has also given rise to social pluralism. China is now an interest-based society, which is characterized by the existence of diversified interests. At a deeper level, such a change is also reflected in the rise of cultural pluralism. With their different interests, social groups have developed diversified cultural values and lifestyles. They no longer simply accept a culture imposed from above. Social pluralism has a political consequence too. Pluralistic interests are now contesting with one another to impact China's state-building, and they all want to influence the direction of China's reform and development according to their own agendas. Indeed, with the decline of official ideology, be it Marxism or Maoism, the state is no longer able to impose any definite ideology onto society. While the state remains reluctant to give up its official ideology, it has actively searched for a new one that is acceptable to both the state and society. This leaves plenty of leeway to social groups to pursue and express their own versions of idealism. China today is once again full of competing and conflicting ideas and ideologies.

This chapter examines several key schools of thought and conflicting ideas in China, including liberalism, nationalism, New Left, and the cultural renaissance movement, in a chronological order. Of course, there is overlapping among these schools. We explore the rise of each school, and its relations with the state and with other schools of thought. Such an examination is important in understanding China and its future since the state alone now cannot dictate the country's development.

Contemporary China: A History since 1978, First Edition. Yongnian Zheng.
© 2014 John Wiley & Sons, Ltd. Published 2014 by John Wiley & Sons, Ltd.

The Rise of Liberalism in the 1980s

Liberalism became the mainstream intellectual discourse in the 1980s. With the end of the Cultural Revolution (CR), Chinese political and intellectual elites were amazed by Western cultural, material, and technological achievements. Their previous belief in the supremacy of socialism was replaced by their new belief in the supremacy of the West. However, liberalism in China did not mean individualism; instead, it was regarded as a means to pursue a stronger China, a very old mentality of strong state which has consolidated throughout China's modern history. As during the May Fourth Movement in the early twentieth century, liberalism in the 1980s is characterized by a strong desire to learn from the West. To reform China by learning from the West became a common pursuit of the reformist leadership and liberal intellectuals.

China's external environment in the 1980s was conducive to the rise of liberalism. In the 1970s, following US President Nixon's visit to China, the two countries established diplomatic relations, and the Sino-Japanese relationship was normalized. The People's Republic of China replaced the Republic of China as the permanent member in the UN Security Council. All these foreign relationship breakthroughs provided China with a benign external environment for its reform and opening-up policy. Between the periods in which China decided to open up and the 1989 Tiananmen crackdown, the West adopted a very friendly attitude toward China. China's opening-up policy led the West to believe that economic liberalization would eventually lead China to democracy.

The domestic environment also tended to be supportive of liberalism. The reformists were dominant within the government despite the strong presence of conservative forces. In the mid-1980s, Deng Xiaoping began to actively promote political reforms.[1] Subsequently, the Party leadership established a political reform discussion group, headed by then Secretary General Zhao Ziyang. Relevant research projects were assigned to different research institutes to be looked into and large numbers of officials were sent overseas to observe and learn from foreign experience.[2] The rapid institutional building up of reformists facilitated the growth of the reform camp, and a heated debate on democratization soon ensued within the government. The 1980s was an era when discussions on political reforms were the most comprehensive and most daring in China's contemporary history. Such top-down reform initiatives effectively mobilized social forces which were in favor of rapid political changes.

The liberalism of the 1980s was also partially the result of attempts on the part of the reformist leadership to draw lessons from the mistakes by the Maoist leadership. Once China opened its door, the Chinese quickly realized that during the times in which China was undergoing Maoist class struggles and other political campaigns, the capitalist countries had developed to a stage unreachable to China; that their notion that the socialist system and communism would be the ultimate system for humanity was nothing more than a self-comforting myth. Skepticism toward their present state and anxiety over the backwardness of their nation caused the intellectuals to cast their eyes toward the West. They hoped that by learning from Western technologies and political thoughts, they could save China and build a strong nation again. The eagerness of Chinese liberals to learn from the West is reflected in various cultural fads China experienced during that decade.

Fascination with Western cultures

During the 1980s, numerous Western classics such as Nietzsche, Kant, Weber, and Kafka were translated into the Chinese language and introduced to the Chinese audience. At the same time, liberal intellectuals produced enormous publications, focusing on Western politics, economy, society, technology, and culture. They initiated a movement that they called the "New Enlightenment." The book series "Marching toward the Future" (*Zouxiang weilai conshu*) saw 74 volumes published within a period of only five years from 1984 to 1988. The book series "Culture: China and the World" (*Wenhua: Zhongguo yu shijie*) and the magazine "Reading" (*Dushu*) also played a major role in this enlightenment movement. The Shanghai-based *World Economy Herald* (*Shijie jingji daobao*), which daringly discussed China's political and economic reforms, had a circulation of 300,000 in its heyday.[3] These publications replaced the old standard communist media and became the bestsellers. In the midst of this great debate, China was engulfed by a reading frenzy for almost 10 years. Books were being sold at volumes unimaginable today.

The university forum craze

After China began its reform, the influence of pro-Western intellectuals grew. These intellectuals had experienced the Maoist dictatorship and developed a deep sense of anxiety for the widening gap between China and the West on all fronts. They believed that the only remedy was to reform the country's political and economic system. The university forums were outlets in which they could express their dissatisfaction with the current situation, criticize the government policy, and promote economic liberalization and political democratization. Liberals such as Liu Binyan, Yan Jiaqi, and Fang Lizhi were popular public intellectuals at these forums and influenced a generation of youths. The organizations and institutions that were active such as Beijing University would have multiple forums within a single day. The thinking of these intellectuals and the cultural fad of that period influenced vast numbers of youths of the day.[4]

A dream for democracy

During the 1980s, what Samuel Huntington called the "third wave of democratization" swept across the globe and affected many countries.[5] China's neighbor South Korea was democratized, Taiwan lifted its ban on political parties and media, while East Germany and the Soviet Union were also changing. Worldwide democratization affected the Chinese government and people and there were heated debates over China's political reforms in both the government and private sectors. In 1988, the *World Economy Herald* raised the idea that if China failed to reform its political system, it would be stripped of its "earth citizenship" (*qiuji*).[6] The heated discussions on China's "earth citizenship" successfully mobilized Chinese nationalistic feeling. The siege mentality of the intellectuals set in and once again became the focal point of China's politics, and the slogan "Saving the Chinese Nation" resurfaced. Many active tertiary institutions became saloons for talks on democracy and discussions on Western democratic systems were the central topic.[7]

Obsession with Western media

The 1980s was a special period in which new ideas clashed with China's own tradition, be it a grand imperial tradition or little communist tradition. On one hand, Western ideas and thoughts were being introduced into China and social forces were mobilized to pursue political changes. On the other hand, the old system was still influential. The domestic media, being the voice of the ruling Party, was regarded as unable to promote reforms, and had also lost credibility among the people with its false, exaggerating, and empty propagandist style of reporting. Hence, foreign broadcasts which covered China such as the Voice of America and BBC became the main source of information for those who cared about politics and contemporary affairs outside China. These foreign media also actively promoted democratic ideas among the Chinese and played an important role in facilitating the expected process of China's peaceful evolution toward democracy.

Ideas matter

Western cultures and ideas influenced both the state and society. Up to the mid-1980s, most Chinese showed their strong preference for Western cultures. According to a nationwide survey in 1987, 75% of the Chinese welcomed the inflow of Western ideas, and 80% of CCP members showed a similar attitude.[8] Understandably, while their identity toward Western ideas increased, their loyalty toward the existing regime declined. Throughout the 1980s, individuals' loyalty to the socialist state was weakened seriously and the ruling Party was criticized. For example, while 30% of the Chinese believed that the CCP's performance was satisfactory, 62% thought otherwise.[9] Popular dissatisfaction exercised increasingly high pressure on the reformist leadership to engage in political reforms and to make the Chinese state more democratic.

Liberalism was forced to retreat after the Tiananmen crackdown, but the rise of social problems since the mid-1990s has again given it an opportunity to regain some public space among intellectuals. Among others, Liu Junning and Yu Youyu at the Chinese Academy of Social Sciences, Qin Hui at Qinghua University, and Zhu Xueqin in Shanghai were the most vocal liberal scholars.[10] Since the early part of this century, liberalism was active. On the eve of the Seventeenth National Congress of the CCP in 2007, Xie Tao, the former vice president of Renmin University, published his article "The Model of Democratic Socialism and China's Future," which argued that for Chinese democracy, the European version of democratic socialism represented by the Swedish model should be the model for China's political reform. Xie's novel way of criticizing the establishment touched a raw nerve with the CCP. *People's Daily* published an "Answer to Readers' Question" on May 10, 1997, claiming that social democrats are not real "Marxists." The topic was largely forgotten by the end of the year as a "welfare state" is far away from the practical concerns in China.[11] However, political liberalism has survived even within the Party leadership. In 2010 and 2011, Premier Wen Jiabao repeatedly emphasized that the country needed political reform in order to promote other aspects of the reform. Following Wen's call, a debate took place among scholars, journalists, and other social groups that aimed to push the reform agenda further. To temper expectations, *People's Daily* published a series of articles to clarify that no reform had been planned, indicating split opinions among the central leaders on this issue.[12]

Nationalism Since the 1990s

The 1990s was marked by a resurgence of nationalism as a reaction against the changed attitude of the West toward China in the aftermath of the 1989 pro-democracy movement and the Chinese intellectuals' idolization of Western democracy during the 1980s.[13]

In 1996, a book, which best represents the new wave of nationalism, *China Can Say No* became an instant best seller and gripped the attention of the international community.[14] The authors were a few youths born in the mid or late 1960s and were then in their 30s. The book prophesied a rise of anti-Americanism among the people and announced the end of their generation's idolism of the West in the 1980s. Another two books soon joined this emotional nationalism, *Behind Demonizing China*,[15] and *The China Road under the Shadow of Globalization*.[16]

Unlike the pro-West liberalism of the 1980s, nationalism of the 1990s was characterized by patriotism which was promoted by the state and followed by social forces. In the 1980s, both the state and society had common interests in their learning from the West. But in the 1990s, both the state and society had an identical goal in resisting the influence of the West. As to liberalism in the 1980s, the rise of nationalism was also due to China's changing external and internal environments.

Externally, changes in the West's China policy favored the rise of a nationalism hostile to the West. After the 1989 Tiananmen crackdown, the US and other Western nations enforced various sanctions against China. Facing increasingly high external pressure, the Chinese government initiated a lasting nationwide educational campaign of patriotism and repeatedly emphasized the use of patriotism to oppose the West's strategy of "peaceful evolution" toward China, a strategy that was perceived to have led to the pro-democracy movement.

China's worsening external environment also led its intellectuals to identify with the government in resisting the influence of the West. In the 1990s, not only was China's human rights record heavily criticized by the West, China's bid to enter the World Trade Organization (WTO) was also interrupted by the US on many occasions. China's bid to host the Olympic Games in 1996 met with opposition from the US. On the Taiwan issue, the US was perceived to have supported Taiwan's pro-independence movement and sold armaments to Taiwan. All these developments contributed to nationalistic resentments among the Chinese youth. Various versions of "China threat" theory circulating in the West during the 1990s further pushed Chinese youth from US lover to US hater.

Meanwhile, China's rapid economic development created an internal condition in favor of patriotism. After Deng's Southern Tour in 1992, China had accelerated the process of reform. The continuous economic growth provided the CCP the legitimacy to rule. Moreover, the failure of Russia's political reforms led Chinese intellectuals to think twice about their own political reforms. The improvement in China's standard of living helped the government's strategy of "economic reform first and political reform later" to gain popular consensus. Economic development also allowed many intellectuals to be incorporated into the vested interests. While many liberal intellectuals were forced into exile in different parts of the West, many others who had previously promoted market economy and democratic politics turned to active support of the government's strategy of reform. Furthermore, the return of Hong Kong and Macau dramatically increased the Chinese sense of nationalistic pride. The combination of humiliation from the West's hard-line China policy and fast rising national pride in China's achievement became the catalyst for this wave of patriotism.

Since the turn of the century, the "Fen Qing" groups (literally, "angry youths") have become the main agent of nationalism.[17] Since the late 1990s, Fen Qing has become a term often used in newspapers and on the Internet. This term refers to youths born after the 1980s who possess both a cynical and critical view of the world and would often express their views on the Internet. As some of these youths were also actively involved in nationalistic movements, the term "Fen Qing" evolved to refer to nationalistic youths.[18]

The Fen Qing-led nationalism gained worldwide attention in the early years of the current century. Examples include the anti-American protests following a Sino-US military airplane collision in Hainan province in 2001 which resulted in the death of a Chinese pilot, nationwide anti-Japanese protests around the same period, and anti-Korean movements following a dispute over the ownership of the Dumpling Festival. In addition, their massive worldwide protests over biased reports on Tibet in the West in 2008 and perceived unfriendly actions toward China's Beijing Olympics shocked the world. For example, the "anti-CNN" website, set up by a 23-year-old graduate of Qinghua University, Rao Jin, used pictures and videos to refute biased reports by Western media such as CNN, Fox, BBC, RTL, and N-TV. This website effectively united Chinese both inside China and overseas to exert pressure on the Western media. Eventually, some foreign media had to correct their reports and some of them even officially apologized.[19]

The Fen Qing nationalism is facilitated by a number of factors. There have existed two psychological gaps among the Chinese, especially the youth. The first psychological gap is the imbalance between the Fen Qing expectation of China's international status and the actual prestige accorded to China by the international community, especially the West. The Fen Qing, being mostly born after 1980, have grown up when China was experiencing exponential economic growth. They share similar consumption patterns with their Western counterparts, with some of them even enjoying a standard of living higher than the average in Western societies. Furthermore, events such as the hosting of the Olympics, the Shanghai Expo, and the successful launch of Shenzhou 7 demonstrated the growth of China's comprehensive national strength. Growing up in such an environment, the Fen Qing have less reason than their two generations of predecessors to idolize Western societies or feel inferior. Given its achievements, the Fen Qing feel that China deserves a high international status. Yet, in reality, many Western societies were not psychologically prepared to accord China such recognition. For more than a century, the Chinese had accepted the fact that they were denied international prestige because China was weak. Today, however, the Fen Qing believe it justifiable to demand more respect from the world. When this respect is not given, the psychological gap between the expectation and reality stimulates nationalistic sentiments.

The second psychological gap is related to the first, but different. It is a psychological gap between the idealistic Fen Qing understanding of the world and the reality. To the average Chinese, the significance of hosting the Olympics is extraordinary, signifying the country's departure from being the "sick man of Asia" to joining the world as an equal major power. The Olympics bear the dreams of several generations of Chinese. One of the main motives of hosting the event was to raise China's international status. The Fen Qing wishfully believed that the world would share their joy in fulfilling their Chinese dream. Yet, the reality is that massive anti-China protests broke out in many Western societies. The anti-China voices became one of the most powerful sources of provocation.

There is also a euphoric factor. After the Global Financial Crisis started in 2008, many in China began to believe that the "Washington Consensus" would finally be replaced by the "Beijing Consensus."[20] Some also believe that the US economy is going downhill from now on and that China will become the next hegemon. The perceived US downfall has generated a strong euphoric moment among the Chinese youth. The book *Unhappy China* clearly demonstrates this arrogance.[21] The authors proposed that China should "rid the world of bullies" and "manage more resources than China currently possesses and bring about happiness to everyone in the world."[22]

Moreover, the Fen Qing nationalism is associated with globalization. The globalization of China's economy has changed its relationship with the rest of the world and has had a major impact on Chinese nationalism. While China's entry into the WTO has brought about economic opportunities and benefits to China, the country has also officially become a trade competitor to many other countries. As trade volume has increased, so have conflicts of interests between China and others. Trade interest conflicts can often cause nationalistic sentiments among the people. Also, globalization has been regarded as a major factor widening income disparities in China. In these cases, nationalists, especially the New Left, often employ the negative effects of globalization to promote their nationalistic course.

The rise of youth nationalism is due to rapid changes inside China. The new generation has grown up in a completely different environment from their parents' generation and as such, the nationalism that they are leading possesses very different characteristics.

Internet savvy youths

In the protests against biased reports on the Tibet issue, many of the web masters were only youths in their 20s. The producer of the YouTube video, "Tibet WAS, IS, and ALWAYS WILL BE a part of China" (with a hit rate of a million in two days and more than 10,000 comments)[23] was a 22-year-old student studying in Canada who goes by the nickname "NZKOF." A young student studying in Germany was responsible for the YouTube video, "Riot in Tibet: true face of the Western media" (the hit rate reached a million within a very short time and there were more than 30,000 comments)[24] and the producer of the video "2008 China stands up" (with a hit rate of a million in 11 days and more than a million positive comments)[25] was CTGZ, a 28-year-old with a philosophy doctorate.

Transnational Fen Qing

During the 2008 protests, the nationalists overseas were in communication with their counterparts in China. They were able to exchange messages via the Internet and provide mutual support and even organize transnational activities. In many of the protests in 2008, while the Fen Qing in China turned up in numbers for protests, the young overseas students were also able to make a great impact due to their linguistic ability and access to Western media. When Western media first produced inaccurate reports on Tibet, it was the overseas students who responded first on the Internet. During the relay of the Olympic Torch, Chinese students in various countries took to the streets to protect the relay. Their actions reflected the transnational nature of this wave of nationalism.

The Internetization of protests

The Fen Qing are made up of people from all walks of life with different educational backgrounds, experiences, and computer literacy levels. Generally speaking, however, the Fen Qing are all able to use the Internet as their common platform. Many protests in 2008 were executed entirely on the Internet. Examples include the anti-CNN signatures protest and the MSN red heart patriotism movement. Since its establishment, the anti-CNN website has already organized many online protests. One of the most common methods of protest is to get every participant to send a protest email to the target.[26] In Internet protests, opposing forces may debate heatedly over an issue and may resort to violent Internet activity such as flaming and hacking into a rival's webpage to edit or disrupt the targeted website. In April 2008, Internet wars of various scales could be observed in both China and overseas Internet forums.

The Fen Qing protests were not limited to cyberspace. They also engaged in street protests which were often planned and organized via the Internet. For example, the boycott of Carrefour in 2008 was organized and mobilized by instant messaging and SMS. Hence, modern communications technology plays a crucial role in the rise of the Fen Qing movement.

The New Left

An even more important intellectual development is the rise of the New Left. The New Left stands for a number of distinct but related intellectual positions and discourses. While overlapping with nationalism and conservatism, it is distinctive in the sense that it has been developed in the course of its dialogue with liberalism.[27]

The New Left emerged in the early 1990s. In 1992, after Deng's Southern Tour, the CCP accepted market economy as the core of its official ideology and the government initiated a new wave of marketization. The rise of the New Left was a reaction to such a fundamental change on the part of the government. As an intellectual movement, the New Left has developed out of several major streams of radicalism, including neo-Marxism, postmodernism, dependency, world system, and postcolonialism. From these perspectives, the New Left is very critical of global capitalism and market economy in contemporary China.

On the international front, the New Left is almost identical with nationalism and has been one of major forces behind the rise of nationalism discussed earlier. In all events including Beijing's failure in 1996 to win its bid to host the 2000 Olympic Games, the 1999 NATO bombing of the Chinese Embassy in Belgrade, the 1997 Asian Financial Crisis, and the 2008 Global Financial Crisis, the New Left joined the nationalistic forces against imperialism and globalization.[28]

It should be noted that the New Left does not want China to return to the Soviet-style economy, even though many of them are suspicious about the market-oriented reform. According to the New Left, while market-oriented reform is inevitable, the state must play an important role in regulating the market. In 1991, Wang Shaoguang published an article in an overseas journal, reflecting on the radical decentralization that Zhao Ziyang initiated in the 1980s. Wang presented a set of strong arguments in favor of centralization which, in fact, took place at that time. After the crackdown on the pro-democracy movement in 1989, the Chinese government enforced a series of measures of recentralization to maintain social stability. Wang concentrated on how economic decentralization had weakened central power. His fear of a possible breakdown of the Chinese state was supported by his comparison between China and other former communist states, especially former Yugoslavia. He believed that radical decentralization had become a major barrier to the formation of an integrated national market economy. He also argued that a highly centralized state was not necessarily totalitarian or authoritarian. Instead, according to him, to build a strong democratic China, the country had to have a centralized state.[29]

After his 1991 article, Wang and his collaborator Hu Angang expanded their arguments and presented a more systematic analysis on the capacity of the

Chinese state. Their book was published in China in 1993 and Hong Kong in 1994. It was widely read by academics and government officials.[30] In 1994, the central government began to implement a new taxation system called tax division in an attempt to recentralize its fiscal power. Though it was uncertain whether there was a direct linkage between the Wang–Hu report and the government's new fiscal measures, the Wang–Hu report undoubtedly justified the efforts by the central government to recentralize its fiscal power.

By the turn of the new century, the voice of the New Left became increasingly heard. What made it influential in China was its stance against an excessive role of the market in China's development. New Left scholars were shocked by polarization resulting from the market-oriented reform and began to question the direction of the reform. They criticized the marketization of housing, education, medical care, and the neglect of rural society as well as heavy dependence on foreign capital, technology, and markets. Wang Hui mounted a strong criticism of the enlightenment movement in the 1980s and Fukuyama's "end of history" assertion as well. He spoke highly of socialist ideas in the process of Chinese modernization. Drawing from different schools of thought in the West, Cui Zhiyuan attempted to revitalize theoretical interests in the concept of socialism. While liberals continue to emphasize the need for deepening marketization, the leftists accuse the government of over-marketization. The New Left believes that China needs a "new round of liberation of the mind" in order to achieve social justice.[31]

In the new century, the New Left has made attempts to shift its philosophical orientation from the West to China. It recognized that China's success cannot be explained by its discourse of socialism; nor can it be explained by the "deregulation" discourse advocated by liberals. To expand its philosophical ground, many New Left intellectuals now turn to the Chinese traditional system for resources of ideas, and they become "neo-conservatives." By doing so, they intend to transcend the leftists and rightists of the Western kind. For example, Gan Yang has attempted to develop a neo-conservative line of thinking of China's development by integrating the Chinese traditional system and some existing institutions borrowed from the Soviet system (such as Communist Party) and Western system (such as Republic).[32] According to him, these three systems are in accordance with the "three traditions" that have existed in China today, including the Confucian tradition, the Maoist socialist tradition, and the Western liberal tradition. He attempted to show what a "Confucian republic" will look like. Of course, neo-conservatism is not new. In the so-called "new authoritarianism" movement in the late 1980s, some scholars began to think about how the CCP regime could draw its source of legitimacy from traditionalism. The "three traditions" argument already appeared in the works of Xiao Gongqin, a Shanghai-based historian.[33]

It is worth noting that the New Left has been hit badly by the Bo Xilai affairs. For years, many New Left scholars had made attempts to associate with the political force represented by Bo Xilai. Such attempts are understandable since their goal is to change the government's policy orientation. But with the fall of Bo, the New Left has lost much of the political ground it had secured in the past decade.

The Cultural Renaissance Movement

In appealing to traditionalism, the New Left joined and promoted the cultural renaissance movement. As discussed earlier, in the 1980s mainstream Chinese intellectuals were in favor of Western cultures, and tended to denounce their own traditional culture. This is exemplified by the then popular TV series "River Elegy" whose authors ascribed China's authoritarianism and its backwardness to Chinese traditional culture and believed that only through wholesale Westernization and the introduction of advanced Western cultures could China develop itself.[34] While some scholars like Xiao Gongqin began to question this theme and appreciate the value of traditionalism, the cultural renaissance only started in the mid-1990s when the Chinese government initiated a campaign of patriotic education.

After the 1989 pro-democracy movement crackdown, Chinese society rapidly lost its faith in communism. To refill the ideological vacuum, the government began to give leeway to traditionalism.[35] An enormous number of books on traditional China in various disciplines of humanities and social sciences were published, and the concern with such knowledge became popular among university students. This led to a wave of what China called the Classical Studies (*Guoxue*) movement. Novels, TV series, movies, etc., thrived by narrating lives in traditional dynasties. China seemed to be falling into a modern version of "ancestor/emperor worship," which stimulated the rise of "neo-traditionalism."

While the *Guoxue* movement focused on classical studies, particularly Confucianism,[36] the New Left, together with other scholars from different disciplines and backgrounds, has pushed it further to form a cultural renaissance movement, exemplified by the rise of the "China model" concept and associated intellectual movements.

In his article "Beijing Consensus" published in 2004, Joshua Ramo highly praised China's development model as opposed to the Western model, namely, the "Washington Consensus."[37] He defines the "Beijing Consensus" as fulfilling three promises: 1) promise of constant experiments with innovation; 2) promise of sustainable development through balancing social needs instead of GDP; 3) promise of autonomous financial and economic system, and resisting external intervention. The "Washington Consensus" concerns an economic reform policy for developing countries, which is supported by the decision-makers in

Washington. It was proposed by John Williamson, an economist in the Peterson Institute for International Economics. Along the line of neo-liberalism, Williamson proposed 10 policy adjustments to Latin America, including: tightening fiscal discipline, reducing subsidy and tax, liberalizing interest rates, currency exchange rates, trade, FDI, privatizing state-owned enterprises, deregulating state interventions, and strengthening legal protection of private property rights.[38]

Since then much scholarly attention in China has been devoted to defining and researching the content of the "China model." While scholars continue to debate what the China model is, this intellectual movement appears more like a cultural renaissance movement than a debate on the China model itself. Over the years, the discussion on the China model has been increasingly popular, especially since the 2008 Global Financial Crisis. More and more prominent scholars of humanities and social sciences have joined in the discussion in one way or another, and dozens of books with "China model" in their titles have been published. For some, it is a convenient platform for evaluating the changes in socioeconomic policies. For many others, it is about a systemic explanation of China's performance. One survey in 2009 showed that nearly 75% of the Chinese intellectuals believe the existence of the "China model;" about 21% of them deny its existence, among whom more than 5% indicated that this model would require "the world's recognition;" and the remaining 4% have "no idea."[39]

However, there is no consensus about the China model among Chinese scholars. From different perspectives, many scholars do not see a clearly defined China model. Liberal economists regard the Chinese policy of liberalization as part of the world's tide of marketization, privatization, and globalization. It implies that the continued success in China hinges on further economic liberalization. Yao Yang, an economist at Beijing University, is representative of this view. In many public occasions, Yao has consistently objected to the term "China model," and insists that the so-called "China model" could only exist in a political sense, namely, a "neutral government" that adopts neo-classic economic policies. Economist Fan Gang also holds a similar view. He attributes nearly all of China's social problems, including corruption, to the lack of deepening marketization.[40] Other scholars see the problem from a political perspective, and argue that to become a model, China needs not only further marketization but also democratization. Li Junru, the former deputy president of the Central Party School, argues that the Chinese institutions are still under reform and evolving, and the so-called China model would dangerously divert the direction of institutional reform to market and democracy and thus stifle the reforms.[41]

For the New Left, the China model not only exists, but is also a legitimate one, in parallel to various other models that existed previously, including those in the West. Realizing that the China model cannot be explained by the dichotomy of authoritarianism and democracy in the West, the New Left has turned to China's tradition and civilization to search for the rationale behind the China model. Pan Wei at Beijing University is representative in this regard. In an attempt at a comprehensive approach, he identified key characteristics of the Chinese system vs. the Western system. According to him, a "system" can be understood as a "trinity" of economic, political, and social subsystems. The "Western system" and "Chinese system" differ from each other in all these aspects. First, the two systems differ in the way of organizing society. In the West, the independent, self-organized, class-based and/or group-based civil societies contend for resources through partisan politics. In China, the network of communities and work units are organically connected with the vertical and horizontal network of bureaucracy. Second, the two differ in the way of organizing politics. In the West, under the principle of majority, an electoral democracy of contending parties forms a flexible balance of governing power, with an independent judiciary to prevent instability. In China, a politically unified and neutral governing group leads a *minben* (literally, people-centered) democracy under the principle of meritocracy, with a division-of-labor mechanism to prevent and correct mistakes. *Minbenism* (literally, people-centrism) means that the very reason for the existence of a government is to serve the entire society, otherwise it should be overthrown. Third, the two also differ in the way of organizing economic life. In the West, free enterprises compete with each other to form a free market economy. In China, two functionally differentiated and mutually supportive sectors – a state sector and a private sector – form a guided market economy, so as to avoid market failures and increase competitiveness in international markets.[42]

Pan also believes that this China model is sustainable since it is a civilization-based one. He argues that the Chinese system is qualitatively different from that of the Soviet system. It is a particularistic, non-missionary, absorbing system, in contrast to those universalistic, missionary, and offensive systems. Originated in a country of great diversities, the Chinese system justifies flexibility with an emphasis on learning from others. Therefore, unlike the Soviet system, the Chinese system claims itself not as an alternative, but a parallel model, fitting into only the Chinese civilization.[43]

Conclusion

At the cultural and ideological front, China has become increasingly polarized since the reform and open-door policy. During the Maoist era, ideology meant something that was imposed onto society from the leadership. In the 1980s, the leadership under Hu Yaobang attempted to introduce changes to the CCP's traditional ideology, namely, Marxism and Maoism. However, the liberal stance of the leadership resulted in the so-called "bourgeois liberalization," and the conservatives in the leadership initiated waves of political campaigns against it.[44] After the crackdown on the pro-democracy movement in 1989, no more ideological debate was allowed and tolerated. When Deng called for radical market-oriented economic reforms after his Southern Tour in 1992, there was a surge of ideological debate on whether China's development should be capitalistic or socialistic. Deng believed that such a debate would go nowhere but slow down the reform process. Therefore, he enforced a "no debate" policy. This policy continues to function today. For instance, the Chinese government has avoided the concept of the China model and abstained from an official discussion of such a model. In fact, government specialists in international relations have suggested not using the concept to avoid offending the West and raising suspicion that China was keen to "export" the concept to underdeveloped countries.[45] The official stance is that the government does not participate in any ideological debates; nor will its existing policy be affected.

While the official policy continues to be "no debate," the government has become more tolerant of popular debates on this issue. The "no-debate" policy has actually accelerated the decline of official ideology. This gives leeway for popular discourses to rise. The rise of social ideologies is thus a reflection of social and cultural pluralism. Among different social ideologies, cultural renaissance has increasingly appeared as a grand trend. China's successful story in the era of the reform and opening-up has resulted in an increasing level of popular confidence in its culture and values.

Like most countries in the world, China today is characterized by cultural and ideological pluralism. Different social groups with diverse values have searched for different ideologies either to influence government policy or to meet their spiritual needs. Different cultural values and ideologies compete with one another, but no cultural value and ideology seems to be absolutely dominant. Moreover, competition at the cultural and ideological front has provided great dynamics for changes in contemporary China.

Notes

1   Chen (1990: 102).
2   Ibid., 106–10. On the role of Zhao Ziyang in China's political reform in the 1980s, see Wu and Lansdowne (2008).
3   <www.hudong.com> (accessed July 28, 2009).
4   Zhao (2007: 45).
5   Huntington (1991).
6   Ibid., 43.

7 The democracy saloon at Beijing University often invited liberal scholars to speak on Western political systems. The saloon played an important role leading to the rise of the 1989 pro-democracy movement.

8 Zheng (1999: 50).

9 Ibid.

10 For a summary of liberalism in the 1990s, see Zheng (2004: Chapter 8).

11 For more details of the debate, see Cao (2008).

12 Zheng (2012: 40).

13 Zheng (1999).

14 Song *et al.* (1996).

15 Li and Liu (1996).

16 Fang *et al.* (1999).

17 See Yang and Zheng (2012).

18 For a survey on Internet-based nationalism in China, see Wu (2007).

19 <http://www.anti-cnn.com/track> (accessed May 16, 2009).

20 "Beijing Consensus" is a term that represents an alternative economic development model to the "Washington Consensus," which was a US-led plan for reforming and developing the economics of third-world countries. While the term had existed since the 1990s, it entered the mainstream political lexicon in 2004 when the UK's Foreign Policy Centre published a paper by Joshua Cooper Ramo entitled *The Beijing Consensus*. In this paper, Ramo laid out several broad guidelines for economic development based on Chinese experience. In China, the New Left has welcomed and accepted this term and has often employed it in framing its discourse on China's reforms. However, liberals have raised serious doubts about this term.

21 Song *et al.* (2009).

22 Ibid., 77.

23 "Tibet WAS, IS, and ALWAYS WILL BE a part of China." <www.youtube.com> (accessed May 17, 2010).

24 "Riot in Tibet: True face of western media." <http://www.youtube.com/watch?v=u SQnK5FcKas&feature=related> (accessed May 16, 2009).

25 Evan Osnos, "Angry Youth: The new generation's neocon nationalists." <http://www.newyorker.com/reporting/2008/07/28/080728fa_fact_osnos?currentPage=all> (accessed May 16, 2009).

26 <http://www.anti-cnn.com/track> (accessed May 16, 2009).

27 There is a growing body of the New Left literature in China. For its reflections on the reform policy and globalization, for example, see Wang (2003) and Wang and Hu (1999), which presented strong arguments for recentralization on the part of the government. For a discussion of the New Left, see Zheng (2004: Chapter 8).

28 For a discussion on the anti-globalization of the New Left, see Zheng (2004: Chapter 8).

29 Wang (1991).

30 For the English version, see Wang and Hu (1999).

31 Li (2010).

32 Gan (2007).

33 Zheng (1999: Chapters 3 and 4).

34 Su and Wang (1988).
35 For a philosophical reflection on Confucianism in today's China, see Bell (2008).
36 On the *Guoxue* movement and the rise of New Confucianism, see Bell (2008).
37 Ramo (2004).
38 Williamson (1990).
39 Zou (2009: 502).
40 Yang (2010) and Fan Gang, "Dangqian zhuyao wenti zaiyu shichanghua gaige bugou shenru" (The Key Problem Today Is that the Market-oriented Reform Is Not Deep Enough), *Ershiyi shiji jingji baodao* (The Economic Herald of the 21st Century), April 4, 2006.
41 Li Junru, "Shenti Zhongguo moshi" (Caution When Raising the China Model), *Xuexi shibao* (Study Times), Central Party School, December 7, 2009. The same issue of the Central Party School journal published four articles against the China model.
42 Pan (2009); also see Pan (2010).
43 Ibid.
44 Goldman (1994).
45 Zhao Qizheng, "Zhongguo wuyi shuchu moshi" (China Does Not Intend to Export Its Model), *Xuexi shibao* (Study Times), December 7, 2009. Zhao is the Director of the Foreign Affairs Committee of the Chinese People's Political Consultative Conference. He argued that the Chinese government does not accept the concept of "China model" and China does not have any intention to export the so-called China model, since such a concept will lead to a sense of "China threat" outside China.

References

Bell, D. 2008. *China's New Confucianism, Politics and Everyday Life in a Changing Society*. Princeton, NJ: Princeton University Press.

Cao, Tianyu, ed. 2008. *Shehui zhuyi haishi minzhu shehui zhuyi* (Socialism or Social Democratism). Hong Kong: Dafeng chubanshe.

Chen, Yizi. 1990. *Zhongguo: shiniangaige yu bajiuminyun* (China: Ten Years of Reform and the Social Movement of 1989). Taipei: Lianjing pinglun chubangongsi.

Fang, Ning, Wang Xiaodong, and Song Qiang. 1999. *Quanqiuhua yinying xia de Zhongguo zhilu* (The China Road under the Shadow of Globalization). Beijing: Zhongguo shehui kexue chubanshe.

Gan, Yang. 2007. *Tong san tong* (Blending Three Traditions). Beijing: Sanlian shudian.

Goldman, M. 1994. *Sowing the Seeds of Democracy in China: Political Reform in the Deng Xiaoping Era*. Cambridge, MA: Harvard University Press.

Huntington, S. P. 1991. *The Third Wave: Democratization in the Late Twentieth Century*. Norman, OK: University of Oklahoma Press.

Li, He. 2010. "Debating China's Economic Reform: New Leftists vs. Liberals." *Journal of Chinese Political Science* 15, 1: 1–23.

Li, Xiguang and Kang Liu. 1996. *Yaomohua beihou de Zhongguo* (Behind Demonizing China). Beijing: Zhongguo shehui kexue chubanshe.

Pan, Wei, ed. 2009. *Zhongguo moshi: jiedu renmin gongheguo liushinian* (China Model: Interpreting 60 Years of People's Republic). Beijing: Zhongyang bianyi chubanshe.

Pan, Wei. 2010. "Chinese System vs. Western System." *EAI Background Brief 530*, East Asian Institute, National University of Singapore.

Ramo, J. C. 2004. *Beijing Consensus: Notes on the New Physics of Chinese Power*. London: Foreign Policy Centre.

Song, Qiang, Zhang Zangzang, and Qiao Bian. 1996. *Zhongguo keyi shuobu* (China Can Say No). Beijing: Zhonghua gongshang lianhe chubanshe.

Song, Xiaojun, Wang Xiaodong, Huang Jisu, *et al.* 2009. *Zhongguo bu gaoxing: dashidai damubiao jiqi women de neiyouwaihuan* (Unhappy China: Grand Age, Grand Goal, and Our Internal Trouble and External Disturbance). Nanjing: Jiangsu renmin chubanshe.

Su, Xiaokang and Luxiang Wang. 1988. *Heshang (River Elegy)*. Beijing: Xiandai chubanshe.

Wang, Hui. 2003. *China's New Order: Society, Politics, and Economy in Transition*, ed. Theodore Huters. Cambridge, MA: Harvard University Press.

Wang, Shaoguang. 1991. "Jianli yige qiangyouli de minzhu guojia – jianlun 'zhengquan xingshi' yu 'guojia nengli' de qubie" (Building a Strong Democratic State: Also on the Distinction Between the 'Form of Government' and 'State Capacity'). In *Dangdai Zhongguo yanjiu zhongxin lunwen* (Essays from the Center of Contemporary Chinese Studies). Princeton, NJ: Center for Modern China.

Wang, Shaoguang and Angang Hu. 1999. *The Political Economy of Uneven Development: The Case of China*. Armonk, NY: M. E. Sharpe.

Williamson, J., ed. 1990. *Latin American Adjustment: How Much Has Happened*. Washington, DC: Institute for International Economics.

Wu, Guoguang and Helen Lansdowne, eds. 2008. *Zhao Ziyang and China's Political Future*. London and New York: Routledge.

Wu, Xu. 2007. *Chinese Cyber Nationalism: Evolution, Characteristics and Implications*. Lanham, MD: Lexington Books.

Yang, Lijun and Yongnian Zheng. 2012. "Fen Qings (Angry Youth) in Contemporary China." *Journal of Contemporary China* 21, 76: 1–17.

Yang, Yao. 2010. "The End of Beijing Consensus: Can China's Authoritarian Growth Survive?" *Foreign Affairs*, February 2.

Zhao, Dingxin. 2007. *Guojia shehuiguanxi yu bajiu beijingxueyun* (The State–Society Relationship and the Beijing Student Movement of 1989). Hong Kong: Chinese University of Hong Kong Press.

Zheng, Yongnian. 1999. *Discovering Chinese Nationalism in China: Modernization, Identity, and International Relations*. Cambridge and New York: Cambridge University Press.

Zheng, Yongnian. 2004. *Globalization and State Transformation in China*. Cambridge and New York: Cambridge University Press.

Zheng, Yongnian. 2012. "China in 2011: Anger, Political Consciousness, Anxiety, and Uncertainty." *Asian Survey* 52, 1: 28–41.

Zou, Dongtao, ed. 2009. *Zhongguo jingji fazhan he tizhi gaige baogao* (Report of China's Economic Development and Institutional Reform), *No. 2, Zhongguo daolu yu Zhongguo moshi (1949–2009)*. Beijing: Shehui kexue chubanshe.

Chapter 8

De Facto Federalism

Economic Reform and *De Facto* Federalism

Changing central–local relations was an important dimension of China's reform and open-door policy from the very beginning. Yet, this dimension is frequently ignored. Changes in central–local relations and the reform and open-door policy are actually two processes which reinforce each other.[1] In this chapter, we scrutinize China's evolvement into a *de facto* federal system and analyze how this system affects different aspects of relations between the center and the provinces and thus the processes of reform and opening up.

Federalism is usually defined in two ways: formal-legalistic and informal-behavioral. From a formal institutional perspective, federalism is often regarded as a form of government that differs from unitary structures in terms of the distribution of power between central and regional governments, the separation of powers within the government, and the division of legislative powers between national and regional representatives.

From this formal institutional perspective, the Chinese state can hardly be considered federal. The country has constitutionally remained a unitary state whereby all local governments are subordinate to the central government. The principle of territorial distribution of power has not been changed since 1949 when the People's Republic was established. According to the Constitution, all provincial governments are local state administrative organs: they must accept the unified leadership of the State Council, implement administrative measures, regulations, and decisions by the State Council, and be responsible and report to the State Council.[2] On the other hand, the State Council can define the specific functions and powers of the local governments, nullify their decisions, locally impose martial law, and direct its auditing agencies to conduct

Contemporary China: A History since 1978, First Edition. Yongnian Zheng.
© 2014 John Wiley & Sons, Ltd. Published 2014 by John Wiley & Sons, Ltd.

inspections related to financial discipline. Similarly, while provincial people's congresses have the right to make local laws, the Standing Committee of the National People's Congress (NPC) can annul these laws if they conflict with national legislation. There is also no clear demarcation regarding the scope and content of the respective legislative authority between the central and provincial congresses.

However, a formal institutional perspective can hardly help understand China's central–local relations properly. China lacks a sound legal infrastructure, and it is still in the process of developing a system which ensures rule of law. Bargaining in different forms between the center and the provinces takes place in the enforcement of laws, regulations, and contracts. Legal fragmentation is an essential part of China's political system. An informal-behavioral perspective can shed better light on China's central–local relations by demonstrating how China has developed *de facto* federalism and how this system is actually functioning today. China's political system is not static. Various factors such as economic development, changes in the power distribution of different levels of government, and changing expectations of different actors within the system ultimately lead to changes in the way the political system is organized. The role of local governments in economic development must be taken into account in making sense of changes in China's central–local relations.

Following the informal-behavioral tradition, we define central–local relations in China as *de facto* or behavioral federalism. The term "Federal China" is gaining popularity among Chinese scholars inside and outside China.[3] These scholars suggest that China should adopt federalism to solve the issues of national unification such as those related to Taiwan, Hong Kong, Tibet, and Xinjiang. In this chapter, we do not deal with these issues. Instead, we examine how *de facto* federalism has evolved within China proper. In other words, we only examine changes which have happened over power distribution between the center and the provinces. Other factors such as ethnicity, Hong Kong identity, and Taiwan nationalism are beyond the scope of this chapter.

In the post-Mao China, *de facto* federalism was a product of intergovernmental decentralization. A *de facto* federal institutional arrangement and high economic performance have reinforced each other. The former has contributed greatly to China's high economic performance while the latter has made the *de facto* federal structure irreversible.[4] However, today the *de facto* federal structure has become a major institutional barrier for meaningful nationwide reforms, which has implications for both the central government and the provinces. The central government tends to be increasingly defensive in political and economic affairs, recentralizing many aspects of power. While all recentralization measures have enabled the central government to sustain its domination over the provinces, they have actually discouraged changes at the provincial level. Some economically powerful provinces are able to initiate local reforms but they are greatly constrained by the political recentralization. The central government can easily nullify their reform initiatives. These rich provinces often turn to use their economic power to resist central policy initiatives. By contrast, the poor provinces are economically too weak to either implement central policy initiatives or initiate their own reform. To reform central–local relations remains a serious challenge for China.

Intergovernmental Decentralization

Political leaders in communist and postcommunist states have widely used decentralization to resolve economic and political problems resulting from overcentralization in the old planning economy. Different ways of decentralization lead to rather different outcomes. Table 8.1 outlines two main types of decentralization and four major dimensions of decentralization. The main form of decentralization in China was intergovernmental. In the 1980s, the reformist leadership under Hu Yaobang and Zhao Ziyang also emphasized state–society centralization, but this has not materialized since local governments at different levels often hijacked power which the central government had wanted to decentralize to society, particularly individual enterprises.

Table 8.1 Two stages of decentralization. Compiled by the author.

Decentralization	Stage I	Stage II
	Intergovernmental	*State–Society (Enterprise)*
Economic	Central–Local	State–Enterprises
	Outcomes:	Outcomes:
	Local or regional property rights	Private property rights
	Jurisdictional competition	Privatization
	Limited marketization	Marketization
	Local intervention	Competition among individual enterprises
	Local protectionism, etc	Less or no government intervention, etc.
Political	Central–Local	State–Society
	Outcomes:	Outcomes:
	Local democracy	Democratization
	Perforated sovereignty and *de facto* federalism	Popular sovereignty and individual rights
	Limited individual rights, etc.	Political participation
	Governmental "NGOs"	NGOs and civil society, etc.

While intergovernmental decentralization led to high economic performance, it had also empowered the provinces, and granted the latter a *de facto* "veto" power in resisting central policies or in selectively implementing them. To recentralize its power, the central government will have to shift its focus from intergovernmental decentralization to state–society decentralization. By doing so, the central government will be able to use social forces to constrain local power and thus increase its capacity to enforce meaningful reforms in the provinces and in central–local relations.

Intergovernmental economic decentralization

Although China's reforms are market-oriented, there have been few serious attempts at providing the central features of private markets, or a system of securing private property rights. Commercial law and an independent court system were virtually non-existent. So, how did China achieve high economic performance in the absence of these factors assumed to be essential for economic growth elsewhere? This is largely due to *de facto* federalism, or market-persevering federalism.[5] Central to *de facto* federalism and market-persevering federalism is intergovernmental decentralization.

After China began its economic reform in 1978 and before the recentralization efforts in the mid-1990s, the leadership repeatedly emphasized devolution of authority from the central to local governments. Intergovernmental decentralization provided an important set of limits on the behavior of all levels of government which was in favor of economic growth. Decentralization directly limits the central government's control over the economy. It induces competition among local governments, serving both to constrain their behavior and to provide them with a range of positive incentives to foster local economic prosperity.[6] Intergovernmental decentralization also rules out the possibility of a single government monopolizing control over the economy. When many regions can choose policies for themselves, all can compare the results, including those which do not wish to initiate reform policies.[7]

Moreover, intergovernmental decentralization provides great market incentives. Efficient markets require two related sets of initiatives for credible commitment by the state – "positive" market incentives that reward economic success, and "negative" market incentives that punish economic failure. The two main features of China's political economic system – decentralization of information and authority and interjurisdictional competition – provide credible commitment to securing economic rights and preserving markets. During the process of economic reform, China's central government deliberately limited its access to certain information in order to prevent the center from repeating the pernicious behavior of the previous reform period. For instance, the center allowed local governments to maintain various "extra-budget" and "off-budget" accounts. Limited knowledge of these budgets ensured that the central government could not tax them. This in turn helped local governments to prosper and generate revenue.

The effect of decentralized allocation of information and authority in achieving credible commitment helps to explain why many local government-owned enterprises, such as township and village enterprises (TVEs) perform better than state-owned enterprises (SOEs) particularly in the 1980s. These local government-owned enterprises have a different governance structure from SOEs and thus face stronger positive and negative incentives. By fully controlling the assets of TVEs, the local governments have access to information not available to the central government, and are thus able to resist state revenue predation in a credible way.

Competition among jurisdictions also forces local governments to represent citizen interests and to preserve markets. Jurisdictional competition among local governments increases efficiency through sorting and matching. It also serves as a disciplinary device to punish inappropriate market intervention by lower government officials. It further helps limit the government's predatory behavior. Mobile resources quickly flee jurisdictions that practice inappropriate behavior. Competition for mobile sources of revenue prevents local political leaders from imposing debilitating taxes or regulations.

Intergovernmental political decentralization

Unlike other communist political institutions, China's political system is flexible, thus offering opportunities for policy innovation. Top leaders in China's political hierarchy have not, as is commonly assumed, always dictated economic decisions. Rather, provincial officials have had an important say in decision-making at the central level. Intergovernmental decentralization has produced "reciprocal accountability," a type of power relationship between top leaders and other Party cadres. According to the Party rules, the relationship between Party leaders and subordinate officials is not a pure hierarchy. The Central Committee has the authority to choose Party leaders, and the Central Committee consists of Party, government, and military officials appointed by Party leaders. The leaders appoint the officials and the officials in the Central Committee choose the leaders. Government officials are both the agents and the constituents of central leaders; local officials are both the agents and the constituents of central leaders. Officials hold their positions at the pleasure of the Party leadership, but Party leaders hold their positions at the pleasure of the officials in the selectorate (e.g., the Central Committee). Such lines of accountability turn a hierarchical relationship into one of "reciprocal accountability."[8]

The relationship of "reciprocal accountability" matters for China's economic performance. It helps the formation of the reform coalition between the central reformist leadership and local governments. On the one hand, since provincial officials seek to be promoted in the political hierarchy, the central authorities could "play to the provinces" to gain the political support of provincial officials by providing them with political incentives through the appointment system. "Playing to the provinces" became an important strategy of the reformist leadership to mobilize local support for the reforms. On the other hand, provincial officials could also "play to the center" because they form the majority of the selectorate and their votes are important to any top leader's political legitimacy. Once the provincial representatives in the Central Committee put the weight of the Party behind the reforms, they are capable of forcing the central leadership into implementing economic reforms in favor of local economic growth. By "playing to the center," provincial officials are able to maintain the reform momentum in favor of local growth.

The centralized political structure

Despite decentralization elements in intergovernmental relations, the centralized structure is maintained. This structure matters for high economic performance since it helps overcome resistance and opposition from the administrative hierarchy itself. Compared with Russia, China's political system has been able to exploit the positive effects of decentralization while overcoming the negative effects. An obvious example is that the local governments in China have actively contributed to the growth of new firms, while the local governments in Russia have typically stood in the way.

While China's central–local institutional arrangements endow local governments with considerable operational autonomy, local officials are agents of the central government. Chinese central authorities have retained a firm grip over the vital aspects of personnel allocation such as selection, promotion, and dismissal. Among others, two institutional factors have contributed to this. First, the Party's principle of management stresses ideological conformity and gives the CCP dominant procedural control over appointment decisions. Second, cadre management is centralized. Though considerable changes have taken place in the cadre management system, the reach of the center is both extensive and deep. Control over personnel allocation is the ultimate trump card that the center wields over the provinces. It is a fundamental constraint faced by all Chinese local officials.[9]

This type of centralized structure is believed to be a precondition for the transition to succeed.[10] While neo-classical political economy tends to focus on market competition in the rewarding of "good" behavior and punishing of "bad" behavior, the market mechanism alone is not enough to explain China's transition from a planned economy to a market one. China's transition has taken place under the tight control of the CCP. The central government has been in a strong position either to reward or punish local administrations. In contrast, Russia's transition came with the emergence of a partly dysfunctional democracy. The central government has not been strong enough to either impose its views or set clear rules on the sharing of the proceeds of growth. As a result, local governments have encountered few disincentives to resist or rein in competition for rents.

The CCP has utilized its power to appoint and fire governors, to support governors whose regions have performed well economically, and to discipline those who have failed to follow its economic policies. Without such a structure, the incentives to pursue regionalist policies are too high, a tendency which cannot be eliminated solely through clever economic and fiscal arrangements. This is evident in Russia's case, where governors were elected, not appointed. As a result, the ability of the central government to reward or penalize governors through administrative and electoral support had been limited.

Decentralization and Its Consequences

Intergovernmental decentralization was very successful in achieving high economic performance, but this came with costs. Although the centralized structure remained, the cost of maintaining this structure became increasingly high. Even though rapid intergovernmental decentralization did not lead to the breakup of China as it did with the Soviet Union, localism or regionalism often became uncontrollable and posed increasingly serious challenges to the central power.

With decentralization, economic power shifted from the central state to local governments at different levels. For example, central revenue shrank from 40.5% of the total revenue in 1984 to 22% in 1993 while central expenditure declined from 52.5% to 28.3% during the same period (Tables 8.2 and 8.3).

Rapid decentralization widened the income gap among provinces and regions. In coastal areas such as Guangdong, Zhejiang, Jiangsu, and Shandong, local officials had developed very strong non-state sectors, which were very profitable and beyond the control of the central government. In inland provinces, owing to various factors such as the lack of financial resources and skilled personnel, local governments had difficulty pushing local growth. Consequently, some provincial governments achieved a high capacity to lead local development and improve local residents' living standards, while others did not. Due to an increase in local diversity, the central government found it difficult to implement unified policies to lead and constrain local governments while local officials could easily nullify central policies.

The decline of central power prevented the central government from coordinating local economic activities effectively. Rich provinces were reluctant to

Table 8.2 Revenues of central and local governments (billion yuan). Compiled by the author from *The Statistical Yearbook of China*, various years.

Year	Total Revenue	Central Government	Local Government	Ratio (%) Central Government	Ratio (%) Local Government
1953	21.32	17.70	3.62	83.0	17.0
1960	57.23	14.28	42.95	25.0	75.0
1965	47.33	15.61	31.73	33.0	67.0
1970	66.29	18.30	48.00	27.6	72.4
1975	81.56	9.66	71.90	11.8	88.2
1976	77.66	9.89	67.77	12.7	87.3
1977	87.45	11.39	76.06	13.0	87.0
1978	113.23	17.58	95.65	15.5	84.5
1979	114.64	23.13	91.50	20.2	79.8
1980	115.99	28.45	87.55	24.5	75.5
1981	117.58	31.11	86.47	26.5	73.5
1982	121.23	34.68	86.55	28.6	71.4
1983	136.70	49.00	87.69	35.8	64.2
1984	164.29	66.55	97.74	40.5	59.5
1985	200.48	76.96	123.52	38.4	61.6
1986	212.20	77.84	134.36	36.7	63.3
1987	219.94	73.63	146.31	33.5	66.5
1988	235.72	77.48	158.25	32.9	67.1
1989	266.49	82.25	184.24	30.9	69.1
1990	293.71	99.24	194.47	33.8	66.2
1991	314.95	93.83	221.12	29.8	70.2
1992	348.34	97.95	250.39	28.1	71.9
1993	434.90	95.75	339.14	22.0	78.0
1994	521.81	290.65	231.16	55.7	44.3
1995	624.22	325.66	298.56	52.2	47.8
1996	740.80	366.11	374.69	49.4	50.6
1997	865.11	422.69	442.42	48.9	51.1
1998	987.60	489.20	498.40	49.5	50.5
1999	1144.41	584.92	559.49	51.1	48.9
2000	1339.52	698.92	640.61	52.2	47.8
2001	1638.60	858.27	780.33	52.4	47.6
2002	1890.36	1038.86	851.50	55.0	45.0
2003	2171.53	1186.53	985.00	54.6	45.4
2004	2639.65	1450.31	1189.34	54.9	45.1
2005	3164.93	1654.85	1510.08	52.3	47.7
2006	3876.02	2045.66	1830.36	52.8	47.2

Table 8.3 Expenditure of central and local governments (billion yuan). Compiled by the author from *The Statistical Yearbook of China*, various years.

Year	Total Expenditure	Central Government	Local Government	Ratio (%) Central Government	Ratio (%) Local Government
1953	21.92	16.21	5.72	73.9	26.1
1960	64.37	27.86	36.51	43.3	56.7
1965	46.00	28.42	17.58	61.8	38.2
1970	64.94	38.24	26.70	58.9	41.1
1975	82.09	40.94	41.15	49.9	50.1
1976	80.62	37.76	42.86	46.8	53.2
1977	84.35	39.37	44.98	46.7	53.3
1978	112.21	53.21	59.00	47.4	52.6
1979	128.18	65.51	62.67	51.1	48.9
1980	122.88	66.68	56.20	54.3	45.7
1981	113.84	62.57	51.28	55.0	45.0
1982	123.00	65.18	57.82	53.0	47.0
1983	140.95	75.96	64.99	53.9	46.1
1984	170.10	89.33	80.77	52.5	47.5
1985	200.43	79.53	120.90	39.7	60.3
1986	220.49	83.64	138.66	37.9	62.1
1987	226.22	84.56	141.66	37.4	62.6
1988	249.12	84.50	164.62	33.9	66.1
1989	282.38	88.88	193.50	31.5	68.5
1990	308.36	100.45	207.91	32.6	67.4
1991	338.66	109.08	229.58	32.2	67.8
1992	374.22	117.04	257.18	31.3	68.7
1993	464.23	131.21	333.02	28.3	71.7
1994	579.26	175.44	403.82	30.3	69.7
1995	682.37	199.54	482.83	29.2	70.8
1996	793.76	215.13	578.63	27.1	72.9
1997	923.36	253.25	670.11	27.4	72.6
1998	1079.82	312.56	767.26	28.9	71.1
1999	1318.77	415.23	903.53	31.5	68.5
2000	1587.94	551.43	1036.51	34.7	65.3
2001	1884.40	575.40	1309.00	30.5	69.5
2002	2205.32	677.17	1528.15	30.7	69.3
2003	2465.00	742.01	1722.99	30.1	69.9
2004	2848.69	789.41	2059.28	27.7	72.3
2005	3393.03	877.60	2515.43	25.9	74.1
2006	4042.27	999.14	3043.13	24.7	75.3

cooperate with one another when they could plan local development independently. Poor and rich provinces were also reluctant to cooperate with one another. Besides the presence of a similar industrial structure, the psychology of being victimized by rich provinces among local officials in poor provinces was also important. The lack of coordination in regional development on the part of the central government was the key factor driving widening income disparities among regions.

This trend was well recognized inside China. By the early 1990s, it was observed that rapid decentralization had given rise to various dukedom economies.[11] The consequences prompted the development of a discourse on recentralization which emphasized the importance of state capacity in regulating the national economy and maintaining the country as a united state. As discussed in the previous chapter, New Leftist scholars such as Wang Shaoguang and Hu Angang presented a strong discourse for recentralization. To counter radical decentralization, the central government started to initiate a recentralization movement around the mid-1990s.

Selective Recentralization

Recentralization does not mean that the leadership intended to reverse the reform and return to the old system. Rather, the leadership wanted to selectively recentralize certain aspects of power, powers which were vital to the administrative hierarchy. In the economic realm, selective centralization was initially concentrated on two major reforms – taxation reform and central banking system reform. Since the early 2000s, recentralization has taken place in a wide range of policy areas such as environment, consumer/product safety, labor, land, and so on, as the central government began to make greater attempts at establishing an effective regulatory regime.

Taxation reform

In 1994, the central government began to implement a new taxation system, a tax-division system or the federal-style taxation system. Before this system, the center did not have its own institutions to collect taxes. All taxes from the provinces were collected by provincial governments first before they were divided between the center and the individual provinces through bargaining.

With the new system, taxes are divided into three categories: central, local, and shared. Central taxes go to the central coffer, local taxes to local budgets, and shared taxes would be divided between the center and the provinces according to prior agreements. Moreover, tax administration is centralized. Instead of authorizing local tax offices to collect almost all the taxes, the center now collects taxes through its own institutions independent of the provinces, meaning that the center has established its own revenue collection agency, the national tax service. The new system also recognizes independent provincial power, that is, provincial authorities and lower governments can collect several types of taxes without interference from above. There are now two parallel and independent systems for tax administration: a national system for central taxes and a local one for local taxes. Shared taxes are collected by the central government first, and then divided between the center and the provinces.[12]

These institutional changes shifted fiscal power from the provinces to the center. Total government revenue increased quite dramatically as a result. The proportion of central collection has increased from lower than 30% to around 50% after the implementation of this reform. If the locally collected revenues that local governments are obligated to remit to the central coffer are included, the central government's share would constitute about two-thirds of total government revenue. Since most revenues are now collected and redistributed by the center, the fiscal dependence of the provinces on the central government has increased substantially. Before the taxation reform, the central government had to rely heavily on the coastal provinces for revenue contribution. The reform has reversed this trend.

Central banking system reform

Similar efforts have been made to reform the central banking system. Before the reform, China's central banking system was highly decentralized. The central bank, People's Bank of China, had branches in every province. However, local branches were often exposed to the political influence of local governments since the personnel of local branches were appointed and their welfare provided for by the local governments. This frequently led to local branches ignoring orders from the central bank and subordinating themselves to local influences. While local branches of the central bank often became an effective instrument for local governments to promote local economic growth, rapid local growth was achieved at the expense of the stability of the national economy. The decentralized central banking system eventually led to the crisis of macro-economic management after Deng's Southern Tour in 1992. After Zhu Rongji became the Premier in 1998, the central government implemented a most daring measure to reform China's banking system: all provincial branches of the central bank were eliminated and nine cross-provincial or regional branches established. This reform has made local interferences in the central banking system impossible.[13]

Political recentralization

Also important are efforts in recentralizing political power. Initial political recentralization took place immediately after the crackdown on the pro-democracy movement in 1989 and the collapse of the Soviet Union in the early

1990s. The central government reinvigorated the old *nomenklatura* system, a traditional method for the communist leadership to control local Party cadres and government officials.[14] It reinforced the system of Party management of cadres, which gives the central government a dominant say over personnel decisions at the provincial and city level.[15] The central government also re-emphasized the cadre transfer system or the cadre exchange system, which enables the center to tighten control over local cadres.[16] Cadres involved in the transfer consist mainly of leading members of Party committees and the government. According to CCP regulations, a leading member of a local Party committee or government should be transferred if he/she has worked in the same position for 10 years. The CCP Constitution mandates a five-year term for Party committee positions at the county level and above. Therefore, if a provincial level cadre has not reached retirement age by the end of his/her second term, he/she has to be transferred. The system of cadre transfer is an effective instrument for the center to constrain localism and prevent local vested interests from becoming too deeply entrenched.

Political recentralization has been effective in constraining the influence of local officials in policy making at the central level. It is true that some regions are always more powerful than other regions in economic terms. In general, the more economically developed regions are also the more politically powerful regions. However, the power of economic regions does not guarantee their political power. Take the Seventeenth Central Committee as an example. In terms of regional distributions, the East Region is dominant with 131 members (35.5%), the North Region is second with 75 members (20.6%), while the South Region has the least representation with only 13 members (3.5%). Unlike previous central committees, members of the Seventeenth Central Committee come from across the regions. The share of the East Region declined from 43.3% of the Fifteenth Central Committee to 40.2% of the Sixteenth Central Committee to 35.5% of the Seventeenth Central Committee. The North Region climbed up from 13.4% of the Fifteenth Central Committee to 15.7% of the Sixteenth Central Committee to 20.6% of the Seventeenth Central Committee.[17]

"Strong economy and weak politics" is particularly true of provinces which are often regarded as being capable of imposing power challenges to the central government. Guangdong and Shanghai are two cases in point. Guangdong has the largest economy in China, but it failed to be dominant at the Seventeenth Central Committee. Only five Seventeenth Central Committee members are from Guangdong Province, down from eight in both the Sixteenth Central Committee and the Fifteenth Central Committee. Seven members of the Seventeenth Central Committee have Shanghai as their home province, but none of them are qualified to be a member of the so-called "Shanghai Gang" formed under Jiang Zemin.

Both Guangdong and Shanghai are economically significant for China. Their economic significance cannot be transformed into political influence. Once the central government feels threatened by growing local political influence, it will make efforts to constrain the latter. Take two examples. During his tenure in Guangdong, Zhang Dejiang took great initiatives to create a development program, namely, the "9 plus 2," which aimed to integrate the economies of nine Chinese provinces surrounding the Pearl River basin with those of Hong Kong and Macao. Given the fact that Zhang was a member of the Political Bureau, he was able to coordinate these provinces and Hong Kong and Macao. Nevertheless, this program was regarded as unjustifiable from the perspective of the national economy. At the Seventeenth Party Congress in 2007, Zhang retained his membership in the Political Bureau and was promoted to Beijing, but played an insignificant role as one of the vice premiers, and his "9 plus 2" program disappeared. In the case of Shanghai, it was extremely powerful during the era of Jiang Zemin, as reflected in the existence of the "Shanghai Gang." The political power of the "Shanghai Gang" was evident when Shanghai Party secretary Chen Liangyu challenged the power of the Hu–Wen leadership. However, prior to the Seventeenth Party Congress, Chen was removed and later jailed for alleged corruption.

State Incapacity

Recentralization and state capacity, however, are hardly identical. These measures have enabled the central government to accumulate its power resources vis-à-vis the provinces. Nevertheless, if power means "getting something done when facing resistance" in a Weberian sense, the power of the central government has been in decline. The central government has failed to produce any significant changes in the provinces. There are ample examples to support this assertion. While its revenue has increased rapidly in the past decades, the central government has not been able to reduce income disparities in various forms. It has yet to provide sufficient public goods such as health care, social security, education, and environmental protection. While fiscal recentralization does not generate expected results, it has led to unexpected consequences. While the central government has accumulated an increasingly large amount of revenues over the years, local governments are in serious deficit.[18]

Intergovernmental decentralization had served as an effective means for China to achieve high economic performance in the early stages of the reform. It was effectively implemented due to great incentives from both the central government and the provinces. The rationale for the central government was that rapid economic development would enable the Party-state to deliver economic goods to the people and thus maintain its political legitimacy. For the provinces, rapid local development would not only bring wealth to local officials, but also help in their political career since local economic growth was the most important indicator for their promotion in the hierarchy of the Party-state. Therefore, intergovernmental decentralization was a win–win game for both the central government and the provinces.

Nevertheless, both the nature of central–local relations and rules of the game between the two changed at a later stage. With intergovernmental decentralization, economic decision-making power shifted to the provinces. Instead of privatization, property rights were decentralized to local governments rather than to individual enterprises or entrepreneurs. Understandably, even though the central government gradually withdrew from the economic affairs of individual enterprises, local governments became highly interventionist. In general, intergovernmental decentralization created an institutional setting and legitimacy for local governments to intervene in economic activities within their jurisdictions. It does not necessarily deny marketization. As a matter of fact, marketization was encouraged due to intense competition among different jurisdictions and enterprises with different forms of ownership. Local protectionism existed in the early stages of economic reform; however, with the growth of market mechanisms, it was constrained. All these factors contributed to high local economic performance.

Intergovernmental decentralization empowered local governments and made them more efficient in responding to social demands and changing socioeconomic circumstances. It thus changed the interaction pattern between the central government and the provinces. With an increase in local responsibilities, central–local relations became interdependent. While in principle the central government still held great power over local governments, cooperation from the provinces became essential. The provinces developed and strengthened their own power bases and created incentives for the central government to adjust its relations with the provinces. The provinces had the power not only to deal with local affairs but also to influence decision-making at the central level.

Intergovernmental decentralization also empowered local governments in their interaction with society. The focus of intergovernmental decentralization was power shifts not between the state and society, but between the center and the provinces. The central leadership did not want to decentralize political power to society; instead, it believed that political participation should be constrained and that mass mobilization would not help in the transition to an efficient government. With intergovernmental political decentralization, the political spaces for free expression and collective actions by individuals and social groups were extended, and limited political participation from below took place, as was the case in the development of semi-competitive local elections. However, intergovernmental decentralization has also produced local regimes of dictatorship, and local high economic performance has been associated with serious human rights violation on the part of the local governments.

Therefore, selective recentralization is justifiable. Selective recentralization was able not only to change the interdependency between the central government and the provinces, but to regain the domination of the central government over the provinces. More importantly, it was to engage state–society decentralization. In order to implement state–society decentralization, the central government has to recentralize power first, since intergovernmental decentralization empowered local governments and powerful local governments often become a barrier to state–society decentralization.

Selective recentralization did enable the central government to regain its domination over the provinces. Nevertheless, selective recentralization did not enable the central government to get things done in the provinces. Among others, a key factor is that state–society decentralization has been greatly constrained by both the central government and the provinces. Without state–society decentralization, the central government does not have a level of legitimacy which would enable it to establish its power to get things done, while society is not enabled to establish its power vis-à-vis the central government or the provinces.

So, the game of power continues to be played between the center and the provinces. Without the participation of social forces, the center still lacks the power to dictate to the provinces, meaning that the central government is not able to ask the provinces to do what it wants them to do. While the central government maintains its official domination over the provinces and has *de jure* power to veto initiatives by the provinces, the provinces also have *de facto* power to veto policy initiatives by the central government. When one party has the power to nullify decisions by another party, a policy deadlock becomes inevitable. This characterizes China's central–local relations today. As long as such a situation prevails, it is unlikely for both the central government and the provinces to engage in any major meaningful reforms.

To avoid such a situation, state–society decentralization is inevitable. In other words, the society must be empowered. Only when its power is mandated by the whole society can the central government gain power over the provinces. When society becomes an active actor in the game, local dictatorships can be constrained and avoided.

The central government had made great efforts to selectively centralize its power. It is also unfair to say that the central leadership is unaware of the importance of state–society decentralization. The purpose of the SOE reform under Zhu Rongji was to empower SMEs, especially in the private sector. Similarly, many measures of social reforms by the Hu–Wen government were intended to empower society as in the case of the development of NGOs and local semi-competitive elections, particularly in rich coastal provinces like Guangdong. All these measures of empowering society, however, were either too reluctant or too cautious. Social changes have forced the Party-state to open its process to social forces, as in the admission of capitalists into the ruling Party. The Party-state, as a well-entrenched vested interest, continues to be resistant to social forces. Before the political process is opened wide to social forces, the game between the central government and the provinces will not lead to drastic political changes.

De facto Federalism and China's Foreign Policy

Scholars have explored the role of the provinces in China's foreign relations.[19] The impact of China's provinces on its foreign relations can be perceived in the context of the *de facto* federalism of central–local relations. Intergovernmental decentralization means to delegate different aspects of power to the provinces. While foreign policy falls nominally under the jurisdiction of the central government, the provinces have become powerful either in influencing decision-making at the central level or in making their own foreign economic policy. The provinces have influenced China's foreign policy behavior in various ways.

Intergovernmental decentralization has "perforated" China's sovereignty. Since the reform and open-door policy, Chinese provinces have bargained, individually or collectively, with the central government for favorable foreign economic policies. Coastal provinces have played an important role in initiating and facilitating China's foreign economic policies. More often than not, the central government has to be serious to take into account the interests of the provinces, simply because without cooperation from the provinces, central policies would go nowhere. The role of the provinces in the border areas is even more evident. China shares borders with 14 countries, including North Korea, Russia, Mongolia, Kazakhstan, Kyrgyzstan, Tajikistan, Afghanistan, Pakistan, India, Nepal, Bhutan, Myanmar, Laos, and Vietnam. The provinces which share borders with these countries have become increasingly para-diplomatic actors in China's foreign trade. The provincial governments promoted rapid growth of foreign trade on the one hand, and constrained the central government's foreign policy-making on the other.[20]

The rapid development of foreign trade at the provincial level has greatly facilitated the globalization of China. It is important to note that economic decentralization from the very beginning was accompanied and facilitated by China's globalization. These two developments resulted in a relatively greater increase in interdependence between the Chinese provinces and the outside world, and a surprising decrease in provincial interdependence. According to a study by the World Bank, as of the early 1990s, internal trade as a percentage of GDP among the Chinese provinces was lower than in the European Community and among the republics of the former Soviet Union. The World Bank thus warned that individual provinces had the tendency to behave like independent countries, increasing external (overseas) trade and reducing trade flows with each other.[21]

While the provinces have been a major actor in pursuing China's high economic performance, they also pose a serious institutional constraint in enforcing laws and regulations, and implementing the agreements that the central government has signed with foreign countries. It was found that *de facto* federalism has enabled low-level officials to methodically circumvent intellectual property rights, ignore product safety standards, and inflict widespread environmental degradation. At each administrative level, enterprising and often corrupt administrators blur the lines between business and government in search of wealth and fame. The provinces consistently place local interests above central government mandates and advance their careers through the relentless and unchecked pursuit of growth. The central government finds itself increasingly powerless to enforce its own treaties, laws, and regulations.[22]

Conclusion

The *de facto* federalism that exists in China today tends to continuously weaken the power of the central government. To regain its power, the central government will have to legalize the division of power between the center and the provinces. However, the leadership is not entirely convinced of the merits of moving beyond *de facto* to *de jure* federalism. To be sure, the Chinese seem to have appreciated the value of federalism as early as the late nineteenth century. What could China do in terms of central–local relations after the collapse of imperial hegemony? This was an important question that many revolutionary leaders including Sun Yat-sen and Liang Qichao considered. By the early years of the twentieth century, federal ideas were so pervasive that they played an important role in the constitutional reforms promulgated by the Qing between 1906 and 1911. The self-government movement reflected many leaders' belief that national strength would be based on local self-government. The 1911 revolution did not lead to the realization of the revolutionary leaders' federal ideal. The breakdown of the Qing dynasty led China to warlordism. During this period federalism was often used as a means for local officials to gain political power.

The CCP employed the appeal of federalism in its struggle for state power. At the CCP's Second National Congress in 1922, the Party declared its intent to establish a federal republic of China, and to unify the main provinces with Mongolia, Tibet, and Hui-Uighur regions on the basis of liberal federalism. The Party also recognized the right of minorities to complete self-determination.[23] But the CCP did not bring a federal system to China. Instead, after it took power, China became a centralized unitary country with the devolution of a significant degree of autonomy only granted to ethnic minority areas.

However, people are not ruled by abstract principles. Soon after the establishment of the PRC, Mao realized that a high degree of centralization involved intrinsic problems and thus initiated two major decentralization movements during the Great Leap Forward and the Cultural Revolution. Even under Mao, whose rule is generally regarded as totalitarian, localities enjoyed autonomy to some degree.

Central to Deng's reforms was intergovernmental decentralization under which China developed a *de facto* federal system. As discussed earlier, great efforts have been made to reconstitute the economic relationship between the center and the provinces, following federal systems elsewhere. Strong demands for institutionalizing *de facto* political federalism also existed, since in practice federalism is often not a free choice, but a function of the political power of territorial leadership when open coercion is excluded as a possible option. The central government's dependence on localities has produced new seeds for political federalism. After the mid-1980s, federalism became a popular topic within the reform leadership and its think-tanks. For instance, in 1986, as initiated by the then Secretary General of the CCP Zhao Ziyang, the central leadership established the Group for Research on Political Institution Reforms. Seven subgroups were organized, with one assigned to focus on decentralization and institutional reforms. A major research theme of this subgroup was whether China could adopt a federal system similar to that in the United States or elsewhere to reform the existing power relations between the central and local governments.[24]

So, why is the Chinese leadership reluctant to rebuild the political relationship between the center and the provinces according to federal principles? To legitimate federalism is not an easy task in China. Ideologically, federalism is contradictory to the spirit of the CCP. The history of warlordism in the early twentieth century links chaos and federalism together. For many, federalism will result in a divided China. Given the fact that federalism has been discussed in the context of Hong Kong, Taiwan, Tibet, Xinjiang, and other territorial issues, the ideological legitimacy of federalism becomes more complicated. Although these territorial factors have pulled China toward federalism, the ideological barrier is not easy to overcome. As long as federalism cannot be legitimized ideologically, a transition from *de facto* to *de jure* federalism is unlikely to take place.

At the practical level, it seems that the timing is not right for the legitimization of federalism. Compared to *de facto* federalism, the advantages of *de jure* federalism are obvious. The institutionalization of *de facto* federalism is favorable for political stability since it reduces the tension between the two actors. Nevertheless, the institutionalization of *de facto* federalism is also likely to render the political system rigid. Given the fact that there are great disparities between provinces, equal rights among them (implicit in federalism) are not likely. Rich provinces prefer a weak center while poor provinces prefer a strong one. Without doubt, top leaders fear that federalism will lead a more diverse China to disintegration. Also, the leadership's priority is to promote economic development rather than to divide power between the center and the provinces and among the provinces. To do so, it has to continuously adjust its relationship with the provinces and mediate relations among the provinces in accordance with changing circumstances. The legitimization of federalism will render such continuous adjustment less likely. In contrast, *de facto* federalism has the advantage of flexibility. What the center needs is creative ambiguity implicit in *de facto* federalism. In other words, the center needs, for the time being, not a clear-cut division between the central government and the provinces, but ambiguity between them. As long as the center maintains its relative power over the provinces, it will be able make adjustments to central–local relations. Nevertheless, in the long run, selective institutionalization of *de facto* federalism will lay an institutional foundation for China's *de jure* federalism.

Notes

1 For different aspects of changing central–local relations, see Yang (1997); Goodman (1997); Goodman and Segal (1994); Hendrischke and Feng (1999); and Fitzgerald (2002).

2 For a survey of China's political system in terms of formal institutions, see Pu (1995: 223).

3 For example, see Yan (1992) and Wu (2004).

4 For a review of this literature, see Zheng (2005).

5 Montinola *et al.* (1995) and Qian (1999).

6 Montinola *et al.* (1995: 79).

7 Ibid., 80.

8 Shirk (1993: 83).

9 Huang (1996).

10 Blanchard and Shleifer (2001).

11 Shen and Dai (1990).

12 For a more detailed discussion of China's fiscal reforms, see Wong and Bird (2008).

13 For a discussion of China's financial system, see Allen *et al.* (2008).

14 Burns (1989).

15 Ibid.

16 *Renmin ribao*, May 17, 1995, 1.

17   The author would like to thank Bo Zhiyue for collecting the data.
18   Lin (2003).
19   Cheung *et al.* (1998); Cheung and Tang (2001).
20   Zheng (1994; 2006: Chapter 7).
21   World Bank (1994). For a summary, see Kumar (1994).
22   Fuller (2008).
23   Ibid.
24   Chen (1990). For a discussion of the revival of the concept of federalism among contemporary Chinese intellectuals, see Lee (2000).

References

Allen, Franklin, Jun Qian, and Meijun Qian. 2008. "China's Financial System: Past, Present, and Future." In Loren Brandt and Thomas G. Rawski, eds., *China's Great Economic Transformation*. Cambridge: Cambridge University Press, pp. 507–68.

Blanchard, Olivier and Andrei Shleifer. 2001. "Federalism With and Without Political Centralization: China versus Russia." *IMF Staff Papers* 48: 171–79.

Burns, J., ed. 1989. *The Chinese Communist Party's Nomenklatura System*. Armonk, NY: M. E. Sharpe.

Chen, Yizi. 1990. *Zhongguo: shinian gaige yu bajiu minyun* (China: Ten Years of Reforms and the 1989 People's Movement). Taipei: Lianjing chuban gongsi.

Cheung, Peter T. Y. and James T. H. Tang. 2001. "The External Relations of China's Provinces." In David M. Lampton, ed., *The Making of Chinese Foreign and Security Policy in the Era of Reform, 1978–2000*. Stanford, CA: Stanford University Press, pp. 91–122.

Cheung, Peter T. Y., Jae Ho Chung, and Zhimin Lin, eds. 1998. *Provincial Strategies of Economic Reform in Post-Mao China: Leadership, Politics and Implementation*. Armonk, NY: M. E. Sharpe.

Fitzgerald, J., ed. 2002. *Rethinking China's Provinces*. London: Routledge.

Fuller, Gregory H. 2008. "Economic Warlords: How de facto Federalism Inhibits China's Compliance with International Trade Law and Jeopardizes Global Environmental Initiatives." *Tennessee Law Review* 75: 545–76.

Goodman, D. S. G., ed. 1997. *China's Provinces in Reform: Class, Community and Political Culture*. New York: Routledge.

Goodman, D. S. G. and G. Segal, eds. 1994. *China Deconstructs: Politics, Trade and Regionalism*. New York: Routledge.

Hendrischke, H. and Chongyi Feng, eds. 1999. *The Political Economy of China's Provinces: Comparative and Competitive Advantage*. New York: Routledge.

Huang, Yasheng. 1996. *Inflation and Investment Controls in China: The Political Economy of Central–Local Relations During the Reform Era*. Cambridge and New York: Cambridge University Press.

Kumar, Anjali. 1994. "China's Reform, Internal Trade and Marketing." *The Pacific Review* 7, 3: 323–40.

Lee, Tahirih V. 2000. "The Future of Federalism in China." In Karen G. Turner, James V. Feinerman, and R. Kent Guy, eds., *The Limits of the Rule of Law in China*. Seattle and London: University of Washington Press, pp. 271–303.

Lin, Shuanglin. 2003. "China's Government Debt: How Serious?" *China: An International Journal* 1, 1: 73–98.

Montinola, Gabriella, Yingyi Qian, and Barry R. Weingast. 1995. "Federalism, Chinese Style: The Political Basis for Economic Success in China." *World Politics* 48: 50–81.

Pu, Xingzu, ed. 1995. *Zhonghua renmin gongheguo zhengzhi zhidu* (The Political System of the People's Republic of China). Hong Kong: Sanlian shudian,

Qian, Yingyi. 1999. "The Institutional Foundations of China's Market Transition." Paper prepared for the World Bank's Annual Conference on Development Economics, Washington, DC, April 28–30.

Shen, Liren and Yuanchen Dai. 1990. "Woguo 'zhuhou jinji' de xingcheng jiqi biduan he genyuan" (The Formation of the Economy of Dukedom, Its Defects and Roots in China). *Jingji yanjiu* 3: 12.

Shirk, S. 1993. *The Political Logic of Economic Reform in China*. Berkeley, CA: University of California Press,

Wong, Christine and Richard Bird. 2008. "China's Fiscal System: A Work in Progress." In Loren Brandt and Thomas G. Rawski, eds., *China's Great Economic Transformation*. Cambridge: Cambridge University Press, pp. 429–66.

World Bank. 1994. *China: Internal Market Development and Regulations*. Washington, DC: World Bank.

Wu, Jiaxiang. 2004. *Lianbang hua: Zhonghua desan gongheguo zhilu* (Federalization: The Road to the Third Republic of China). Hong Kong: The Mirror Press.

Yan, Jiaqi. 1992. *Lianbang Zhongguo gouxiang* (The Conception of a Federal China). Hong Kong: Minbao chubanshe.

Yang, Dali. 1997. *Beyond Beijing: Liberalization and the Regions in China*. New York: Routledge.

Zheng, Yongnian. 1994. "Perforated Sovereignty: Provincial Dynamics and China's Foreign Trade." *The Pacific Review* 7, 3: 309–21.

Zheng, Yongnian. 2005. "Institutional Economics and Central–Local Relations in China: Evolving Research." *China: An International Journal* 3, 2: 240–69.

Zheng, Yongnian. 2006. *De Facto Federalism in China: Reforms and Dynamics of Central–Local Relations*. Singapore and London: World Scientific.

Chapter 9

Social Policy Reform

While the market-oriented reform in China has promoted rapid economic growth, it has also generated enormous social problems, such as widening income disparities, increasing social injustice, and rising social protests, which called for effective social reforms. In the early periods of reform, social policy did not emerge as an independent policy concept. It was only when economic development incurred heavy social costs and social grievances that social policy acquired prominence due to its importance to social stability and sustainable economic growth. The Hu Jintao–Wen Jiabao administration in particular first made social policy an important realm of the reform under the grand project of the so-called "harmonious society."

In terms of policy dynamics, social policy-making has been an exclusive process within the Party-state leadership. Thus whenever social reform programs coincided with the political priority of economic growth, they were implemented promptly, such as marketization of higher education, health care, and housing. Otherwise, social policy was generally slow to respond to overwhelming social grievances and potential social instability. Although public participation in policy-making remains low and underinstitutionalized, the realm of social policy has become increasingly open to different voices and social forces, as the result of the great social transformation and the emergence of the middle class.

This chapter examines the progress of social policy reform and explores its political dynamics. We first provide an overview of the social policy reform, and then explain the dynamics and the lack of dynamics of social policy reform in several key areas, including social insurance, social protection, welfare provision, education, health care, and housing. We will show the progress that China has achieved and the challenges that lie ahead in all these reform areas.

Contemporary China: A History since 1978, First Edition. Yongnian Zheng.
© 2014 John Wiley & Sons, Ltd. Published 2014 by John Wiley & Sons, Ltd.

Social Policy under Jiang

In the Maoist era, the Chinese lived in a highly centralized and closed system, where economic, social, and political functions were all intermingled and integrated in the administrative framework of the state. In compensating for low levels of wage income, the state provided a range of fringe social goods including housing, health care, childcare, and education through work units in urban areas and, to a lesser degree, in rural areas. All employees of urban work units and their households enjoyed a measure of communal health care, publicly funded education, and heavily subsidized public housing among other price subsidies.[1] In rural areas, a minimum measure of communal welfare was provided via the commune system, in particular in the areas of basic education and health care. There was an implicit social contract between the state and society in which the former provided a minimum social protection to the latter and the latter accepted the rule of the state. Under such a condition, there was no dynamic for change and development.

However, the low level of social welfare proved to be unsustainable. The Maoist system experienced a series of crises after the reform began in the late 1970s, first in the rural and then urban areas. In the rural areas, the rise of the household responsibility system (HRS) marked the end of rural grassroots welfare provisions, since the collapse of the People's Commune deprived the rural welfare system of its formal institutional foundation. Initially, some welfare functions were transferred to the TVEs and local governments. With the decline of the TVEs and fiscal demise of the local and grassroots authorities, the rural welfare system further slipped into disrepair. In the cities, social reform encountered more complicated institutional and historical contexts. The initial reforms, which intended to liberalize the SOE sector and invigorate the urban market, in fact enhanced rather than undermined the employment-based urban welfare provision.[2] However, after the Zhu Rongji administration deepened reforms in the SOE and financial sector in the mid-1990s, social reform became an inevitable follow-up to economic reform, as the old system continued to lose much of its former institutional strength based in the traditional SOE system.

It came as no surprise that the first sets of social policy reforms were instituted in the immediate aftermath of the SOE reform in the early 1990s. In order to cope with the consequences of massive lay-offs from bankrupt SOEs, the central government implemented the first round of social reform in pensions and unemployment benefits. This part of social policy, which primarily dealt with retrenched SOE workers, began to be institutionalized as complementary measures to economic reform and social stability. In 1993, the Minimum Standard of Living Scheme (MSLS, also known as the Minimum

Living Standard Guarantee) was introduced, initially targeted at laid-off elderly workers resulting from the SOE reform in Shanghai.[3]

Under the Zhu administration, social reform focused on setting up social insurance. The aim of reform was to establish social insurance as a more socially-based system to replace the old SOE-based system. Various employment-related insurances were set up, first in employment, medical care, old age pensions, work injury, and maternity leave. Beginning as programmatic responses to the SOE reform, the old age insurance – a key social insurance scheme – was first instituted in 1991 and applied to all urban enterprises in 2005 as a concrete and standardized scheme.[4] As part of the rapidly progressing financial reform, this part of social policy reform gradually found its institutional embodiment in new state agencies, namely, the Ministry of Labor and Social Security (later changed to Ministry of Human Resource and Social Security) and the Social Security Management Fund.

As the socialist principles gradually gave way to the complementary paradigm of social instability, basic social policy concerns such as welfare provision and social protection also found their embodiments as institutional complements to the market-oriented social reform in the mid-1990s. In terms of policy design, marketization in the sphere of social welfare is not intended to rule out the important policy goal of social protections. For example, in the housing sector, the central government has set in place systems such as Low Rent House (LRH) and Economic Housing (EH) for the low and middle income families.[5]

Meanwhile, the market-oriented approach of social reform also met its limits. Politically powerful institutions tended to protect their members from potentially destructive policies, while fully embracing policies of social protections and insurance. Most significantly, marketization in the housing sector was firmly resisted by the politically powerful state sector. The downsized state sector agencies and large monopoly enterprises, thanks to their growing fiscal sinews, also provided the most generous subsidies and subscribed to the most comprehensive insurance programs.

Overall, when Hu Jintao and Wen Jiabao came to power, their administration faced three distinctive institutional legacies in the area of social policy reform. The first one is economic. China's welfare and social provision system is now very similar to the liberal model, with very limited scope for state involvement and market-based provision of welfare, and a very high level of societal self-reliance. China's social policy reform involved a systemic shift from a statist model of citizenship-based minimum coverage to a predominantly liberal model, where means-tested welfare schemes and social insurances offer the bulk of social protection.[6]

The second and perhaps the most salient institutional legacy is a very unequal distribution of state-subsidized welfare provisions across different social groups defined chiefly by sectoral and regional identities rather than individual needs or merits. In the aftermath of the sweeping reform in the state sector in the late 1990s, the central government, central monopoly SOEs, and various government organizations emerged as powerful corporate entities retaining some key features of the old system of heavily subsidized welfare provision.[7] This left the institutionally downsized state sector a bastion of corporate welfare programs compared with all other sectors, with state employees among the most protected social groups. At the regional level, the household registration system (HRS) and the associated discriminatory policies against migrant workers is another set of major institutional hurdles that has constituted an inbuilt status-based welfare inequality between rural and urban, migrant workers and indigenous residents.[8]

The third major legacy is the Maoist past. Although institutional vestiges remained of the Maoist paternalistic state, its ideology has inculcated in the Chinese psyche a widely shared value of basic social justice. Immediately after Hu assumed office, among the first things he did was to pay homage to the revolutionary sites and reaffirm his allegiance to selective ideas from Mao. Maoist paternalistic socialism also made an important imprint on Chinese political discourses, especially for the politically vocal New Left, which was discussed in Chapter 7. At the practical level, the memory of the Maoist legacy also provided ideological supports to many forces, ranging from government think-tanks and grassroots activists all the way to many disadvantaged social groups.

Social Policy Reform under Hu

As Hu succeeded Jiang as the CCP Secretary General in 2002 and Wen succeeded Zhu as Premier in 2003, China entered the Hu–Wen era, and social policy reform as a coherent agenda began to rise in reform priority. The Hu–Wen approach to social policy is characterized by a mixed strategy of further market-oriented reforms combined with more state engagement as regulator of the market and protectors of social stability. In the "scientific development outlook" and "harmonious society" projects, the new administration avowed its ideological commitment to protect society and achieve a basic measure of social equality and justice in the distribution of benefits and costs of the economic development.

The new social policy initiative is twofold. First, it sought to strengthen and expand the elementary institutions of social protections already put in place in the late days of the Jiang–Zhu era, such as the five employment insurances. Second, efforts were made to address the excesses of earlier market-oriented approaches to introduce a higher degree of equality and justice through direct state subsidy in the provision of education, health care, and public housing. In short, the Hu–Wen social policy reform is tasked with delivering social welfare with higher quality, lower prices, and more equal access. Closely related to these two areas of social reforms was a proposal in 2010 to curb the skewed income distribution in the interest of most urban workers.

The first major task of social policy reform went relatively smoothly thanks to the fact that it did not involve the adjustment of interests of the parties involved and entailed only limited increase in the government's fiscal commitment. Continued robust economic growth in this period ensured a fairly stable rise in corporate and governmental revenue. The administration saw significant rise in the coverage rate, total enrollment, and accumulated fund in various social insurance schemes, with the most substantial rise in the extent of coverage in health care and old age (pension) insurance, the two most important items in the whole social insurance scheme, from less than half to two-thirds coverage in the urban areas (Figure 9.1).

The Hu–Wen administration has achieved significant progress in expanding the scale and raising the level of coverage of direct social protection. The MSLS, first put in place in 1993, only became an effective national institution in the new millennium. In particular, the administration effectively extended the MSLS to rural areas. From 2003 to 2009, the rural MSLS had grown from non-existence to cover 43.1 million rural poor. The new administration oversaw a significant increase in coverage of all five major insurances and others (Figure 9.2).

The second area of social policy reform involves important changes in the market-oriented approach in social welfare provision. Most reform schemes hope to address the critical problems of high price, exclusion, and inequality in the delivery of education, health care, and housing via market channels. Little concrete success has been achieved on these accounts. There remains significant inequality and exclusion in the provision of health care, education, and housing for the ordinary citizen.

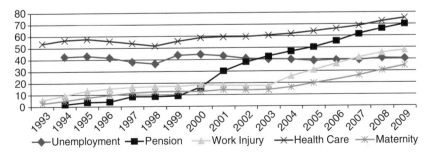

Figure 9.1 Coverage rates of the five social insurance schemes. Compiled by the author from *The China Statistical Yearbook*, various years.

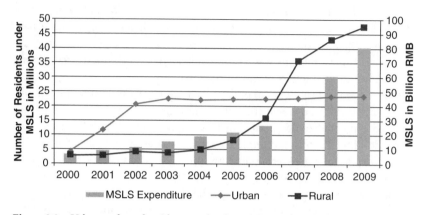

Figure 9.2   Urban and rural residents under the Minimum Standard of Living Scheme. Compiled by the author from Ministry of Civil Affairs data, various years.

The government approach was to bring back the state in basic welfare provision, specifically in addressing the issue of exclusion and high price in welfare provision while keeping household income on the rise. The level of exclusion is most severe in the health care sector. In 2003, 23–36% of patients in different areas declined hospital treatment, as much as 75% of them in rural areas citing high costs as the primary factor.[9] The new plan of health care reform has a clear mission to build state-subsidized and tightly regulated public hospitals and a network of grassroots medical centers to cover basic needs.[10] On the whole, the administration has been able to align the financial burden of health care, education, and housing with the average urban household income, with the share increasing from 15% to 32% in the last period of urban reform, and with this share dropping slightly to 29% by 2008 (Figure 9.3).

However, present welfare programs have yet to find comprehensive solutions to the issues of inequity and exclusion, especially for those choosing to accept the market price. Despite achievements in checking excessive growth in welfare costs in general, the government is faced with many more significant problems as the new generation of the 1970s and 1980s comes of age and the old generation of the 1950s and 1960s approaches retirement age. The resulting surge in welfare demand poses serious threats to the government still struggling to cope with an unbearable rise in costs. The upsurge of social grievances against fast rising housing price among the young generation is a clear sign of this change.

The present welfare system is characterized by different approaches and varying degrees of policy continuity. Some policy reforms have been more systemically implemented throughout, such as the steadily increasing coverage of social insurance. Other policy reforms have been less satisfactory and some-

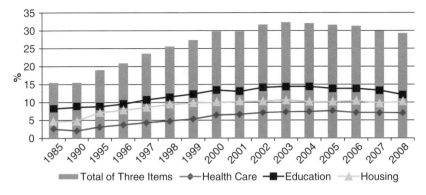

Figure 9.3   Share of welfare items in household consumption. Compiled by the author from *The China Statistical Yearbook*, various years.

times ridden with rent-seeking activities, such as the welfare housing programs LRH and EH. Some reform programs have been implemented more or less consistently since the start, such as the MSLS programs, whereas other programs have been characterized by ad hoc approaches, some of them even contradictory to each other, such as the repeated game of central controls and local activism in the housing market.

These differences derive from the different political dynamics for social policy reform which vary widely across specific policy domains. Some of the reform programs are direct continuations of earlier modernization projects. This pattern is common for policy domains without major contentions and resistance from special interests. The institution of employment-related insurances, arguably among the more successful urban social policies, encountered the least resistance and rapidly achieved full coverage. The effort to repair the state-subsidized grassroots obligatory education system which focused on elimination of high school fees and equalizing educational opportunity in the rural areas was also implemented relatively smoothly from 2005. These reform efforts culminated in the new Labor Law and amendments of the Compulsory Education Law, respectively.

Another type of reform measures are domestic responses to crisis situations and the external pressures of globalization. The best example is the SARS crisis in 2003, which through a series of global engagements initiated a serious rethinking on China's public health conditions and motivated the state to reform the public health and information sector.[11] In 2010, the reforms of the income distribution system and the state monopolies gained momentum as domestic social grievances intensified.

Despite the role of social policy reform in the "harmonious society" project, the ongoing reform is still primarily determined by the paramount agenda of economic development and market reform. Whenever global or regional economic downturns threaten domestic GDP growth, social sectors will be opened up to stimulate domestic demands irrespective of possible social consequences such as distributive justice and the affordability of basic welfare benefits. The market-oriented reforms of higher education and health care in 1998, although long under consideration, found their immediate cause in the Asian Financial Crisis (1997–98). The post-2008 Global Financial Crisis policy has created irrational exuberance in the real estate market, which has only succeeded in fueling a relentless build-up in the housing price, not only threatening economic and financial stability, but also generating immense social grievances and undermining the political base of the regime.

In the domain of social welfare, where strong corporate and local interests are at stake, social policy reform runs into a number of structural constraints. In the Hu–Wen era, as in earlier years of reform, while the legal hurdles for social mobility have been gradually removed, the substantive divides have on the contrary increased in terms of the distribution of social and economic costs and benefits of the reform. The new policy package in the Hu–Wen era, which is strictly guided by gradualism and constrained by the overwhelming concern for social stability, has so far achieved only limited progress in these respects. This has allowed institutionally conditioned social inequalities, such as the lack of basic welfare provision for migrant workers and their family members, to persist.

Most projects planned by the Hu–Wen social policy reform are still at an early stage. The social policy has so far eschewed any abrupt and fundamental changes. Significant headways have been made in that employment-related social insurance coverage and labor protections have been extended to include most urban workers including migrant workers. But much less progress was made toward universal basic health care, fair access to education beyond the minimum number of years, and affordable housing for those in need. Likewise, equality in welfare provision has deteriorated, making China one of the least equitable nations in the world in the delivery of welfare services such as health care.

Dynamics of Social Policy Reform

Social policy reform has progressed unevenly across different policy areas. This is largely due to different political dynamics across policy areas. The social policy process is a strategic reaction of the government to social grievances and social problems from different social groups under various institutional constraints. Social grievances and pressures can come from both inside and outside the state apparatus. Those who are directly working in various state agencies are insiders, such as Party and government organizations and to a lesser degree government sponsored institutions and large SOEs, especially those managed by the central government. The social policy process thus runs on two levels. At one level, organized interests of the state agency, and especially central leadership, can directly influence policy. At another level, less organized or unorganized social forces can input their grievances into the political system primarily through media, in particular the Internet.

In planning social reform, the government is motivated by two factors, namely the collective voice from society demanding reform and the costs of reform, including resistance from institutional constraints and direct costs of state subsidy or transfer. In each case the resultant voice from all social groups affected, which is interpreted as the political cost for delay or inaction in social reform, is compared with the direct costs and institutional resistance involved in possible social policy reform. The institutional resistance in most cases comes from the direct providers of social welfare, in most cases corporatized agencies under the political control of the state. If the demands of social forces outweighs institutional constraints, the government is more likely to launch reform and make the necessary investment; otherwise the government will refrain from reform and make little investment.

Social insurance

Social insurance includes five work-related insurances associated with employment, namely, old age pension, medical insurance, unemployment insurance, work injury insurance, and maternity insurance. In addition, social insurance includes the housing provident fund (HPF). The bulk of the urban labor force participates in the five insurance schemes and the HPF. Compared with other forms of welfare provision, social insurance has a number of features facilitating its implementation.

Targeted primarily at the urban labor force holding secure jobs as opposed to the unemployed and part-time workers, social insurance enjoys very wide political support among urban working class. Employees in state enterprises and work units are the first to benefit. Though vocal as political forces, the regular employees of private enterprises, increasingly aware of their legal rights, tend to organize themselves for collective action. This tendency was further strengthened as labor-related social protests and massive incidents raised the urgency of labor protection.

Since everyone in the workforce is exposed to various types and levels of risks, the exit option is unavailable for any risk-averse employees for work-related social insurance, especially the state sector under the direct political control of central and local governments. For instance, prior to the implementation of the new Labor Law, there was already wide social support for better protection of migrant workers by legislating for their basic insurance. Considering the instability and volatility of the lower-end labor market in China, unemployment is a most pressing political concern on the part of the Chinese government.

The pooling and sharing of risk in social insurance schemes, except for the HPF, also serves to unite both strong and weak voices in the direction of expanding the coverage rate to achieve universal coverage. While risks may vary across different individuals, there is no clear variation and stratification of risks based on social status (except for work-related injury). This relatively uniform distribution of risks aligns the interests of all urban employees from all social strata in support of a nationwide insurance system.

The social insurance system today still lacks equality and sometimes suffers from many blind spots in its coverage. A major source of inequity between the enterprise and government sectors is the dual-track pension scheme. Since the SOE reform, enterprise sector pensions are fully privatized and delinked from the state. However, pensions of civil servants and government-funded agencies are provided by the state, creating a dual-track pension system. The HPF contribution in particular displays very sharp government sector inequality due to unspecific regulations over its upper bounds.[12] As the politically more vocal section of the workforce currently enjoys a measure of exit from the insurance-based system, there is a clear lack of political dynamics to increase the level of old age insurance and a resistance toward reform of the dual-track system. The main constraints of social insurance come from the financial conditions of the individual enterprises. Many of China's small and medium enterprises have always been living on a meager profit margin. Even as the new Labor Law made the enterprise contribution to insurance premiums a legal requirement, significant numbers of migrant workers are still undercovered by social insurance due to a lack of corporate funding and law enforcement capacity.

Social protection

Social protection is the direct redistribution of income through the state. The classic example is the MSLS and to a lesser extent the institution of a minimum wage. In China, following the neo-liberal model of limited protection for the very needy, only means-tested marginal social groups are eligible for minimum welfare support from the state.

The politics of social protection works by a simple mechanism. Since there is no exit for the very needy, the low-income group has a very strong attachment to state transfer payments. However, lacking in channels of expression and organizational capacity, the voice from below is likely to be very weak and would most probably have to rely on a social agency for its articulation. Thus, social protection for the very needy might be a long way off from being institutionalized, such as a rural MSLS. While impoverishment has been a long-standing issue in both urban and rural China, it was not until 2005 that the government began to call for a nationwide implementation of a rural MSLS to aid the desperate poor, long after the scheme was first introduced in urban industrial centers.

The urban poor are relatively better protected in the social reform. This is not just because they are politically less marginal. Thanks to urban corporate reform, China's poverty relief enjoyed a relatively early start in the urban industrial region. The MSLS was first institutionalized as a social policy to cope with the social consequences of SOE reform, which resulted in massive urban unemployment in the industrial city of Shanghai in 1993. Later it spread with the deepening of the SOE reform into inland provinces.

In a similar light, the Hu–Wen administration set up the minimum wage system in 2003 and made it a legal requirement in the new Labor Law in 2008, primarily to protect migrant workers in coastal provinces. This institution of labor protection is part of the administration's concerted efforts to address social inequality, especially the urban–rural income gap. Since the global financial crisis in 2008, the minimum wage scheme has extended its coverage and become better enforced, but the level of minimum wage, as in the case of the MSLS, remained at a very low level and sometimes appeared inflexible to adjustment in some regions.

The key issue of social protection lies in the level of protection. Politically, China's working and non-working poor fall snugly into the least vocal social groups. A weak and limited voice from a marginal social class often induces state inaction and constrains the extent and level of China's social protection. This is further delayed by local authorities, often without political and fiscal incentives to aid the poor, especially migrant workers. This policy lag can be very significant in that heavy state fiscal commitment only occurs long after relevant institutions are first set up.

Welfare provision

Welfare provision, covering the areas of housing, health care, and education, is perhaps the most complicated and contentious domain of social policy in China. The domain of welfare provision is first and foremost about the distribution of economic costs and benefits of the reform, since commodification and marketization of housing, health care, and education have transformed these social spheres as important sectors of the economy. The issue of welfare provision involves, among others, the key economic and social interests of China's emerging middle class as a politically strategic social group.

The market-oriented allocation of housing, education, and health care are predominantly urban issues. In particular, the price and quality of these social goods are most consequential in the most urbanized part of China where both the elite and middle class are largely concentrated. The highly differentiated distribution of voice and exit options between the elite and middle class has so far created serious tensions in all relevant policy domains, especially in the field of housing. For all three sectors concerned, the fault line between elite and middle class is the availability of exit option and the level of voice.

In today's China, the social elite have every means to circumvent and take advantage of market mechanisms where the middle class, despite its considerable political weight and growing voice in the media, has no alternative but to accept the terms of the market. Market allocation is strictly based on "dollar vote," in that prior access to limited supply of social goods is given to the highest bidders. With the surging market price for education, health care, and housing, some middle-class bidders are effectively crowded out of the market. The crowded out social groups have the most incentive to reject the pricey welfare regime and resort to more violent means, whereas those who are not completely out of the game will have incentives to speak out against poor quality and high price of the welfare goods and services.

The game of welfare provision is thus typically played out among the central and local governments, the political and economic elite with exit option, the middle class with dollar votes, the government agents with a stake in pricey commodified welfare products, and the crowded out marginal groups. In terms of gain and loss, the elite enjoy absolute personal gain at little personal costs, the middle class relative social and personal gain at considerable personal costs, and the marginal group absolute social and personal loss. The government agents are often rent-seekers and are resistant to any reform. Forms of voice also vary across this social spectrum, from minor complaints to serious social grievances and violent retributions, while the channels of voice also shift from official government bodies to violent personal protests.

Education

For years, educational policy has attracted much media attention as one of the most problematic sectors across all social policy domains. There is constant social grievance about the percentage of government spending on education which has yet to reach the international standard of 4%. However, in terms of equity of access and distributive justice, the educational sector has outperformed both health care and housing.

At the level of basic education, China has made significant progress since the reform, both in terms of participatory rates and average years of schooling. Two important factors are at work. First, there is no exit for any social class from the government-funded social policy domain of obligatory education, from elites to marginal groups. Second, the obligatory stage of education is not as commercialized as other domains of welfare policy and enjoys a unique legal protection. In the reform era, the idea of basic education for all has gained wide social consensus and unswerving political support from the central leadership. The legalization of the Nine Year Obligatory Education means no exit for any social class at the stages of primary and junior high school education.

The government has overall been successful in expanding basic education and improving the general quality of education. These progresses notwithstanding, distributive inequity remains critical. Marginal social groups such as migrant workers are poorly served by the state-run urban basic education system and financial and human resources vary widely among rural and urban, poor and rich regions. Since the weaker social groups have only limited voices, there has been a lack of dynamic reform for years. As in the case of other domains of social services, the predominant choice for marginal groups is to opt for involuntary exit at some point beyond the mandatory years of education.

The marketization of higher education has spawned the phenomenal growth of China's higher education sector. Further, the process of marketization also means a shift of access criteria from purely academic merits to monetary resources. In other words, the better-off now have a higher chance of entering college while poor households face the daunting cost of fees. Broadening channels of higher education enrollment also means a larger playground for the political and social elite who have privileged access to the extra quotas. Since there is an obvious exit option for poor households, it is not surprising to find a declining proportion of undergraduates from rural backgrounds.[13]

Another significant development is the effect of globalization on education. The opportunity to study abroad has widened the exit option for the social elite, especially the top cream. The exit of elite households and students from the domestic higher education sector naturally deprives the system of the most powerful voice. Without these potential powerful voices exercising constant checks on the service provided by the higher education sector, the institutions of higher education will face much lesser criticisms and pressures and, as a result, the quality of higher education is adversely affected. Thus it is fair to argue that the availability of this elite exit option has become one of the factors contributing to the lagging or deteriorating quality of higher education in China.

Despite comparative underfinancing, China's education system, and especially its higher education sector, has overall enjoyed more profuse and generous state funding than other social welfare domains.[14] Increasing inequity and declining quality of education amidst the expansion in higher education enrollment have become the most critical issues in China's higher education sector, both closely related to the marketization and globalization of higher education in the last decade. In terms of benefits and costs, higher education reform redistributes higher education resources from lower income groups to the economically well-off, whereas the welfare position of the middle class is ambiguous.[15] The weak voice of the disadvantaged social groups means that they will find little support, not to mention any organized body, to assert their interests in promoting a more merit-based and less commercialized system.

Education reform is tasked to a self-contained educational system comprising various levels of educational institutions, local bureaucracy, and the Ministry of Education. In the current framework of administrative control, the higher education sector occupies a prominent political position as an independent unit from the local administration, whereas primary and high schools are locally controlled institutions. Among the independent institutions of higher education, universities with central ministerial affiliations even rank as powerful vice-ministerial administrative units. Such an organizational structure implies that the higher education system will continue to absorb more resources and pose more obstacles to reforms than primary and high schools. The competitive expansion and the pursuit of scale rather than quality, which is in accordance with the vital corporate self-interests of the higher education system, are still hard to reform.

Health Care

Health care policy directly involves the well-being of every individual member of society. In terms of voice and exit, the interests involved are more complicated than education but not as complex as housing provision. The access to health care is characterized by the existence of wide-ranging privileges for special social groups and almost no legal protection for marginal social groups. At the top of the pyramid sit the social groups which do not need to worry about medical bills. For incumbent and retired senior officials in the state sector, their health care spending is fully or for the most part covered by the state budget. The rich capitalists and entrepreneurial class can seek an exit from the market system by seeking health care abroad. Thus, exit options from the health care market are available for both top political and economic elites. At this level, there is no incentive for these privileged groups to voice any grievances as they are the direct beneficiaries.

At the next level are social groups such as the civil servants and the upper middle class whose socioeconomic positions and financial resources are sufficient to secure for themselves and their family members full or substantial levels of government or corporate-funded medical insurance. These two classes enjoy at least certain protection from the rising costs of health care services. Like the elite class, they have limited incentive to voice their displeasure against the current arrangement. But with at least partial self-contribution, they are still likely to comment on the quality of services.

Most of the middle class, with limited access to state subsidies and only minimum insurance coverage, are left with the sole choice of obtaining health services from the market partially financed by their savings. These social groups have strong incentives to challenge the present system since they have to pay a heavy price for most health care services. Collectively, they have little direct influence over the actual agenda-setting, but their strong preference for state-funded public hospitals over continued marketization is likely to produce an accumulative effect.

At the lowest social rung, some social groups are completely excluded from the health care market and basic insurance due to the prohibitive level of costs relative to their incomes and the incomplete social security system. As their collective voice is very weak, most of them choose a voluntary exit from medical care. However, the scale of exclusion is larger and more consequential, as hundreds of millions of rural households are virtually cut off from any medical benefits.

Like education, inequity and exclusion are major problems in the present health care system. But both problems have been much more severe in the case of health care than education. The key factor at issue is the cost of medication, followed by the undercoverage of basic medical insurance. Compared with education, the government has been more reluctant to increase direct health care expenditure than to expand medical insurance. Health care expenditure fell from 6% in 1994 to 2.6% in 2001. But more significantly for the middle class, rent-seeking and the resultant poor quality of service in hospitals are even more rampant and obnoxious than in education.

While linked to various levels of government as semi-autonomous institutions, public hospitals are mostly locally based, politically less significant corporate and administrative entities. In consequence, systemic reforms to deal with rent-seeking behavior will encounter less resistance than with education reform. Considering the social distribution of benefits and costs, health care reform is also unlikely to produce a serious conflict between an elite already enjoying full coverage and the excluded class desperately in need of basic coverage. In 2009, the government began to build a mini-NHS to deal with this issue. The whole process will take a long time, especially in providing equal service, as long as the elite insiders do not have compelling incentives to pursue such a direction on account of their own fully protected interests.

Housing

In many respects, housing policy is the most critical of all China's social policy domains. The problem is predominantly that of prohibitively high housing price and the interests involved are more complicated than any other spheres of social policy.

Housing policy is not as much a concern for China's older generation as it is for the younger generation since the last two rounds of reform only monetized, not marketized, housing, offering housing as part of the welfare provisions of work units rather than full private goods. Since the 1990s, the central government has implemented several welfare schemes to provide housing on state subsidy and ensure the price is within the affordable range. However, the pervasive tendency of rent-seeking at local levels soon led to effective impasse in these subsidized housing programs.

Since the social provision of housing is highly marketized for most in need of urban dwelling, the most clear-cut division in housing allocation is between those who have been exempted from the high-price market and those who must bid in the market. The former covers employees of organizations that could provide cheap housing as a part of the welfare package, including civil servants, government affiliated sectors, and employees of some monopoly SOEs. The latter group cover the rest of the population who have no such privileges.

As in any other welfare provisions, exit options are only available to the politically powerful class. However, there is an added twist that makes the housing issue an exception from the rule, namely the capacity of the marketized housing to absorb tremendous speculative capital sums as investment goods. Since control on housing market investment was removed in 2003, the housing price in China's major urban areas has risen to exorbitant levels, far exceeding the gradual increase in middle-class income. In consequence, the crowding-out effect is much more severe in the housing market than in any other sectors of welfare provision. The middle class, having no means of exit, have no alternative but to face the dilemma of a risky and costly investment on the one hand and forced exit from the market altogether on the other hand.

Exclusion in housing is particularly politically destabilizing since much of the middle class are primarily victims of crowding-out. The subsequent social grievances are not distributed linearly according to relative economic and social status, as in the case of health care and education. Rather, grievances are concentrated in aspirant middle classes, mostly the young generation of university graduates as well as middle-class urban migrants in the non-state sector. Denied direct access to government bodies, they represent nevertheless the most vocal voices in the media, wielding significant power in shaping public opinion, particularly on the Internet. The indirect political pressure on the central government to tackle the housing price hike and perhaps undertake a wave of new reform is strong and well-represented at the political periphery.

To make the problem more complicated, the interests and appeals of the middle class mired in housing price bubbles have powerful potential allies and foes within the political and economic elite. With respect to housing policy, the elite tend to be divided by the preferences for short-term and personal gains against the prospect of long-term economic and social bubbles. Rising housing prices raise the risks of bubbles and subsequent non-performing loans in the state banking sector, and could further give rise to economic insecurity. On the other hand, land-selling local governments and the political and economic elite with multiple properties obviously prefer continuous rising housing and land prices. In this case, both local governments and developers as agents of welfare provision are both opposed to reform. Housing, unlike education and health care, could easily be politicized to provide opportunities for internal as well as external contentions.

Conclusion

If examined from historical perspectives, most of the social grievances have their origins in the social policy reform both in the narrow sense of welfare reform and in a broader sense of the restructuring of state–society relations. Much of the social injustice discussed above is rooted in the inequality and injustice in the distribution of social welfare. For example, the new burdens of expensive medication, education, and housing are sources of grievances among various groups of middle and lower class in China today. High rates of crime, erosion of social cohesion, and moral decay are likewise largely the result of basic educational inequity and the lack of social protection. The failure of social policy reform to reduce the costs of the essential welfare goods and provide protection for the majority is likely to result in further social instability.

Social policy reform is not only complementary but key to further economic reforms. A chronic structural issue in the Chinese economy is the lack of effective domestic consumption. This structural weakness in turn leads to over-reliance on domestic investment and overseas markets, two basic causes for China's internal and external economic imbalance. Social policy reform is an important remedy to this imbalance, since effective social reform will help to relieve average households of overpriced housing, health care, and education and directly boost consumption. Studies have indicated that most middle-class Chinese families substantially cut their consumption budget in response to the predominant need to save and then spend for a housing mortgage.[16]

The absence of social infrastructure that protects and empowers individuals and households to fully participate in the labor market has an equally distorting effect on the economy as the other major sources of socioeconomic rigidity, such as state monopoly over key factors of production and market access. A resultant lack of effective domestic demand, private sector entrepreneurship, and social sources of economic growth since the late 1990s in turn necessitates heavy state investment and government intervention. Such structural constraints often force the Chinese economy into the dilemma of industrial overcapacity, underemployment, inflation, and asset bubbles.

The Hu–Wen administration has made social policy an important and independent aspect of the public policy agenda. By expanding the coverage of social insurance, strengthening social protections for the poor, and reforming market-oriented social provisions, the current social reform has achieved varying degrees of progress in all social policy domains. But the lack of reform dynamics is clearly a key obstacle. To a large extent, reform is still limited in scope and short of general public expectations. At a more profound level, further social policy reform will also require a broadened agenda to include a readjustment in state–society relations. Such necessary shifts constitute the political dimension of social reform.

Today, state–society relations in China are plagued by a myriad of special privileges and stakes for the social elite in the name of the state. Such widespread exit options are causing a serious lack of, and delay in, reform dynamics. In this sense, further reform will need to transform exclusive state-sponsored privileges and special interests into various forms of universal rights, such as transparent and legally approved employer-specific welfare compensations, in addition to a legally administered bundle of rights on social insurance, social protection, and state-subsidized welfare provision for all eligible (means-tested) citizens across all social classes and professional boundaries.

In particular, special welfare rights of civil servants and employees in monopoly SOEs have to be adjusted and curtailed. With the exit options withdrawn from the political elite and a measure of universal citizen rights introduced to state-sponsored social welfare, the voice for inexpensive and quality welfare provisions will be significantly strengthened. The broadened social reform agenda will thus have to include, among others, creating rights of equal access to state-sponsored social provisions under a program of universal citizenship.

Meanwhile, social policy reform needs to be incorporated into fiscal reform, through increased central responsibility and a more transparent and democratic budgeting process. The first mechanism is a continuation of the Hu–Wen administration's effort to expand social spending by both increasing central shares and central–local transfers for welfare programs. Moreover, as an essential part of the social policy reform, the budgeting process of national social spending has to be open to wider public scrutiny.

China's economic success is critically contingent on the mutual reinforcement between the dual dynamics of economic growth and social stability. But the current uneasy coupling of an economic growth model based on a GDP-centered approach and a static form of social stability enforced by direct state control is replete with contradictions. A key source of contradiction is the lack of clearly envisioned and timely implemented social policies to compensate and protect social groups whose welfare positions are adversely affected by economic reform and existing socioeconomic institutions. The slow progress of social policy reform has led to increasing distrust between the state and society and the disloyalty of the majority of social groups, with profound political implications. As discussed in Chapter 6, social protests are closely associated with social injustice. Without proper social policy reform among other major reforms to address the fundamental structural dilemmas, both social and economic development ahead will be unsustainable and will fall prey to a vicious circle.

Notes

1 Walder (1986: 59–67).
2 Naughton (1995: 101–03).
3 Tang (2010).
4 Chan *et al.* (2008: 62–64).
5 Ibid., 173–75.
6 Esping-Andersen (1990: 24–27).
7 Chan *et al.* (2008: 62–63, 141, and 185).
8 Liu (2005).
9 Zhao (2006: 478).
10 Zhao and Huang (2009).
11 Chan *et al.* (2010).
12 In most enterprises, although social insurances meet legally required minimums, the level of protection remains relatively low and stagnant, especially enterprise pension based on old age insurance, which is only 20% of the prevailing wage level. The comparable figure in the government sector could be as high as 60–80%. Since the HPF does not involve social risk sharing and requires heavy funding, the fund is mostly concentrated in the government and monopoly SOEs.
13 "Declining Proportion of Rural Undergraduates Endangers Social Harmony." *China Youth Daily*, January 24, 2010.
14 China's spending on education, like government financing for health care and public housing, has declined over the years. Its share of education expenditure in the overall government budget declined from 17.6% in 1994 to 13.4% in 2006. However, the decline has been much more severe in health care, social protection, and public housing. Compared with developed welfare states, China's underfinancing of health care and social protection is also more severe than that of education.
15 The net welfare effect of the marketization of higher education depends on benefits gained from the expansion of access to higher education set against its deteriorating quality and the increase in financial burden on each household. On average, marketization has the effect of distributing the opportunities and fruits of education from poor meritocratic students to rich mediocre students by making the system less meritocratic and more plutocratic.

16   "Beixiaoshi de zhongchanjieji" (The Disappearing Middle Class). *China News Weekly*, January 13, 2010.

References

Chan, Chan Kwan, King Lun Ngok, and David Phillips. 2008. *Social Policy in China: Development and Well-being*. Bristol: The Policy Press.

Chan, L. H., L. Chen, and J. Xu. 2010. "China's Engagement with Global Health Diplomacy: Was SARS a Watershed?" *PLOS Medicine* 7, 4: e1000266.

Esping-Andersen, Gøsta. 1990. *The Three Worlds of Welfare Capitalism*. Princeton, NJ: Princeton University Press.

Liu, Zhiqiang. 2005. "Institution and Inequality: The Hukou System in China." *Journal of Comparative Economics* 33, 1: 133–57.

Naughton, B. 1995. *Growing Out of the Plan: Chinese Economic Reform, 1978–1993*. Cambridge: Cambridge University Press.

Tang, Jun. 2010. "Chengxiang dibao zhidu: lishi, xianzhuang yu qianzhan" (Urban and Rural MSLS: History, Present Status and Future Prospects). Beijing: Institute of Sociology, Chinese Academy of Social Sciences.

Walder, A. G. 1986. *Communist Neo-Traditionalism, Work and Authority in Chinese Industry*. Berkeley, CA: University of California Press.

Zhao, Litao and Yanjie Huang. 2009. "China's Moves to Reform Its Healthcare System." *EAI Background Brief* 486, East Asian Institute, National University of Singapore.

Zhao, Zhongwei. 2006. "Income Inequality, Unequal Health Care Access, and Mortality in China." *Population and Development Review* 32, 3: 461–83.

Chapter 10

Bureaucracy and Governance

The last chapter discussed how China has embarked on social policy reforms to cope with social changes resulting from rapid market-oriented economic transformation. This chapter will examine how the Chinese government has engaged in bureaucratic restructuring to lay down an institutional foundation for market economy. Specifically, the reform aimed to achieve three related goals: reducing the role of government; promoting the role of market forces; and governing an increasingly market-oriented economy. Capitalist economic development has rapidly facilitated China's transition from a planned to a market economy, which requires a set of economic institutions that are compatible with market-led economic activities. Needless to say, such institutions are not spontaneous products of economic development, but have to be created by the government.

This chapter shows how the Chinese leadership has transformed a bureaucratic system under the Maoist planned economy in the pre-reform era to one which is compatible with a market economy. The transformation was incremental. It was divided into three distinctive stages. The first stage was during the era of Deng Xiaoping, from the early 1980s to 1997, during which each restructuring was characterized by the transition from the planned economy to the "socialist market economy." As discussed in Chapter 3, the economic reform in the 1980s and early 1990s was characterized by radical decentralization, meaning that the central government decentralized its economic power to both local governments and enterprises. To achieve that goal, the central government introduced bureaucratic reforms to reduce its institutional intervention in some economic fields, and gradually withdrew from them to let

Contemporary China: A History since 1978, First Edition. Yongnian Zheng.
© 2014 John Wiley & Sons, Ltd. Published 2014 by John Wiley & Sons, Ltd.

market forces function. The second stage started with the 1998 bureaucratic restructuring designed by Premier Zhu Rongji which was characterized by and served the market economy. Radical decentralization in the previous decade had seriously undermined the institutional framework of the planned economy. To govern a decentralized economy, the government overhauled the whole bureaucratic structure and set up new institutions to support the economy. Since the early 2000s, China has entered the third stage of bureaucratic reform. The government has shifted its reform focus to building a regulatory regime for better economic governance.

Dynamics of Restructuring the Bureaucratic State

After the PRC was established in 1949, Chinese leaders made great endeavors to establish a modern bureaucratic system. Due to endless political campaigns by Mao, the bureaucratic apparatus was extremely unstable in the pre-reform years. In the post-Mao era, the leadership has shifted its emphasis from political movement to economic development. Accordingly, the restructuring of the state bureaucratic system has shifted from serving "revolutionary" tasks to "constructing" goals, with the aim of rationalizing the bureaucratic state to make it more efficient. A consensus among the reformers is that the bureaucratic reforms were needed for reducing, even eliminating, shortcomings such as inefficiency, dysfunction, overstaffing, corruption, and so on.[1]

In the context of market economy, bureaucratic restructuring has sought, more than anything else, to provide an institutional foundation for the development of an increasingly market-oriented economy. To let market forces function, the state will have to reduce its institutional intervention in and even withdraw from economic affairs. However, as a major economic actor, the state is reluctant to do so. The reformist leaders thus have to restructure the bureaucratic system to withdraw institutional support for state interventions on one hand, and to provide institutional support for market forces on the other hand. Certainly, the development of market forces does not mean that China wants to have a laissez faire economy. Instead, with the development of market forces, the government has also introduced institutional changes aimed at establishing a regulatory regime to govern the market.

In performing all these tasks, the reformist leaders are constrained in planning and restructuring the state bureaucracy. Every reform, be it to reduce the role of government or to increase the role of market forces, involves politics, and is thus subject to bureaucratic interests and their resistance. Although every reform planner has claimed that restructuring seeks to rationalize the state bureaucratic system and to increase its efficiency, the results of every restructuring are very different. Since organizational staffing, structure, and operations affect the distribution of political power and strongly influence the formation of public policy on a wide range of issues, restructuring frequently becomes a political game among different power-holders.

This also applies to top leaders. Every bureaucratic restructuring affects their individual power interests. Power politics is carried out by institutional reorganization. Each leader needs his own institutional means to carry out his policies and to govern the economy. Therefore, we have seen that every bureaucratic restructuring is accompanied by the coming of a new "premier-select."[2] In China, though the leadership collectively designs bureaucratic reforms, "the premier-select" plays an extremely important role in planning the restructuring. In planning each restructuring, the premier-select has to consider how to use it to consolidate his power position and strengthen his institutional capacity to make and enforce his policies. Although the premier-select does not have much freedom in changing the structure of the state bureaucracy, and in particular the State Council, since other leaders also have a say in the restructuring plan, he has the power to set up new institutions to formulate and implement policies that are more in line with his own policy orientation rather than those of other leaders. So, under Zhao Ziyang (1982–87) and Li Peng (1988–92), there was the State Commission for Economic System Restructuring (SCESR); under Zhu Rongji, there was the State Economic and Trade Commission (SETC); and under Wen Jiabao, there is a National Development and Reform Commission (NDRC). These institutions are not only organizational power bases, but also implement new policies set by the new administration, and are thus called the "mini-State Council."

The 1982 Restructuring by Zhao Ziyang

In the late 1970s and early 1980s, many senior government officials who were ousted during the Cultural Revolution (CR) returned to the political scene. With their reappearance and the policy shift from Maoist class struggle to Deng's economic modernization, more ministries, many of them in charge of specific industrial sectors, were added to the State Council. Consequently, the number of organizations under the State Council increased rapidly from 76 in 1978 to 100 in 1981.

When the leadership started its ambitious bureaucratic reform program in 1982, it wanted to improve both the efficiency and the responsiveness of state institutions. The reforms ran headlong into entrenched local units, and factional interests. In that year, the National People's Congress (NPC) passed a proposal for restructuring which reduced the number of vice premiers from 18 to 3 and that of organizations from 100 (48 ministries and 52 commissions) to 61 (43 ministries and 18 commissions).

The 1982 restructuring is a reflection of the fusion of a planned economy and a market one. This was done in accordance with ideological change. In 1982, the CCP held its Twelfth Congress, during which the leadership claimed that China's economic reform was aimed at establishing a mixed economic system, with the planned economy as its main pillar, and the market economy as its supplement. This is reflected in the institutional changes from the 1982 restructuring. Several ministries and commissions designed for promoting socialist economic development were created either from scratch or by taking over others. For instance, the State Economic Commission (SEC) took over five state commissions, one task group, and five state bureaus and became a powerful commission in charge of promoting market forces – to counterbalance the State Planning Commission, an institution of the old planned economy. The Ministry of Commerce took over two other ministries that were the product of the planned economy. Meanwhile, many ministries that were typical of the planned economy remained unchanged or had no big change, or even just changed their names, such as the Ministry of Metallurgical Industry, Ministry of Nuclear Industry, and Ministry of Coal Industry.

Very importantly, Premier Zhao Ziyang himself was in charge of the new SCESR. Zhao wanted his own institution to design the restructuring of the economic system to develop elements of a market economy. The commission was the think-tank for the administration during Zhao's term.

The new administration retained the Planning, Economic, and Scientific and Technology Commissions, with a vastly expanded brief going to the SEC which absorbed parts of the planning and policy coordination functions of five abolished commissions – Agriculture, Energy, Machine Building, Finance, and Capital Construction. Long-term capital construction planning, however, went to the State Planning Commission, while the management of capital construction projects came under a new ministry called Ministry of Urban and Rural Construction and Environmental Protection. The hundreds of factories directly under the abolished Capital Construction Commission were now attached to this new ministry. These changes made the SEC responsible for agriculture, industry, capital construction (short-term planning), railroads and transportation, finance and monetary affairs, some aspects of foreign trade, and the production of an annual national economic plan.

Reorganization of the state commissions was only part of the 1982 reform plan. In March 1982, Zhao announced that the number of commissions and ministries would be reduced from 52 to 39, but by May, he revised this figure upward to 41, and by the end of 1982, to 43. These changes indicated resistance from some ministries. However, despite these retreats, the reforms trimmed the State Council staff by approximately 17,000.[3] While Zhao was not able to change the planned system, he was able to create many new organizations. These two sets of institutions ideally needed time to adapt to each other.

However, to implement his economic reform Zhao needed continually to abolish some old ministries and create new ones. For instance, the Auditing Administration and the Ministry of State Security were created in 1983, the Ministry of Supervision and some state bureaus in 1986. Meanwhile, the Ministries of Machinery Building and of Armaments were merged to form a Commission of Machinery Industry.

After the restructuring, there were 61 organizations in the State Council, of which there were 43 ministries and 18 commissions. Unfortunately, five years later, the organizations increased again to 72, of which there were 45 ministries and 27 commissions. From 100 organizations in 1981 to 61 in 1982 to 72 in 1987, the restructuring experienced a cycle of contraction and expansion.

The 1988 and 1993 Restructurings by Li Peng

In 1987, the CCP held its Thirteenth Congress during which the Party leadership raised a new concept of "combining planned and market economies," and claimed that China was still at a primary stage of socialism. This conceptual change indicated that the market economy attained a position equal to that of the planned economy in the Party's ideology. Li Peng became the premier-select at that congress, meaning that he would succeed Zhao in 1988 when the Seventh NPC convened. The change in the CCP's ideology created a suitable political environment for the 1988 restructuring. Li Peng became the planner of the 1988 restructuring. His conservative stand significantly affected the essence of the restructuring. After Zhao's market-oriented economic reforms met with serious difficulty in the mid-1980s, the conservatives assumed the upper hand. Beside Li, Yao Yilin, one of close allies of Chen Yun, was recruited into the Standing Committee of the Political Bureau and became Vice Premier in 1988.

During this restructuring, ministries and commissions were reduced from 45 to 41. The Ministry of Energy was created by merging three ministries. The greater part of these abolished ministries became state companies, for example, the Petroleum and Gas Company of China. This was a move toward a market economy. The creation of the Ministry of Materials was, however, a step back to the planned economy. The ministry was put in charge of planning, manufacture, and distribution of commanded materials.[4]

One particularly significant merger was the takeover of the SEC by the State Planning Commission to strengthen an already oversized State Planning Commission, with about 1,300 staff. This reorganization was no doubt partly motivated by the conservatives' desire to throttle the reformist entrepreneurship of the SEC. The SEC had led the efforts to expand enterprise autonomy since 1979, whereas the State Planning Commission had defended the authority of the plan. When the SEC ceased to exist and became only a set of bureaus under the State Planning Commission, the reforms lost their highest-ranking bureaucratic advocate.

After Deng's Southern Tour in 1992, the CCP's Fourteenth Congress that year formally legitimized the market economy, and established it as the goal of China's economic reform. The leadership decided to initiate a new wave of bureaucratic restructuring and adjust the state bureaucratic system to a market economy. The Fourteenth Party Congress, however, also decided that Li would continue his second term of premiership, meaning that the Li team would plan the 1993 restructuring. One could expect that the restructuring after Deng's Southern Tour would be drastic and most of the state institutions that had supported the planned economy would be abolished and new ones set up to support and promote the market economy. Nevertheless, such expectations did not materialize. Given the fact that the conservative Premier Li continued his second term, the restructuring was seriously constrained. By then, Li had consolidated his power with the previous restructuring, and he lacked any motivation to introduce any drastic changes.

As a result, the bureaucratic structure did not change much. Overall, only one ministry, the Ministry of Energy, was abolished. But in fact, it was split into two ministries (Coal Industry and Power Industry) that were considered as Li's power base. Correspondingly, the Ministry of Machinery and Electrical Industry, seen as Jiang Zemin's power base, was similarly expanded. The only noticeable development in the move toward the market economy was the creation of the SETC, chaired by the new Vice Premier Zhu Rongji. The commission later became the institutional base of Zhu's radical economic reform.

The 1998 Institutional Reform under Zhu Rongji

A market economy does not evolve spontaneously from planned economy. Without doubt, Deng Xiaoping played a major role in pushing for market-oriented economic reform and establishing "building a market economy" as the goal of the CCP. But measured by the restructuring of the state bureaucratic system, China's market economy has not developed evenly under different leadership periods.

Figure 10.1 shows the trend of the restructuring. We can see that the two most radical changes took place under Zhao Ziyang and Zhu Rongji. After the restructuring in the early 1980s, the number of state bureaucracies remained unchanged until Zhu's reform began in 1997/8. Indeed, the two waves of the restructuring under Zhao and Zhu have been regarded as milestones in China's economic reforms. However, there is a difference between the two. Zhao's reform was achieved by establishing new operational mechanisms in accord-

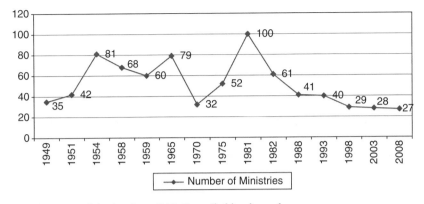

Figure 10.1 Ministries since 1949. Compiled by the author.

ance with the market economy, while leaving the old structure largely intact. In contrast, Zhu's reform was characterized by an institutional rebuilding favoring the market economy, meaning that many old institutions were abolished while new ones were established. After entering the Hu–Wen era in the present century, the leadership has given the highest priority to social policy reform, as discussed in the last chapter. In the area of economic reform, the government has shifted its emphasis from restructuring to building a regulatory regime.

During its Fifteenth Congress in 1997, the CCP leadership declared that state-owned enterprise (SOE) reform would be the most important political agenda for the new administration. At that congress, Zhu became the premier-select for the next NPC in 1998, meaning that Zhu would be the major planner of the 1998 restructuring of the state bureaucratic system. As expected, during the Ninth NPC in 1998, Zhu declared that his new administration would accord the highest priority to the reform and reorganization of the State Council and its various ministries. Under Zhu's restructuring plan, the existing 40 commissions and ministries were to be slashed to 29. The existing 8 million civil servants were also to be cut by half. Certainly, such large-scale bureaucratic reform had not been seen since the early 1980s.

It is worthwhile highlighting some major changes under Zhu's reform scheme. First of all, the SCESR was restructured. The commission was set up in 1982 by Zhao in order to plan China's economic reform and it soon became an important formal bureaucracy under the State Council. Nevertheless, after Zhao was promoted to take charge of Party affairs in 1987, the commission turned very conservative under Li Peng. Even when Zhu came to be in charge of China's economic reform, he did not use the commission to initiate and implement his reform policies since it was still under the control of Li. Only after Zhu became Premier was the commission unable to avoid being sidelined.

Zhu, however, had to make a compromise, and he was not able to ignore it completely. Instead, he transformed it. It is now no longer a formal bureaucracy, but a high-level consultative institution under the State Council. Zhu became its director and various ministers were its members.

A second major change occurred to the State Planning Commission. The commission was not abolished, but renamed the State Development Planning Commission. The old commission had been a symbol of the planned economy and its reform had not been easy. Overall, after two decades of economic reform, its power had weakened considerably. Nevertheless, it was still not ready to disappear. There had been much debate among major leaders on what it should do and how it should evolve. It was strengthened under Li Peng and Yao Yilin. Under Zhu, by giving it a new name, its power was institutionally weakened, and it became only a research institute focusing on China's long-term development plans.

Third, the number of sectoral ministries was reduced from 12 to three, a most radical change from all previous restructurings. This change was in line with the objective of separating the government from enterprises, which had been regarded by the reformist leadership as the solution to the problems saddling SOEs. Accordingly, a new organization, the Ministry of Labor and Social Security, was created.

Fourth, a particularly significant reform measure that Zhu undertook was business de-militarization. The State Commission of Science, Technology, and Industry for National Defense took over the governmental functions from the military companies. This reform certainly weakened the military businesses and marked the first step by the Chinese government to delink the military from business activities.

Since the very early days of the PRC, the Chinese military had been involved in various types of businesses such as food production, equipment repair, transport, mining, services, and provision of other day-to-day necessities of the military.[5] Most enterprises were run by the General Logistics Department and its local units. The General Staff Headquarters and the General Political Department also ran enterprises of their own. The military–business link intensified after the onset of the economic reform. The expansion of the military business was initially due to budget constraints.[6] Originally, the purpose of these enterprises was to serve the needs of the military and promote self-sufficiency and their activities were almost entirely restricted to the armed forces. The 1980s, however, saw major changes in their role. Over the years, the military had become one of the few military establishments in the world that was extensively engaged in a wide range of commercial activities in both domestic and international markets, including mining, footwear and garment manufacturing, pharmaceuticals and chemical products, hotels and vacation resorts, real estate, automotive industry, transportation, telecommunications, and others.

In many ways, the military–business links had greatly affected the military's combat capability as a modern military institution. It also raised doubts on other aspects such as professional ethics, the degree of internal cohesion, military morale, and disciplinary problems. What worried the leadership was that civilian laws generally could not be extended to cover military companies that were mostly controlled by princelings; and that the military–business links undermined the operation of the national economy and had become a barrier to the development of a market economy.

Among other negative effects, the most damaging ramification of the military's involvement in profit-making activities was the way that such activities were inevitably intertwined with the political economy of cities and towns where such commercial activities were located. Military business deals were instrumental in fostering regional and local political and economic powers as against the national government's. In parts of China, especially in coastal areas, the military's economic welfare was tied closely to local economic development. The relationship between the local military forces and local governments became interdependent. Local military forces often helped local government officials to engage in questionable economic activities. The collusion between the military and local commercial establishments tended to reinforce local defiance toward the national government.

Understandably, the new administration, supported by the CCP leadership, initiated a major campaign to delink the military from business activities. In July 1998, Jiang Zemin outlined steps to implement the campaign.[7] Major leaders such as Zhu Rongji, Hu Jintao, Wen Jiabao, and Wei Jianxing all took part in the process of restructuring the military–business connection. Zhu repeatedly stressed that all military expenses needed to come from the central coffers.[8] In early November 1998, the Chinese leadership set up a task force to handle the businesses of the military. The group was chaired by Zhu himself, with Hu Jintao and General Zhang Wannian as his deputies. The group reported directly to the Standing Committee of the Political Bureau. The formation of this powerful task force helped to accelerate the process of delinking the military from business activities. By the end of the year, the group announced that the PLA and Armed Police had formally renounced their control of previously owned business establishments.[9]

Finally, a far more important change in the 1998 restructuring concerned the SETC. The commission took over 7 existing commissions and ministries, two councils, and two large-scale SOEs. This change made the commission the most powerful organization within the State Council. The formation and development of the SETC was closely associated with Zhu's market-oriented economic reform, particularly his plan to radically reform SOEs.

Many forces pushed Zhu to initiate this radical reform. First of all, it seemed to Zhu that a large government structure and slow process of bureaucratic reform should be blamed for the difficulty of the SOE reform problem.[10] China's SOEs were the result of the planned economy, which enabled government officials to intervene in SOEs legitimately. Zhu recognized that a precondition to reforming SOEs was to separate the government from enterprises. But without abolishing the old institutions that had been involved in SOEs, any measures to reform SOEs would be ineffective. Certainly, in order to reform SOEs, the old Leviathan had to be tamed first. Most ministries liquidated by the 1998 restructuring were economic bureaucracies. Second, internal and external pressures at that time called for a rather radical institutional rebuilding. Internally, with the progress of the SOE reform, unemployment was increasing drastically and posed a serious threat to social stability. Externally, the 1997 Asian Financial Crisis had sent the Chinese leadership a strong signal that without rapid reform of China's SOEs and its financial system, China would not be able to avoid the misfortune that many other Asian countries had experienced. Third, without such a large-scale reform, a strong and efficient government would be in doubt. Close relations between government bureaucracies and enterprises would render any anti-corruption measures ineffective. Certainly, serious corruption had weakened the government's capacity in implementing policies and winning the confidence of the people.

Zhu became Premier with a new set of reform ideas, and he wanted to play a new game with new rules. To strengthen his power required the implementation of these new rules, which in turn required a new type of institution in which Zhu could mobilize various resources. Reorganization of the State Council, especially the SETC, undoubtedly provided Zhu with an opportunity to construct his own power base to implement his reform policies. The restructured SETC was empowered by incorporating six former ministries including Power Industry, Coal Industry, Metallurgical Industry, Machine-Building Industry, Chemical Industry, and Internal Trade. After their incorporation, these ministries were downgraded to bureaus and they no longer managed SOEs. With this change, the new commission became the most powerful coordinating organ in the country. More importantly, by doing so, Zhu wanted the commission to play a role similar to Japan's MITI in leading China's future economic development. China's main strategy to reform large-scale SOEs was to organize large industrial conglomerates similar to those of South Korea's *chaebols*. The new commission was to play an important role in such a transition. As a matter of fact, the new commission served as Zhu's major power base which enabled him to make and implement his plan of the SOE reform.

The 2003 and 2008 Reforms by Wen Jiabao

The CCP held its Sixteenth Congress in 2002. Power was transferred from Jiang's third generation of leadership to Hu's fourth generation. Associated with the power succession was a major policy shift from pro-capital to pro-people. The shift was inevitable. Since Deng's Southern Tour, the leadership had given the highest policy priority to economic growth, and a mentality of what China called "GDP-centrism" was formed among government officials. While the country achieved rapid economic growth, enormous undesirable and unexpected consequences followed. There were increasingly heavy human costs. For instance, according to official statistics, over 263,500 people died in industrial accidents in two years (2004–05). In the coal mining sector alone, nearly 6,000 miners died in 2005.[11] Another example is the large number of serious food safety incidents since the early years of this century.

The Hu-centered leadership decided to address emerging daunting social problems resulting from the policy of single-minded economic growth and it shifted its reform priority to social policy, as discussed in the last chapter. This was also reflected in the government's efforts in establishing a regulatory regime to govern the market.[12] Indeed, some initiatives were already taken by the Zhu administration. For example, as mentioned earlier, the Ministry of Labor and Social Security was established during the 1998 reform. When Wen Jiabao became the premier-select in 2002, he began to plan the 2003 reform. Although the 2003 reform was not radical, the intention to establish a regulatory regime was apparent. The number of ministries and commissions was reduced to 28 from 29, and several key regulatory agencies were established, including the State-owned Assets Supervision and Administration, the China Banking Regulatory Commission, the Ministry of Commerce, and the State Food and Drug Administration.

The most important reform by Wen was the creation of the NDRC in 2003, by integrating the State Development Planning Commission, State Economic and Trade Commission, and several other functions. The NDRC is a milestone in China's transition to a market-oriented economy, and its role extends to almost every aspect of the Chinese economy, from development planning and reforming the economic system to industrial policy, orchestrating major investment projects or programs, price stabilization, climate change, resource conservation, social development, employment and income distribution, regional development, foreign trade and investment, poverty and disaster reliefs, and so on; it also participates in formulating fiscal and monetary policies and plays a key role in implementing them.

While the market economy has been in place for years in China, the central government often finds that it has to resort to direct administrative control to achieve its macroeconomic objectives. The NDRC is an indispensable tool for that. It has a tendency of conducting macro-regulatory policies through micro-management of economic issues. Apart from promulgating rules and regulations, its power and influence come from three sources: project screening (approving or rejecting an investment project), the pricing of key commodities and services, and allocation of budgetary investment funds. In March 2008, some of its role in industrial policy was transferred to the new Ministry of Industry and Information Technology.

At the Seventeenth Congress in 2007, the CCP leadership established "building a harmonious society" as the goal of China's next step of development. The "super-ministries" reform (*dabuzhi gaige*), aimed at improving governance, became the top policy agenda in the area of institutional reform. This reform integrated minor ministries and departments with similar functions under the State Council into larger ones, or "super-ministries." The 2008 reform cut cabinet-level agencies from 28 to 27. Five "super-ministries" were established, including the Ministry of Industry and Information, the Ministry of Environmental Protection, the Ministry of Transport, the Ministry of Human Resources and Social Security, and the Ministry of Housing and Urban–Rural Construction.

The promotion of the State Environmental Protection Administration to a full-fledged environment ministry was expected to give its representatives the power to influence cabinet-level decisions on green issues. Compared with its predecessor, the Ministry of Construction, the Ministry of Housing and Urban–Rural Construction relinquished its functions on public transport to the Ministry of Transport, and its functions on urban water utilization to the Ministry of Water Resources. The new ministry was expected to focus on urban housing development amidst public complaint about the property price hike. The Ministry of Energy and the Ministry of Finance were not affected, while the Ministry of Railways was still independent of the Ministry of Transport. The reform tried to define clearly the responsibilities and powers of each department, clarify the relationship of responsibilities among departments, and improve the mechanism for interdepartmental coordination and cooperation.

To establish a regulatory regime takes time. The Chinese leadership has made continuous efforts toward that goal. During the 2007 Party Congress, Li Keqiang became candidate for the next Premier (confirmed by the 2012 Party Congress, to take effect from March 2013). Since then, Li (as Vice Premier) has been assigned the task of overseeing continuous reforms toward a regulatory regime. In December 2008, the State Council established a small leading group on deepening medical and health reform. Li was the head of this group, assisted by deputy heads comprising a group of senior officials in the State Council. This group is tasked to consider major principles, policies, and measures on deepening reforms of the medical and health system and coordinate the work on major issues of medical and health reforms.[13] In January 2010, the State Council established another coordinating mechanism on energy, the National Energy Commission. Premier Wen was chairman, and Vice Premier Li was vice chairman. Li, in fact, has been in charge of energy policies since then.[14] China also established the Food Safety Commission of the State Council with Li as its chairman and Vice Premiers Hui Liangyu and Wang Qishan as its vice chairmen.[15] The commission is tasked to evaluate the present food safety situation, plan and coordinate work on food safety, make major policies on food safety regulation and supervision, and supervise the implementation of food safety regulations.

Conclusion

China's bureaucratic reform has been driven and constrained by various factors. The reform has proceeded in accordance with shifts in ideological stance on the part of the CCP. Only after the establishment of the "socialist market economy" in 1992 did Chinese leaders become certain as to how the bureaucratic system should be restructured to embrace a market economy. Furthermore, individual leaders' policy preference also plays an important role in designing a particular reform policy. Li Peng did not succeed in reforming the state in 1993 because of his dominant conservative mindset and other factors. Only after Zhu Rongji became Premier and was in full charge of economic reform in 1997 was radical restructuring carried out.

The restructuring of the state bureaucracy was aimed at accommodating the needs of a growing market-oriented economy. Zhu's restructuring was in accordance with market principles and the state bureaucracy was increasingly geared to market requirements. Indeed, Zhu and the reformist leadership made ever greater efforts to provide an institutional environment for a market economy to grow.

The restructuring of the state bureaucracy was also a part of the efforts by the Chinese leadership to rebuild a modern economic state. Embedded in what Zhu and the reformist leadership did was the idea that the restructuring would help China modernize its bureaucratic system and make it more efficient in governing an increasingly complicated market society. How central power was to be established over the economy and society was a major consideration when the leadership introduced major reform measures. This is the rationale behind the efforts to establish a regulatory regime under the Wen administration. This rationale explains why China's bureaucratic restructuring has been incremental on the one hand, and consistent on the other throughout the reform period.

Notes

1   Burns (1983).
2   In China, constitutionally, the Premier is nominated by the State President and approved by the National People's Congress. But in reality, the CCP leadership

selects the Premier and the National People's Congress only confirms the CCP's decision.

3   Burns (1983).

4   Su and Han (1993: 92).

5   Zhang (1989: 15–16).

6   For more detailed analysis of budget problems and the PLA's enterprises, see Bickford (1994).

7   "PLA Told to Close Down All Its Firms." *China Daily*, July 23, 1998.

8   Willy Wo-Lap Lam, "PLA to Get $28b for Businesses." *South China Morning Post*, August 3, 1998; Lam, "PLA Chief Accepts 47b Payout." *South China Morning Post*, October 9, 1998.

9   *Ming Pao*, Hong Kong, December 15, 1998.

10 Luo Gan, "Guanyu guowuyuan jigou gaige fangan de jidian shuoming" (Some Explanations to the Plan of Organizational Reform of the State Council). *Wen Hui Bao*, Hong Kong, March 7, 1998, A7.

11 Xinhua News Agency, "Li Yizhong zai quanguo anquan shengchan gongzuo huiyi shang de jianghua" (Speech by Li Yizhong on National Conference on Work Safety), <www.xinhuanet.com> (accessed January 26, 2006). Li is the Director of the State Administration for Work Safety.

12 On the evolution of the Chinese regulatory state, see Yang (2004) and Hsueh (2011).

13 *People's Daily*, March 17, 2010, <http://cpc.people.com.cn/GB/64093/64094/11158118.html> (accessed January 6, 2011).

14 For more details, see Bo (2010).

15 <http://news.xinhuanet.com/politics/2010-02/10/content_12962299.htm> (accessed January 6, 2011).

References

Bickford, T. J. 1994. "The Chinese Military and Its Business Operations: The PLA as Entrepreneur." *Asian Survey* 34, 5 (May): 460–76.

Bo, Zhiyue. 2010. "China's New National Energy Commission: Policy Implications." *EAI Background Brief* 504, East Asian Institute, National University of Singapore.

Burns, J. P. 1983. "Reforming China's Bureaucracy, 1979–82." *Asian Survey* 23, 6 (June): 692–722.

Hsueh, Roselyn. 2011. *China's Regulatory State: A New Strategy for Globalization*. Ithaca, NY: Cornell University Press.

Su, Shangxiao and Wenwei Han. 1993. *Zhonghua renmin gongheguo zhongyang zhengfu jigou* (Central Government Organizations of the People's Republic of China). Beijing: Jingji kexue chubanshe.

Yang, Dali. 2004. *Remaking the Chinese Leviathan: Market Transition and the Politics of Governance in China*. Stanford, CA: Stanford University Press.

Zhang, Zhenlong, ed. 1989. *Jundui shengchan jingying guanli* (Management of Military Production). Beijing: Jiefangjun chubanshe.

Chapter 11

Democratization

China's democratization has been a major concern even since the country opened its door to the outside world in the late 1970s. When Eastern European dissident voices became louder at the end of the 1980s and the one-party systems collapsed in the early 1990s, the Western academic community delightfully (re)embraced the concept of civil society. Scholars firmly believe that the peaceful overthrow of the authoritarian one-party systems in Eastern and Central Europe was the result of the protest and tacit resistance of a large range of associations and informal organizations such as Solidarnosc in Poland and the Monday Demonstrations in Leipzig. The enthusiasm behind the political changes in Eastern and Central Europe revived liberal-democratic ideas about citizens' participation and political action from below. In the past decade, such bottom-up revolutions have continued to take place in different parts of the world, in Georgia first, and more lately in the Arab world.

Will China follow in the footsteps of what happened in Eastern Europe and elsewhere in terms of the transformation of Party–state relations and state–society relations? We have examined key aspects of social change in China such as civil society, netizens, middle classes, NGOs, and social protests. The ultimate question is: will all these changes lead China to become a modern democratic state? This question can further be divided into two questions: first, will the Chinese state become modern? And second, will the Chinese state become democratic? To answer the first question, we have to look into changes in the Party–state relationship. To answer the second, we have to look into changes in the state–society relationship. Based on discussions in the previous chapters, this chapter aims to answer these two related questions. It will show the nature of the Chinese political system from two perspectives, namely, the Party–state relationship and the state–society relationship.

Contemporary China: A History since 1978, First Edition. Yongnian Zheng.
© 2014 John Wiley & Sons, Ltd. Published 2014 by John Wiley & Sons, Ltd.

The Party–state relationship matters since it conditions the modernization process of the state. While in principle the state is subordinate to the Party, the Party and its state belong to two different fields. While the CCP has the ultimate political power, the government takes care of daily social and economic affairs. The interest of the Party and that of the government might not be identical. The Party is not necessarily able to exercise effective control over the government, and the government will not necessarily voluntarily take orders from the Party. Therefore, to maintain its domination over the government, the Party has to design various formal and informal institutions and procedures to control the government. However, the Party domination over the state does not mean that the latter is a completely helpless actor; instead, it has own unique sources of power and autonomy within the framework of the Party-state.

At the level of the state–society relationship, this chapter focuses on how the Party-state maintains and reinforces its domination over social forces. Although conflicting interests exist between the Party and the state, their interests become identical in the face of social forces. It is a more complicated and difficult task for the Party-state to maintain and reinforce its domination over social forces. In dominating social forces, the Party-state has to justify its domination. The relationship of the Party-state and social forces is thus a dual process of domination and legitimation while the purpose of legitimation is effective domination. We define this dual process as "hegemonization."

The process of political changes in contemporary China is characterized by hegemonization. By making sense of this dual process, we can better understand the Chinese political system. In this chapter, we explore changes in the Party–state relationship first, and then in the state–society relationship to answer the two questions raised above. By examining changes in the Party–state relationship, we will show how this relationship has been rationalized and how the Chinese state has been modernized. By examining changes in the state–society relationship, we will show how the CCP has been able to sustain itself by accommodating democratic elements while resisting Western types of democracy. This will help to deepen our understanding of how the Chinese political system has been evolving in accordance with socioeconomic changes.

Socioeconomic Transformation and Political Changes

Tensions between the Chinese Party-state and society have increased. There is a growing disconnect between a vibrant, dynamic economy and society, on the one hand, and a rigid, anachronistic system of governance and political control, on the other hand. The CCP is seen by many groups and individuals in society as largely irrelevant in their daily lives, an annoyance to be avoided where possible and endured when necessary.[1] If one compares the CCP today with the CCP several decades ago, it is not difficult to find that the CCP has been in a state of progressive decline in terms of its control over various aspects of the intellectual, social, economic, and political life of the nation. According to David Shambaugh, "the CCP's traditional instruments of control – propaganda, coercion, and organization – have all atrophied and eroded considerably over time. . . . Globalization and China's multifaceted interactions with the outside world have further undermined the Party's control over society. The CCP today also faces pressing challenges of increasing social stratification and inequality, widespread corruption, pervasive unemployment, rising crime, and rural unrest."[2]

Scholarly works like this, plus frequent journalistic accounts,[3] often lead people to believe in the imminent collapse of the CCP and even China as a nation-state. The logic is simple: the CCP will fall because it cannot meet social demands. Political parties, including communist ones, are like plants, and they need to adapt to changing environments in order to survive and develop. The CCP is apparently not such an organism. As Shambaugh noted, "Leninist systems are not well equipped to respond to the changing demands and needs of society – precisely because they are intrinsically top-down 'mobilization' regimes rather than possessing the feedback mechanisms to hear and respond to aggregated social needs and demands."[4]

China's political development, however, does not follow the former Soviet Union and Eastern European communist states. Many scholars have observed that Chinese social forces only enjoy very limited autonomy from the state, and many civil organizations are hybrid organizations in which state and society are interwoven and thus do not meet the minimal definition of a civil society, whose component organizations exist outside and independent of the state.[5] While in Eastern Europe civil society organizations are often perceived as agents of democratization, civil organizations in China often act as the state's instrument of control over social forces rather than as mechanisms for expressing and pursuing the interests of the latter.[6] Apart from some underground organizations and loosely networked dissent groups, Chinese civil organizations "do not serve as forums for critical public discussion of political affairs" and they usually "have neither an explicit nor an implicit democratic programme."[7]

Indeed, the Party-state so far has been able to maintain its domination over society. It certainly has not given up using force in stopping popular demonstrations expressing discontent at its practices and suppressing political organizations threatening its authority. However, force alone cannot explain the Party's hold on power. Scholars have attempted to answer the question why the CCP is different from other formal communist parties. Many have attempted to look at changes in relations among the Party, state, and society in explaining the level of political legitimacy that the CCP has enjoyed.

While scholars often refer to China's model of the Party-state's relationship with society as corporatism which highlights the dominant role of the Party-state over social forces, they have used different labels to refer to the Chinese variant in order to differentiate it from corporatism in other places, such as "state-socialist corporatism,"[8] "socialist corporatism,"[9] "corporatism Chinese style,"[10] and "local corporatism," "departmental corporatism," and so on.[11] It is argued that "the principal attraction of corporatist models is their ability simultaneously to acknowledge the pluralizing socioeconomic changes induced by market reforms and the continued dominance of the Leninist Party-state" in China.[12]

Within this overall framework, some scholars have focused on the CCP's capability to adapt itself to new socioeconomic environments. Early on Bruce Dickson argued that the CCP was in a phrase of what Samuel Huntington called "adaption." But Dickson also believed that unlike the Kuomintang in Taiwan, the CCP would not follow the path to democratization.[13] In his more recent work, however, Dickson contends that the initiative of the CCP to recruit private-sector entrepreneurs is consistent with the evolution of other East Asian ruling parties. This initiative is an effort to "adapt" itself in order to save itself. He believes that this initiative is a pragmatic, adaptive measure, and the CCP's strategy of "co-optation" is working.

Nevertheless, Dickson doubts whether the CCP is able to accommodate genuine civil society and the organized aggregation of social interests, since Leninist parties are by nature intolerant and incapable of ceding such power to autonomous social groups.[14] In her study on China's private entrepreneurs, Kellee Tsai also shares this view and contends that private entrepreneurs and the emergent middle class are not going to demand regime change. Her study explores a variety of "adaptive informal institutions" that have permitted the CCP to rebuild and sustain its rule.[15]

The utility of the corporatist paradigm, however, is not without problems in explaining the relationship between the Party-state and society in China. Even scholars in the corporatist paradigm have found the limitations of this model in explaining civil society in China. White, Howell, and Shang pointed out that the associations they came across in their research exhibit a diversity of relationships with the state, with some organizations being more autonomous and voluntary than others, so they are best described as forming an organizational continuum stretching from a state-dominated extreme to a civil society extreme.[16] Shue also wrote about a "state-corporatist continuum" of civil associations in China.[17] Pearson observed that "socialist corporatism does not exist uniformly in all business sectors," with some associations enjoying more autonomy than others, although she still thinks that "there are sufficiently similar characteristics to consider them all part of a new socialist corporatist strategy."[18] According to Yep, corporatism is essentially a system of interest representation that involves political exchange between the state and organized social interests. For corporatism to work, there must be effective mechanisms for aggregating and communicating social interests. In addition, the specific social group that enters into corporatist exchange with the state needs to have a strong internal cohesion. On both counts Yep found that business associations in China fall short of the corporatist definition. They are too dominated by the state to be able to play effective interest aggregation and communication roles. Instead of promoting horizontal integration within the business sector, these organizations actually hinder such integration, as business managers are disaggregated into different associations according to types of ownership and the scale of their enterprises. In this sense, Yep argued that "there may be forms of corporatism emerging in China, but not in essence."[19]

The corporatist model has also been criticized from a rather liberal perspective. For example, Tony Saich, while disagreeing with the civil society model, faulted the corporatist model for overestimating the capacity of the state to enforce its will upon civil organizations and underestimating the ability of civil organizations to circumvent or deflect state intrusion. According to him, civil organizations in China are able to negotiate their own niches with the state, and they often "subordinate" themselves to the state of their own volition, as this allows them to have more impact on policy making and to pursue their members' interests and organizational goals more effectively than if they remained completely autonomous.[20]

Whether one argues for a corporatist model, a continuum from corporatism to civil society, or a particular mix of the two, it all boils down to a state-versus-society framework, what Elizabeth Perry has termed the "state-society paradigm."[21] This state–society dichotomy has formed the basis for most existing studies of Chinese civil organizations, even though many scholars acknowledge that the boundaries between state and society are often blurred. Under the influence of the state-versus-society framework, scholars become preoccupied with discussing the degree of autonomy from the state enjoyed by civil organizations. Perry thus suggested that a deeper understanding of Chinese politics requires that researchers move beyond the state–society dichotomy by disaggregating the crude and unwieldy categories of "state" and "society."[22]

The continuing dominant role of the CCP requires scholars to rethink China's Party–state and state–society relations. While China has differentiated itself from the Soviet Union and Eastern European communism, it does not conform to either the civil society or the corporatist paradigm. In the past three decades, China has achieved unprecedented, rapid socioeconomic transformation; but rather than loosening its grip, the CCP has reinforced its domination over society. While maintaining its Leninist structure, the CCP has been able to adapt to changing socioeconomic conditions by introducing modern state institutions and even incorporating democratic elements. China's political development so far seems to indicate that despite dramatic socioeconomic changes, China will not necessarily move toward democracy, as understood by many scholars in the West; neither will it collapse, as predicted by some others.

Hegemonization: Domination and Legitimation

Changes in the relations between the Party and the state and between the Party-state and society have been a process of hegemonization. The term of "hegemonization" connotes three basic meanings. First, the CCP wants to maintain its domination over the state on the one hand and social forces on the other. Second, it maintains its domination over the state by giving more space to the latter and over social forces by accommodating them and soliciting their loyalty. And third, hegemonization is therefore an effective tool of legitimation. In this context, we argue that the rationalization of the Party–state relationship and the development of civil society is a dual process of domination and legitimation.

By defining hegemonization as an effective mode of legitimation, we place our emphasis on the interaction between the Party and the state and between the Party-state and social forces. We attempt to highlight the following points. First, the interaction between the Party and the state and between the Party-state and social forces is not always a zero-sum game. Although hegemonization implies the process of the Party dominating the state and the Party-state dominating social forces, this does not mean that either the state or social forces are completely powerless since otherwise the Party and the Party-state will not be able to acquire legitimacy. Second, the state and social forces are active agents in this process, just as the Party and Party-state are. Politics is relational, so is power. Legitimation means that the Party-state solicits loyalty from social actors through non-coercive means, and social forces somehow voluntarily accept the domination of Party-state power. Both processes of domination and legitimation are struggles between the Party-state and social forces. In their interactions with each other, both the Party-state and social forces struggle for power. Third, hegemonization is thus a dynamic process of mutual transformation of the Party-state and social forces. To acquire legitimacy through hegemonization does not mean that the Party-state can simply impose its will onto social forces; neither does it imply that social forces accept Party-state domination without resistance or negotiations with the state. It is an interactive process between the two actors, and their continuous interactions lead to mutual transformation.

Figure 11.1 elaborates the dual process of domination and legitimation, a process through which the CCP establishes and maintains a hegemonic political order. The left side represents the dual process of domination and legitima-

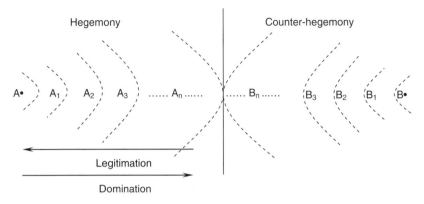

Figure 11.1 Hegemonization: domination and legitimation.

tion of the CCP over social forces. "A" represents the Party-state, and A_1, A_2, A_3 . . . represent social forces such as mass organizations (e.g., the Chinese Communist Youth League, the All China Federation of Trade Unions, and the Women's Federation), and other social forces (e.g., chambers of commerce and various forms of non-governmental organization). By accommodating social forces into the boundary of the hegemony, the Party-state solicits loyalty from social forces; and by accepting Party-state domination, social forces become part of the political process.

Moreover, the CCP is a part of society, which is the sphere in which it organizes consent and hegemony. According to Gramsci, if one organization is to become hegemonic, it has to combine the interests of other organizations and social forces with its own interests so as to create a national-popular collective will.[23] Similarly, the CCP cannot achieve national leadership, and become a hegemonic organization, if it confines itself only to its own organizational interests or the interests of the social forces upon which it has built its hegemonic position. Instead, to sustain and reinforce its hegemonic position across different historical periods, the CCP has to transcend these interests by taking into account the aims and interests of other social forces, linking these with its own interests so as to become their "universal" representative. By doing so, the CCP realizes a dual process of domination and legitimation in its relations with social forces.

Society, however, is also the sphere in which the subordinate social forces may organize their opposition, struggle for power, and construct an alternative hegemony – a counter-hegemony. The right side of Figure 11.1 points to a possible counter-hegemony. When the CCP is challenged or perceives that it is challenged by different actors within a possible counter-hegemony (e.g., B, B_1,

B_2, B_3 . . .), it tends to use coercive measures against these actors. It is at this juncture that the CCP departs from all political organizations in the liberal-democratic model where political pluralism is the norm. The CCP does not allow a counter-hegemony to develop. To achieve that goal through coercive measures is not always effective, and indeed often counterproductive due to changing socioeconomic environments. Therefore, while not surrendering the option to use coercive measures at any point in time, the CCP actively engages social forces and transforms social forces by accommodating them. In this same process, the CCP realizes self-transformation.

Rationalizing Party–State Relations

In order to maintain its domination over the state, the CCP has made great efforts to rationalize its relationship with the state. Over the years, both the Party and the state are not satisfied with the structure of their relationship. The parallel system of the Party and the government from the national to local levels has led to political inefficacy and administrative inefficiency. While the boundary between the Party and the government has blurred, the two are in constant conflict. During a crisis, such internal conflict could paralyze the governance system. This seems inevitable since the blurring of boundary between the Party and the government makes less clear the responsibility between the two. Therefore, many reform measures have been carried out to rationalize the Party–state relationship while establishing the rule in which the Party maintains its domination over the government.

The three-in-one system

The three-in-one system refers to the offices of the State President and the Chairmanship of the CMC being tied to the position of the Secretary General of the CCP. In other words, today the Secretary General (the head of the ruling Party) is concurrently the head of the state (State President) and the highest commander of the military (Chairman of the CMC). This system somehow resembles the semi-presidential system in other countries.

Prior to Jiang Zemin's accession to the post of State President in 1993, the office was insignificant and was usually filled by a political noble or revolutionary elder. Previous office-holders included Madam Sun Yat-sen (Soong Ch'ing-ling), Li Xiannian, and Yang Shangkun. In an attempt to institutionalize Party–state relations, both State Presidency and Vice State Presidency have now become very important positions in the Chinese leadership. Hu Jintao was the Vice State President for several years before he succeeded Jiang. Institutionalization has not only brought about some level of "division of functions" between important public offices, it also has the benefit of legitimizing the Party's command over the military. While the basic principle of "the Party commands the gun" remains largely unchanged, this power is now vested in a formal office, which acts on behalf of the Party. This is evident in the institutional arrangement of the CMC. While the CMC is one organization, it actually refers to two institutions, namely, the Party's CMC and the state's CMC.

The positions as the State President and the Chairman of the state's CMC give the Secretary General and his office a legitimate base to perform executive functions. There is an informal "division of labor" between the State President's office and the State Council. The State President's office has been in charge of foreign affairs, national defense, national security, and public security, despite the formal ministries of Foreign Affairs, National Defense, National Security, and Public Security being located in the State Council, while the State Council is in charge of economic and civil affairs. That implies that major decisions in the former areas are made by the Party (Secretary General's office) in the name of the State President's office. Of course, the State Council often bears the responsibility of policy implementation.

Party secretary as the head of people's congress

At the provincial level, the secretary of the provincial Party committee concurrently acts as the head of the people's congress in most of China's provinces and cities. While this arrangement is often interpreted as an effort on the part of the CCP to strengthen its control over provincial people's congresses, the underlying rationale behind it can also be explained in terms of the Party–state relationship.

According to China's Constitution, the National People's Congress (NPC) is "the highest organ of state power" (article 57); and "the NPC and the local people's congresses at various levels are the organs through which the people exercise state power" (article 2).[24] However, in reality, the NPC and local people's congresses are often rubber stamps of the Party, meaning that Party organizations make major decisions first and then ask the NPC and local people's congresses to "approve." In both Mao's and Deng's eras, the NPC and local people's congresses were usually headed by a powerless retired senior Party cadre and government official.

This situation has changed since 1989. During the pro-democracy movement in 1989, many NPC leaders showed their sympathetic attitude toward the movement. Hu Jiwei, then editor of *People's Daily* and a member of the Standing Committee of the NPC, even attempted to use the NPC to nullify the State Council's martial law. After the crackdown, the Party leadership began to strengthen the Party's control over the NPC and local people's congresses. Since the early 1990s, the NPC Standing Committee has been headed by a member of the Political Bureau Standing Committee, including Qiao Shi, Li Peng, and Wu Bangguo. At the provincial level, the people's congress is headed by the secretary of the provincial Party committee.

This arrangement, however, can also be interpreted in the following way. According to Zhao Ziyang, the idea to have this arrangement was initiated in the 1980s when political reform became the important agenda of the Party leadership. This arrangement was expected to be helpful to reconcile the two contradictory sources of power: the NPC as the highest organ of state power in theory and the CCP as the actual highest power in reality.[25] Zhao implies that the Party secretary as the head of the people's congress gives the Party a legitimate means to influence the government. During the 1980 debate on political reform, the separation of the Party from the government became the focus. If the Party and the government became two separate bodies, then the question was: how could the Party exercise its control over the government? In this regard, the Party and the NPC (and local people's congresses) have similar functions since, according to China's Constitution, the NPC and local congresses are to supervise the government at different levels. So, by being actively involved in the activities of the NPC and local people's congresses, the Party at different levels establishes a legitimate means to "supervise" and maintain its domination over the government. Therefore, this new tie-in has led the CCP to exercise direct control over provincial people's congresses on one hand, and there is also little doubt on the other hand that provincial Party secretaries, as representatives of the central leadership, now come face-to-face with local people's representatives, and need to listen to and take the representatives' opinions into consideration before the provincial Party committees can make important decisions.

More space and greater autonomy for professionalism

Ideological correctness is slowly giving way to allow more professionalism in the ranks of government officials. To boost effective governance, the CCP, since the mid-1990s, has begun to loosen its grip on the state to give professionals more autonomy in the day-to-day running of the country. In other words, the state has been allowed to become powerful in its own "field."

The most visible signs are those within the State Council. Over the years, the State Council has become a body of economic and social management by professionals. The posts of Premier, Vice Premier, State Councillor, ministers, and vice ministers are now filled by professionals. This is especially so for positions at the ministerial and vice-ministerial levels. The rise of professionalism largely reflects the increasing need for expertise to deal with the complexities of new social and economic issues. In 2007, China had the first two non-communist cabinet appointments, namely, Wan Gang, Minister of Science and

Technology, and Chen Zhu, Minister of Health. While the political implications of these two appointments should not be exaggerated, these cases do mean that professionals now play an increasing role in handling daily state affairs.

Professionalism has also been injected into both the NPC and local people's congresses. The NPC is largely an inefficient platform due to its massive size, which hovers at around 3,000 representatives. It convenes for only a very short period annually, usually 10–14 days. Moreover, the structure of its meeting, which is made up of full-day plenary sessions, is not suited for lengthy deliberations. To overcome these shortcomings, NPC reforms since the early 1990s have focused on expanding the Standing Committee and establishing special committees.

Over the years, the Standing Committee has been expanded to its present strength of 176 members. The expanded Standing Committee functions as a "miniature NPC." Its small size allows more frequent and efficient consultations as compared to the NPC as a whole, yet it is large enough to accommodate different social and political bases, particularly those who are non-CCP members. The expansion of this group of "first-among-equals" serves to raise the quality of motions tabled during annual NPC conferences, and allows follow-up on NPC decisions when the need arises.

Currently, the NPC has nine special committees in the areas of Foreign Affairs, Finance, Education, Minorities, and Agricultural and Rural Affairs. Special committees usually draw their members from two sources: government officials who have previously served in various state organizations, and specialists in particular fields. These special committees provide expertise and public office experience both in the law-making process and in supervision of the daily functioning of the government (the State Council and its various ministries). Professionalization has altered the role of the NPC from that of a "rubber stamp" to one that is capable of overseeing governmental operations.[26]

Hegemonization and Social Participation

While China has witnessed the rise of civil society, middle classes, social protests, and other aspects of social developments, drastic social changes so far have not lead to democratization, as has happened in other parts of the world. All the changes in the relationship between the Party-state and society do not weaken the power of the Party-state. As a matter of fact, all the changes are within the process of hegemonization of the Party-state over social forces. It is important to situate hegemonization in the context of China's development which is directed by the Party-state. This implies three important points. First, the rise of social forces is a consequence of China's development. The fact that the Party-state has directed China's development implies that maintaining its domination over social forces is an integral part of this development. Second, this fact also means that the Party-state is not reactive but pro-active in responding to changing social forces, and thus reinforcing its domination over society. Third, this process of reinforcement is also an outcome of the constant interplay between the Party-state and society, and the Party-state is undergoing change while transforming society.

When drastic socioeconomic changes take place, the Party-state has to transform itself and redefine its relations with social forces in order to maintain its hegemonic position and domination over social forces. The interactive process between the state and society is mutually transformative. Despite the mutually transformative nature, all changes in these relations do not lead to democratization of any Western type. The Party-state has been very active in reinforcing its domination and maintaining hegemonic position through its active engagement of different social forces. During this process, the Party-state has accommodated democratic elements. Political participation has taken place at different levels, as represented by rural democracy and accommodation of capitalists. These aspects of development are important since they have created dynamics for democratization. However, there is no sign to indicate that social participation will lead to democratization in a Western sense. Opening up the political process to social forces is a means to enable the Party-state to exercise its hegemony over society.

Developing different forms of local democracy

China has implemented local democracy for years. Local democracy refers to rural village elections for village committees since the late 1980s, and township elections for the heads of townships since the 1990s. China's rural reform in the late 1970s, which was characterized by radical decentralization and was based on the household responsibility system, soon led to the collapse of the old system of governance (the production brigade system), and eventually the collapse of the commune system. The Party-state leadership decided to restructure the governance system at the basic level. In 1987, the NPC passed the "Village Committee Organic Law of the PRC (Experimental)." According to the law, "village committees should be established in China's rural areas in order to safeguard farmers' opportunities and rights of political participation. The control over village cadres by farmers and the level of villagers' self-government will be improved through direct election of the directors, deputy directors and members of the villagers' committees, thus upgrading the quality of farmers' political participation." By 2001, this system had spread to the whole country.

This top-down reform did not mean in any sense that the Party-state wanted to give up its rule in countryside; instead, it was aimed at strengthening the rule of the Party in rural areas by accommodating democratic elements.[27] While the village committee was elected by villagers, the CCP branch at the village level continued to exist. The rapid spread of rural democracy, however, soon created contradictions between the elected body and the Party branch in the same village. While the elected village committee can draw its legitimacy from villagers, the Party branch often faced challenges in dealing with the former. To solve this contradiction, many provinces have developed a system of "two ballots" in which the Party secretary in a village is subject to a popular vote, meaning that in these places both the Party secretary and village head are elected.[28] The parallel system of the Party and the village branch has continued, but their relation with each other has been transformed.

The CCP has also begun to implement direct elections at the township level – the basic level of administration – on an experimental basis. In the mid-1990s, China experienced its first cases of township elections for key township officials. Since then, the new election practices have spread to many townships in many counties in a number of provinces. The positions open to election have been extended from township vice mayors to township mayors, and sometimes even township Party secretaries. The number of cases increased from a dozen in the mid-1990s to several hundreds in the late 1990s, and to several thousands by the early 2000s. Compared to village elections, township elections are more constrained by various factors and thus were referred to as "semi-competitive elections" by the scholarly community.[29]

Township elections are policy products, not legal ones. As a matter of fact, township elections have not been justified in Chinese laws, and remain controversial even though they are now widespread.[30] The political support from the leadership, both at the central and local levels, is the key factor which has facilitated the implementation of this system.

Beside village and township elections, China today is experimenting with different kinds of democratic elements such as the election of urban community committees, allowing independent candidates to run for local people's congresses, the emergence of what is referred to in China as "rights-democracy," and social movements.[31] Politically, bottom-up social democracy (or people's democracy) has been identified by the CCP at the Seventeenth National Congress of the CCP in 2007 as one of the key areas for China's political reform in terms of democratization.

While the scholarly community is doubtful whether China's one-party system can accommodate democracy, the CCP has been sophisticated in introducing democratic elements to reform the old system of governance in rural and urban areas. "Democratization" has served as a means of legitimation for the CCP at the local levels. The process of democratization has been well choreographed, since the CCP leadership needs to make sure that every step of "democratization" will not undermine its domination. While it is uncertain whether China will be able to develop a democracy, as understood in the West, the CCP has surely managed to hegemonize local residents by accommodating "democracy."

Expanding the social base

The Party-state has also demonstrated its capability to accommodate new social classes, as exemplified by its accommodation of capitalists or private entrepreneurs. Accommodating capitalists will most likely be regarded as a milestone in the history of the CCP. Historically, all communist parties were hostile to capitalism and capitalists. The old CCP Constitution stated that the goal of the Party was to eliminate capitalism and the capitalist class. Despite the de-emphasis of the role of ideology in the post-Mao era, the issue of whether capitalists or private entrepreneurs should be allowed into the Party had been controversial for a long period of time. The private sector began to play an important role in the 1980s, first in the economic area, and then in the political realm, as shown in the pro-democracy movement in 1989 during which many private entrepreneurs not only contributed financial resources to the movement, but also played a leadership role.[32] In the aftermath of the 1989 crackdown, the Central Committee of the CCP issued a regulation on August 28, 1989, entitled "A Notice on Strengthening Party Building" (document no. 9, 1989). The regulation stated, "Our Party is the vanguard of the working class. Since it is an exploitative relationship between private entrepreneurs and workers, private entrepreneurs cannot be recruited into the Party."[33] Jiang Zemin, then Party secretary, was one of the major political forces behind this regulation.[34]

The private sector, however, continued to provide much dynamism for the Chinese economy after the 1989 pro-democracy movement's suppression. Deng's Southern Tour in 1992 triggered a new wave of radical economic liberalization which in turn promoted rapid expansion of the private sector. The privatization program after the mid-1990s provided a further boost for the development of the private sector. Understandably, private entrepreneurs soon became a formidable force in the country's economic life. At the same time, liberals within the CCP began to propose that the Party should allow private entrepreneurs to join and thus expand the Party's social bases. Such liberal arguments elicited strong reactions from the leftists. Despite the controversies and the sensitivity of the issue, the leadership decided to go one step further to formally allow private entrepreneurs to join the Party.[35] In early 2000, the Party leadership under Jiang raised a new concept of *san ge dai biao* (literally, "Three Represents"). According to this concept, the CCP represents the "most advanced mode of productive force, the most advanced culture, and the interests of the majority of the population."[36] The "three representatives" theory was regarded as the CCP's affirmation of the non-state sector in the economy. More importantly, it also shows that the CCP began to consider how the interests of newly rising classes and social groups can be represented.

The CCP has an aversion to bottom-up initiatives; it is more comfortable with the top-down approach through which it is able to keep developments in check. For many years, the CCP has been accountable for continuing tight political control, and crackdowns on budding social movements. Yet there are also moves taken by the CCP to broaden its social base by pro-actively engaging different social groups that have emerged in China's changing socioeconomic environment. Effective governance requires the CCP to solicit political loyalty from these groups.

In order to solicit loyalty from the rising entrepreneur class, the CCP leadership is pragmatic enough to accommodate it. The decision to recruit private entrepreneurs into the Party implies that the CCP is adjusting itself to China's changing political reality. Capitalist economic development has rapidly changed China's social structure. When the traditional communist ruling classes such as workers and peasants decline, the role of the entrepreneur class becomes increasingly important. Embracing the new social classes certainly has enabled the Party to expand its social bases. The decision also reflects the fact that the Party is developing a new way to rule the country. When class struggle was used by Mao to take over the country, political mobilization became important and inevitable. In order to mobilize social forces against its enemies, the Party leadership then had to rely on the workers and peasants. But now that the Party is the only ruling party it has to represent as many social interests as possible. To a great extent, whether the Party can maintain its domination over an increasingly diversified society depends on whether it can stand above all social forces and coordinate these different and often conflicting interests. Needless to say, this is also a process of hegemonization. To maintain its domination over capitalists while reinforcing its legitimacy, the CCP has to represent the interests of this newly rising social force and "allocate" a certain space for them within the regime.

This is clearly manifested by the profound changes that have occurred in the CCP's membership. During Mao's era, the CCP was a genuine revolutionary party with its members overwhelmingly comprising workers and peasants. For example, in 1956 83% of Party members came from these two groups. The figure still remained high in 1981, at 64%. After Deng Xiaoping came to power, he initiated the so-called technocratic movement, replacing workers and peasants in the Party with technocrats. Worker and peasant Party members were reduced to 48% in 1994,[37] and continued to decline to 29% in 2005.[38]

These changes are also reflected on the legal front. The Second Session of the Ninth National People's Congress (NPC) in 1999 passed a constitutional amendment which, for the first time since the establishment of the People's

Republic, provides constitutional protection for the private economy. In 2008, the Eleventh NPC passed the Property Law to guarantee private property rights. The Property Law marked an important step in China's transition to a market economy. The travails faced in securing passage of the new law underscored the difficulties Chinese leaders face as they attempt to put in place a coherent legal and financial system for the country. It had taken 13 years and eight readings (when only three are technically – and in most cases, practically – required) for the property bill to come into force. This law was originally scheduled to be passed in 2006, but was dropped after Party conservatives started a signature campaign against it, protesting that it would undermine the country's socialist system. The Property Law elaborated on the creation, transfer, and ownership of property in China.

Conclusion

We have so far discussed how the development of a market economy and globalization has led to the transformation of the Chinese Party-state. Political transformation is the result of China's transition to a market economy and the country's integration into the world market and global capitalism. Despite difficulties, the Party-state has made enormous efforts to adjust the governance structure to accommodate a market economy while facilitating the process of China's integration into the global system. The leadership has adjusted China's political order to accommodate a rising interest-based social order and rebuild the state bureaucratic system and economic institutions to promote capitalistic economic development and nurture a nascent market economy. All these reform measures appear to have moved China closer toward internationally accepted norms of the modern state.

Why is market-oriented economic development not able to democratize China? Apparently, the Party-state has engaged in state transformation in order to benefit from market development and globalization with no intention of giving up its monopoly on power. The Party-state struggles for its continuous domination over society, especially vis-à-vis newly rising social forces. Effective domination, however, is also a process of legitimation. Without legitimacy, the Party-state will have to rely on coercion which is increasingly costly and unsustainable. There are many ways of legitimation. In this case, legitimation is realized through accommodating social forces within the boundary of the regime. Democratic measures are not excluded during this process.

The development of civil society has been an important feature of Chinese politics since the reform and open-door policy. Yet, when civil society comes to China, it is transformed. Civil society has so far neither promoted political pluralism nor is it contradictory to democracy. In other words, the development of civil society has facilitated great political changes and even democratic development, but political changes do not necessarily lead to a liberal democracy as seen in the West.

Such developments have some implications on the current study of civil society in China where scholars place their emphasis on either the Party-state or social forces. The mutually transformative nature of relations between Party-state and society is often underestimated. This chapter has highlighted a few points. There are different social forces with different preferences and interests. With the hegemonization of the Party-state over social forces, some social forces are more autonomous and politically more influential than others, and some are more organized than others. For example, well-organized commercial interests are able to exercise more political influence over the Party-state than less organized workers and disorganized farmers. Accordingly, the political behavior and the power capabilities of social forces vary. Even for the same social group, its political action and influence is contingent upon the political weight that the Party-state assigns to it at any given time.

The Party-state and social forces are mutually transformative via their interactions. To overemphasize civil society as a mere area in which the domination of the Party-state over social forces is realized will lead us to misconstrue the real-world power struggles between the Party-state and social forces. The results of the engagement and disengagement of the Party-state with social forces are tangible and even momentous, but the outcomes rarely reflect the ultimate aims of either. Their interactions cumulatively reshape the Party-state and social forces. The Party-state might be able to impose its own version of domination onto social forces, but not always. It might do so to some social forces, not others. More often than not, the Party-state has to adjust itself in order to accommodate social forces. Likewise, social forces might find that they need to adjust their interactions with the Party-state. In all cases, the Party-state and social forces are transforming each other and it is during such interactions that the process of hegemonization takes place.

The mutual transformative relationship between the Party-state and social forces opens up different possibilities for political change in China. The dual process of domination and legitimation enables the CCP to adapt to a changing socioeconomic environment which is in favor of democratization while reproducing its domination over social forces. In this way, the hegemonic structure of power relations between the Party-state and society remains while the Party-state regime becomes increasingly accommodating of democratic elements. Therefore, the regime is neither a totalitarian or authoritarian one in its traditional sense nor a democratic one as understood in the West.

Notes

1 Baum (2004).
2 Shambaugh (2008: 3–4).
3 For example, Chang (2001).
4 Shambaugh (2008: 7).
5 This literature is growing fast, for example, see Shue (1994); Nevitt (1996); Howell (1998); Unger and Chan (1996); White (1994); and Whiting (1991).
6 Yep (2000); and White *et al.* (1996).
7 Howell (1998: 71–72).
8 Shue (1994).
9 Pearson (1997).
10 Unger and Chan (1996).
11 White *et al.* (1996).
12 Baum and Shevchenko (1999: 348).
13 Dickson (1997).
14 Dickson (2005).
15 Tsai (2007).
16 White *et al.* (1996).
17 Shue (1994).
18 Pearson (1997: 134–35).
19 Yep (2000: 548).
20 Saich (2000, 2001).
21 Perry (1994).
22 Ibid.
23 Simon (1991: 48–52).
24 *Constitution* (1994).
25 Zong (2007: 147).
26 For example, see Tanner (1998) and Peerenboom (2002).
27 Zhong (2012) and Li and O'Brien (2000).
28 Li (1999: 103–18).
29 Lai (2008).
30 See Dong (2008).
31 The "rights-democracy" refers to citizens from the marginalized or disadvantaged social groups asserting or defending their rights through a variety of means. For a discussion of all these forms of democracy, see Li (2008).
32 Goldman (1994).
33 Office of Documentary Research (1991: 456).
34 Ibid., 442.
35 Zheng (2004: Chapter 4). For the complicated role of private entrepreneurs in Chinese politics, see Dickson (2003, 2008) and Chen and Dickson (2010).
36 "Jiang Zemin tongzhi zai quanguo dangxiao gongzuo huiyi shan de jianghua" (Comrade Jiang Zemin's Talk in National Party Schools Working Conference), June 9. *People's Daily*, July 17, 2000.
37 Wibowo (2001).

38 Xinhua News Agency, "Professions of CCP Members, 2005," <www.xinhuanet.com> (accessed February 12, 2007).

References

Baum, R. 2004. "Systemic Stresses and Political Choices: China's Road to Soft Authoritarian Reform." In *U.S.–China Relations and China's Integration with the World*. Washington, DC: Aspen Institute, pp. 15–20.

Baum, R. and A. Shevchenko. 1999. "The 'State of the State'." In M. Goldman and R. MacFarquhar, eds., *The Paradox of China's Post-Mao Reforms*. Cambridge, MA: Harvard University Press, pp. 333–62.

Chang, Gordon. 2001. *The Coming Collapse of China*. New York: Random House.

Chen, Jie and B. Dickson. 2010. *Allies of the State: China's Private Entrepreneurs and Democratic Change*. Cambridge, MA: Harvard University Press.

Constitution. 1994. *Constitution of the People's Republic of China*. Beijing: Foreign Languages Press.

Dickson, B. 1997. *Democratization in China and Taiwan: The Adaptability of Leninist Parties*. Oxford: Clarendon Press.

Dickson, B. 2003. *Red Capitalists in China: The Party, Private Entrepreneurs, and Prospects for Political Change*. Cambridge: Cambridge University Press.

Dickson, B. 2005. "Populist Authoritarianism: China's Domestic Political Scene." Paper presented at the Third American-European Dialogue on China, Washington, May 23.

Dickson, B. 2008. *Wealth into Power: The Communist Party's Embrace of China's Private Sector*. Cambridge: Cambridge University Press.

Dong, Lisheng. 2008. "Grassroots Governance and Democracy in China's Countryside." In Zhengxu Wang and Colin Durkop, eds., *East Asian Democracy and Political Changes in China: A New Goose Flying?* Singapore: The Konrad Adenauer Stiftung, pp. 155–68.

Goldman, M. 1994. *Sowing the Seeds of Democracy in China: Political Reform in the Deng Xiaoping Era*. Cambridge, MA: Harvard University Press.

Howell, J. 1998. "An Unholy Trinity? Civil Society, Economic Liberalization and Democratization in post-Mao China." *Government and Opposition* 33, 1: 56–80.

Lai, Hairong. 2008. "The Causes and Effects of the Development of Semi-Competitive Elections at the Township Level in China since the 1990s." PhD thesis, Department of Political Science, Central European University, Budapest.

Li, Fan. 2008. "Is Democratic Development in China Sustainable." In Zhengxu Wang and Colin Durkop, eds., *East Asian Democracy and Political Changes in China: A New Goose Flying?* Singapore: The Konrad Adenauer Stiftung, pp. 135–51.

Li, Lianjiang. 1999. "The Two-Ballot System in Shanxi Province: Subjecting Village Party Secretaries to a Popular Vote." *The China Journal* 42 (July): 103–18.

Li, Lianjiang and Kevin O'Brien. 2000. "Accommodating 'Democracy' in a One-Party State: Introducing Village Elections in China." *The China Quarterly* 162 (June): 465–89.

Nevitt, C. E. 1996. "Private Business Associations in China: Evidence of Civil Society or Local State Power." *China Journal* 36 (July): 25–43.

Office of Documentary Research of the Central Committee of the CCP. 1991. *Xinshiqi dang de jianshe wenjian xuanbian* (Selected Documents of Party Building in the New Era). Beijing: Renmin chubanshe.

Pearson, M. 1997. *China's New Business Elite: The Political Consequences of Economic Reform.* Berkeley, CA: University of California Press.

Peerenboom, R. 2002. *China's Long March toward Rule of Law.* Cambridge: Cambridge University Press.

Perry, E. 1994. "Trends in the Study of Chinese Politics: State–Society Relations." *The China Quarterly* 139: 704–13.

Saich, Tony. 2000. "Negotiating the State: The Development of Social Organizations in China." *The China Quarterly* 161: 124–41.

Saich, Tony. 2001. *Governance and Politics of China.* New York: Palgrave Macmillan.

Shambaugh, D. 2008. *China's Communist Party: Atrophy and Adaptation.* Washington, DC and Berkeley: Woodrow Wilson Center Press and University of California Press.

Shue, V. 1994. "State Power and Social Organization in China." In J. S. Migdal, A. Kohli, and V. Shue, eds., *State Power and Social Forces: Domination and Transformation in the Third World.* Cambridge: Cambridge University Press, pp. 65–88.

Simon, R. 1991. *Gramsci's Political Thought: An Introduction.* London: Lawrence and Wishart.

Tanner, M. S. 1998. *The Politics of Lawmaking in Post-Mao China: Institutions, Processes, and Democratic Prospects.* Oxford: Oxford University Press.

Tsai, Kellee. 2007. *Capitalism without Democracy: The Private Sector in Contemporary China.* Ithaca, NY: Cornell University Press.

Unger, J. and A. Chan. 1996. "Corporatism in China: A Developmental State in an East Asian Context." In B. L. McCormick and J. Unger, eds., *China after Socialism: In the Footsteps of Eastern Europe or East Asia.* Armonk, NY: M. E. Sharpe, pp. 95–129.

White, G. 1994. "Prospects for Civil Society: A Case Study of Xiaoshan City." In D. S. G. Goodman and B. Hooper, eds., *China's Quiet Revolution: New Interactions between State and Society.* Melbourne: Longman Cheshire, pp. 194–218.

White, G., J. Howell, and X. Shang. 1996. *In Search of Civil Society: Social Change in Contemporary China.* Oxford: Oxford University Press.

Whiting, S. 1991. "The Politics of NGO Development in China." *Voluntas* 2, 2: 16–48.

Wibowo, Ignatius. 2001. "Party Recruitment and the Future of the Chinese Communist Party." Unpublished manuscript, East Asian Institute, National University of Singapore.

Yep, R. 2000. "The Limitations of Corporatism for Understanding Reforming China: An Empirical Analysis in a Rural County." *Journal of Contemporary China* 9, 25: 547–66.

Zheng, Yongnian. 2004. *Globalization and State Transformation in China.* Cambridge and New York: Cambridge University Press,

Zhong, Yang. 2012. *Political Culture and Participation in Rural China.* London: Routledge.

Zong, Fenming. 2007. *Zhao Ziyang ruanjin zhong de tanhua* (Zhao Ziyang: Captive Conversations). Hong Kong: The Open Press.

Selected Bibliography

Allen, Franklin, Jun Qian, and Meijun Qian. 2008. "China's Financial System: Past, Present, and Future." In Loren Brandt and Thomas G. Rawski, eds., *China's Great Economic Transformation*. Cambridge: Cambridge University Press, pp. 507–68.

Anheier, H., M. Glasius, and M. Kaldor. 2005. *Global Civil Society 2004/5*. London: Sage Publications.

Averill, Stephen C. 1981. "The New Life in Action: The Nationalist Government in South Jiangxi." *The China Quarterly* 88: 594–628.

Balasubramanyam, V. N., S. Mohammed, and D. Sapsford. 1996. "Foreign Direct Investment and Growth in EP and IS Countries." *Economic Journal* 106: 92–105.

Baum, R. 1993. "The Road to Tiananmen: Chinese Politics in the 1980s." In Roderick MacFarquhar, ed., *The Politics of China 1949–1989*. Cambridge: Cambridge University Press, pp. 340–472.

Baum, R. 1994. *Burying Mao: Chinese Politics in the Age of Deng Xiaoping*. Princeton, NJ: Princeton University Press.

Baum, R. 2000. "Jiang Takes Command: The Fifteenth National Party Congress and Beyond." In Hung-Mao Tien and Yun-han Chu, eds., *China under Jiang Zemin*. Boulder, CO: Lynne Rienner, pp. 15–32.

Baum, R. 2004. "China's Road to Soft Authoritarian Reform." In *U.S.–China Relations and China's Integration with the World*. Washington, DC: Aspen Institute, pp. 15–20.

Bell, D. 2008. *China's New Confucianism, Politics and Everyday Life in a Changing Society*. Princeton, NJ: Princeton University Press.

Bergère, Marie-Claire. 1998. *Sun Yat-sen*. Translated by Janet Lloyd. Stanford, CA: Stanford University Press.

Bernstein, T. P. and Xiaobo Lu. 2000. "Taxation without Representation: Peasants, the Central and the Local States in Reform China." *The China Quarterly* 163: 742–63.

Bian, M. 2005. *The Making of the State Enterprise System in Modern China: The Dynamics of Institutional Change*. Cambridge, MA: Harvard University Press.

Contemporary China: A History since 1978, First Edition. Yongnian Zheng.
© 2014 John Wiley & Sons, Ltd. Published 2014 by John Wiley & Sons, Ltd.

Bickford, T. 1994. "The Chinese Military and Its Business Operations: The PLA as Entrepreneur." *Asian Survey* 34 (5): 460–76.

Bickford, T. 1999. "A Retrospective on the Study Chinese Civil–Military Relations since 1979." Paper to CAPS/RAND Conference. Washington, DC.

Blanchard, Olivier and Andrei Shleifer. 2001. "Federalism With and Without Political Centralization: China versus Russia." *IMF Staff Papers* 48 (special issue): 171–79.

Bo, Zhiyue. 2006. *China's Elite Politics: Political Transition and Power Balancing.* Singapore and London: World Scientific.

Bo, Zhiyue. 2010. "China's New National Energy Commission: Policy Implications." *EAI Background Brief 504.* East Asian Institute, National University of Singapore.

Brahm, L. J. 2002. *Zhu Rongji and the Transformation of Modern China.* Singapore: John Wiley & Sons.

Bray, D. 2005. *Social Space and Governance in Urban China: The Daiwei System from Origins to Reform.* Stanford, CA: Stanford University Press.

Brodsgaard, K. E. and S. Young, eds. 2000. *State Capacity in Japan, Taiwan, China and Vietnam.* Oxford: Oxford University Press.

Brook, T. and B. M. Frolic, eds. 1997. *Civil Society in China.* Armonk, NY: M. E. Sharpe.

Bulag, U. E. 2000. "Ethnic Resistance with Socialist Characteristics." In Elizabeth J. Perry and Mark Selden, eds., *Chinese Society: Change, Conflict and Resistance.* London and New York: Routledge, pp. 178–97.

Burns, J. P. 1983. "Reforming China's Bureaucracy, 1979–82." *Asian Survey* 23 (6): 692–722.

Burns, J. P., ed. 1989. *The Chinese Communist Party's Nomenklatura System.* Armonk, NY: M. E. Sharpe.

Burns, J. P. 1994. "Strengthening Central CCP Control of Leadership Selection: The 1990 Nomenklatura." *The China Quarterly* 138: 458–91.

Calhoun, C. J. 1994. *Neither Gods nor Emperors: Students and the Struggle for Democracy in China.* Berkeley, CA: University of California Press.

Cao, Tianyu, ed. 2008. *Shehui zhuyi haishi minzhu shehui zhuyi* (Socialism or Social Democratism). Hong Kong: Dafeng chubanshe.

Cavey, Paul. 1977. "Building a Power Base: Jiang Zemin and the Post-Deng Succession." *Issues and Studies* 33 (11): 1–34.

Chan, Chan Kwan, King Lun Ngok, and David Phillips. 2008. *Social Policy in China: Development and Well-being.* Bristol: The Policy Press.

Chang, Gordon. 2001. *The Coming Collapse of China.* New York: Random House.

Chen, Jie and B. Dickson. 2010. *Allies of the State: China's Private Entrepreneurs and Democratic Change.* Cambridge, MA: Harvard University Press.

Chen, Runyun. 1988. *Xiandai Zhongguo zhengfu* (Modern Chinese Government). Jilin: Jilin wenshi chubanshe.

Chen, Yizi. 1990. *Zhongguo: shinian gaige yu bajiu minyun* (China: Ten Years of Reforms and the 1989 People's Movement). Taipei: Lianjing chuban gongsi.

Cheng, Joseph Y. S. 1998. "Power Consolidation and Further Economic Reforms." In Joseph Y. S. Cheng, ed., *China Review 1998.* Hong Kong: The Chinese University of Hong Kong Press, pp. 25–60.

Cheng, Tiejun and Mark Selden. 1997. "The Construction of Spatial Hierarchies: China's Hukou and Danwei System." In Timothy Cheek and Tony Saich, eds.,

New Perspectives on State Socialism in China. Armonk, NY: M. E. Sharpe, pp. 23–50.

Cheung, Peter T. Y. and James T. H. Tang. 2001. "The External Relations of China's Provinces." In David M. Lampton, ed., *The Making of Chinese Foreign and Security Policy in the Era of Reform, 1978–2000.* Stanford, CA: Stanford University Press, pp. 91–122.

Cheung, Peter T. Y., Jae Ho Chung, and Zhimin Lin, eds. 1998. *Provincial Strategies of Economic Reform in Post-Mao China: Leadership, Politics and Implementation.* Armonk, NY: M. E. Sharpe.

Cohen, Paul A. 1988. "Post-Mao Reforms in Historical Perspective." *Journal of Asian Studies* 47 (3): 519–41.

Davis, D. and F. Wang, eds. 2009. *Creating Wealth and Poverty in Post-Socialist China.* Stanford, CA: Stanford University Press.

Davis, D. S., Richard Kraus, Barry Naughton, and Elizabeth J. Perry, eds. 1995. *Urban Spaces in Contemporary China: The Potential for Autonomy and Community in post-Mao China.* Washington, DC / Cambridge: Woodrow Wilson Center Press / Cambridge University Press.

Deng, Xiaoping. 1993. *Deng Xiaoping wenxuan* (Selected Works of Deng Xiaoping), *vol. 3, 1982–1992.* Beijing: Renmin chubanshe.

Dickson, B. 1997. *Democratization in China and Taiwan: The Adaptability of Leninist Parties.* Oxford: Clarendon.

Dickson, B. 2003. *Red Capitalists in China: The Party, Private Entrepreneurs, and Prospects for Political Change.* Cambridge: Cambridge University Press.

Dickson, B. 2008. *Wealth into Power: The Communist Party's Embrace of China's Private Sector.* Cambridge: Cambridge University Press.

Dikötter, Frank. 2010. *Mao's Great Famine: The History of China's Most Devastating Catastrophe, 1958–62.* London: Bloomsbury.

Dillon, M. 1999. *China's Muslim Hui Community: Migration, Settlement and Sects.* Richmond, UK: Curzon Press.

Donaldson, John A. 2011. *Small Works: Poverty and Economic Development in Southwestern China.* Ithaca, NY: Cornell University Press.

Dong, Lisheng. 2008. "Grassroots Governance and Democracy in China's Countryside." In Zhengxu Wang and Colin Durkop, eds., *East Asian Democracy and Political Changes in China: A New Goose Flying?* Singapore: The Konrad Adenauer Stiftung, pp. 155–68.

Economy, E. 2004. *The River Runs Black: The Environmental Challenges to China's Future.* Ithaca, NY: Cornell University Press.

Eichengreen, B. and H. Tong. 2006. "Fear of China." *Journal of Asian Economics* 17 (2): 226–40.

Esping-Andersen, Gøsta. 1990. *The Three Worlds of Welfare Capitalism.* Princeton, NJ: Princeton University Press.

Fairbank, J. K. 1983. *The United States and China*, 4th edition. Cambridge, MA: Harvard University Press.

Fairbank, J. K. and M. Goldman. 1998. *China: A New History.* Cambridge, MA: Harvard University Press.

Fang, Ning, Wang Xiaodong, and Song Qiang. 1999. *Quanqiuhua yinying xia de Zhongguo zhilu* (The China Road under the Shadow of Globalization). Beijing: Zhongguo shehui kexue chubanshe.

Feuerwerker, Albert. 1968. *China's Early Industrialization: Sheng Hsuan-Huai (1844–1916) and Mandarin Enterprises.* Cambridge, MA: Harvard University Press.

Fewsmith, Joseph. 1994. *Dilemma of Reform in China.* Armonk, NY: M. E. Sharpe.

Finkelstein, D. M. and K. Gunness, eds. 2007. *Civil–Military Relations in Today's China: Swimming in a New Sea.* Armonk, NY: M. E. Sharpe.

Fitzgerald, J., ed. 2002. *Rethinking China's Provinces.* London: Routledge.

Fuller, Gregory H. 2008. "Economic Warlords: How de facto Federalism Inhibits China's Compliance with International Trade Law and Jeopardizes Global Environmental Initiatives." *Tennessee Law Review* 75: 545–76.

Gan, Yang. 2007. *Tong san tong* (Blending Three Traditions). Beijing: Sanlian shudian.

Garcia-Herrero, A. and D. Santabarbara. 2005. "Does China Have an Impact on Foreign Direct Investment to Latin America." *China Economic Review* 18 (3): 266–86.

Garnaut, Ross and Ligang Song, eds. 2007. *China: Linking Markets for Growth.* Canberra: National University of Australia Press.

Gittings, J. 1965. *The Role of the Chinese Army.* Oxford: Oxford University Press.

Gladney, Dru C. 1991. *Muslim Chinese: Ethnic Nationalism in the People's Republic.* Cambridge, MA: Harvard University Press.

Goldman, Merle. 1994. *Sowing the Seeds of Democracy in China: Political Reform in the Deng Xiaoping Era.* Cambridge, MA: Harvard University Press.

Goldman, M. and R. MacFarquhar, eds. 1999. *The Paradox of China's Post Mao Reforms.* Cambridge, MA: Harvard University Press.

Goodman, D. S. G., ed. 1997. *China's Provinces in Reform: Class, Community and Political Culture.* New York: Routledge.

Goodman, D. S. G. and G. Segal, eds. 1994. *China Deconstructs: Politics, Trade and Regionalism.* New York: Routledge.

Gu, Edward X. 1999. "From Permanent Employment to Massive Lay-Offs: The Political Economy of 'Transitional Unemployment' in Urban China (1993–8)." *Economy and Society* 28 (2): 281–99.

Guthrie, D. 1999. *Dragon in a Three-Piece Suit: The Emergence of Capitalism in China.* Princeton, NJ: Princeton University Press.

Hamrin, Carol Lee and Suisheng Zhao, eds. 1995. *Decision-Making in Deng's China: Perspectives from Insiders.* Armonk, NY: M. E. Sharpe.

Han, Minzhu, ed. 1990. *Cries for Democracy: Writings and Speeches from the 1989 Chinese Democracy Movement.* Princeton, NJ: Princeton University Press.

Harding, Harry. 1987. *China's Second Revolution: Reform after Mao.* Washington, DC: The Brookings Institution.

Heberer, T. 1989. *China and Its National Minorities: Autonomy or Assimilation?* Armonk, NY: M. E. Sharpe.

Hendrischke, H. and Chongyi Feng, eds. 1999. *The Political Economy of China's Provinces: Comparative and Competitive Advantage.* New York: Routledge.

Hishida, Masaharu, Kazuko Kojima, Tomoaki Ishiii, and Jian Qiao. 2010. *China's Trade Unions: How Autonomous Are They? A Survey of 1,811 Enterprise Union Chairpersons.* London and New York: Routledge.

Howell, J. 1998. "An Unholy Trinity? Civil Society, Economic Liberalization and Democratization in post-Mao China." *Government and Opposition* 33 (1): 56–80.

Hsueh, Roselyn. 2011. *China's Regulatory State: A New Strategy for Globalization*. Ithaca, NY: Cornell University Press.

Huang, Yasheng. 1996. *Inflation and Investment Controls in China: The Political Economy of Central–Local Relations during the Reform Era*. Cambridge: Cambridge University Press.

Hunt, Michael. 1993. "Chinese National Identity and the Strong State: The Late Qing-Republic Crisis." In Lowell Dittmer and Samuel S. Kim, eds., *China's Quest for National Identity*. Ithaca, NY: Cornell University Press, pp. 62–79.

Hunter, Alan and Kim-kwong Chan. 1993. *Protestantism in Contemporary China*. Cambridge: Cambridge University Press.

Huntington, Samuel P. 1991. *The Third Wave: Democratization in the Late Twentieth Century*. Norman, OK and London: University of Oklahoma Press.

Joffe, E. 1987. *The Chinese Army after Mao*. Cambridge, MA: Harvard University Press.

Kaldor, M., H. Anheier, and M. Glasius, eds. 2003. *Global Civil Society 2003*. Oxford: Oxford University Press.

Karmel, Solomon M. 1995–96. "Ethnic Tension and the Struggle for Order: China's Policies in Tibet." *Pacific Affairs* 68 (4): 485–508.

Kuhn, Philip A. 1975. "Local Self-Government under the Republic: Problems of Control, Autonomy, and Modernization." In Frederic Wakeman, Jr. and Carolyn Grant, eds., *Conflict and Control in Late Imperial China*. Berkeley, CA: University of California Press, pp. 257–98.

Kumar, Anjali. 1994. "China's Reform, Internal Trade and Marketing." *The Pacific Review* 7 (3): 323–40.

Lai, Hairong. 2008. "The Causes and Effects of the Development of Semi-Competitive Elections at the Township Level in China since the 1990s." PhD thesis, Department of Political Science, Central European University, Budapest.

Lai, Hongyi. 2004. "Surge of China's Private and Non-state Economy (I)." *EAI Background Brief 187*. East Asian Institute, National University of Singapore.

Lam, Willy Wo-lap. 1993. "Leadership Changes at the Fourteenth Party Congress." In Joseph Y. S. Cheng and Maurice Brosseau, eds., *China Review 1993*. Hong Kong: The Chinese University of Hong Kong Press, pp. 17–67.

Lardy, Nicholas R. 1992. *Foreign Trade and Economic Reform in China, 1978–1990*. Cambridge: Cambridge University Press.

Lardy, Nicholas. 1998. *China's Unfinished Economic Revolution*. Washington DC: The Brookings Institution.

Lardy, Nicholas R. 2002. *Integrating China into the Global Economy*. Washington, DC: The Brookings Institution.

Lau, Lawrence J., Yingyi Qian, and Gerard Roland. 2001. "Reform Without Losers: An Interpretation for China's Dual-Track Approach to Transition." *Journal of Political Economy* 108 (1): 120–43.

Lee, Ching Kwan. 1999. "From Organized Dependence to Disorganized Despotism: Changing Labor Regimes in Chinese Factories." *The China Quarterly* 157: 44–71.

Lee, Hong Yung. 1991. *From Revolutionary Cadres to Party Technocrats in Socialist China*. Berkeley, CA: University of California Press.

Lee, Hong Yung. 1993. "Political and Administrative Reforms of 1982–1986: The Changing Party Leadership and State Bureaucracy." In Michael Ying-Mao Kau and

Susan H. Marsh, eds., *China in the Era of Deng Xiaoping: A Decade of Reform.* Armonk, NY: M. E. Sharpe, pp. 41–48.

Levenson, Joseph. 1964. *Modern China and Its Confucian Past: The Problem of Intellectual Continuity.* New York: Anchor Books.

Li, Cheng, ed. 2010. *China's Emerging Middle Class: Beyond Economic Transformation.* Washington, DC: The Brookings Institution.

Li, Cheng and Lynn White. 1998. "The Fifteenth Central Committee of the Chinese Communist Party: Full-Fledged Technocratic Leadership with Partial Control by Jiang Zemin." *Asian Survey* 38 (3): 231–64.

Li, He. 2010. "Debating China's Economic Reform: New Leftists vs. Liberals." *Journal of Chinese Political Science* 15 (1): 1–23.

Li, Lianjiang. 1999. "The Two-Ballot System in Shanxi Province: Subjecting Village Party Secretaries to a Popular Vote." *The China Journal* 42: 103–18.

Li, Lianjiang and Kevin O'Brien. 2000. "Accommodating 'Democracy' in a One-Party State: Introducing Village Elections in China." *The China Quarterly* 162: 465–89.

Li, Xiguang and Liu Kang. 1996. *Yaomohua beihou de Zhongguo* (Behind Demonizing China). Beijing: Zhongguo shehui kexue chubanshe.

Liang, Xiaosheng. 1998. *Zhongguo shehui ge jieceng fenxi* (An Analysis of Social Strata in China). Beijing: Jingji ribao chubanshe.

Lieberthal, Kenneth. 2004. *Governing China: From Revolution through Reform*, 2nd edition. New York and London: W.W. Norton & Company.

Lin, Shuanglin. 2003. "China's Government Debt: How Serious?" *China: An International Journal* 1 (1): 73–98.

Liu, Zhiqiang. 2005. "Institution and Inequality: The Hukou System in China." *Journal of Comparative Economics* 33 (1): 133–57.

Lü, Xiaobo and Elizabeth J. Perry, eds. 1997. *Danwei: The Changing Chinese Workplace in Historical and Comparative Perspective.* Armonk, NY: M. E. Sharpe.

Lu, Xueyi, ed. 2010. *Report on Social Class Study in Contemporary China, Social Structure of Contemporary China.* Beijing: Institute of Sociology, Chinese Academy of Social Sciences.

Lu, Xueyi and Jing Tiankuai, eds. 1994. *Zhuanxing zhong de Zhongguo shehui* (Chinese Society in Transition). Harbin: Helongjiang renmin chubanshe.

MacFarquhar, R. 1974. *The Origins of the Cultural Revolution 1: Contradictions among the People, 1956–1957.* Oxford: Oxford University Press.

MacFarquhar, R. 1983. *The Origins of the Cultural Revolution 2: The Great Leap Forward 1958–1960.* Oxford: Oxford University Press.

MacFarquhar, R. 1997. *The Origins of the Cultural Revolution 3: The Coming of the Cataclysm, 1961–1966.* Oxford: Oxford University Press.

MacFarquhar, R. and John K. Fairbank, eds. 1991 *The Cambridge History of China*, vol. 15, *The People's Republic, Part 2: Revolutions within the Chinese Revolution, 1966–1982.* Cambridge: Cambridge University Press.

MacFarquhar, R. and M. Schoenhals. 2006. *Mao's Last Revolution.* Cambridge, MA: Harvard University Press.

Mertha, Andrew C. 2008. *China's Water Warriors: Citizen Action and Policy Change.* Ithaca, NY: Cornell University Press.

Montinola, Gabriella, Yingyi Qian, and Barry R. Weingast. 1995. "Federalism, Chinese Style: The Political Basis for Economic Success in China". *World Politics* 48: 50–81.

Mulvenon, J. C. and R. H. Yang, eds. 1999. *The People's Liberation Army in the Information Age*. Santa Monica, CA: Rand.

Murphy, Rachel. 2002. *How Migrant Labor is Changing Rural China*. Cambridge: Cambridge University Press.

Nathan, A. J. and Perry Link, eds. 2001. *The Tiananmen Papers*. New York: Public Affairs.

Naughton, Barry. 1995. *Growing Out of the Plan: Chinese Economic Reform, 1978–1993*. Cambridge: Cambridge University Press.

Naughton, Barry. 2008. *The Chinese Economy: Transition and Growth*. Cambridge, MA: MIT Press.

Nevitt, C. E. 1996. "Private Business Associations in China: Evidence of Civil Society or Local State Power." *China Journal* 36: 25–43.

OECD. 2008. *Investment Policy Review: China 2008*. OECD.

Oi, J. C., S. Rozelle, and X. Zhou, eds. 2010. *Growing Pains: Tensions and Opportunity in China's Transformation*. Stanford, CA: Stanford University Press.

Oksenberg, M., L. R. Sullivan, and M. Lambert, eds. 1990. *Beijing Spring, 1989: Confrontation and Conflict: The Basic Documents*. Armonk, NY: M. E. Sharpe.

Pan, Wei, ed. 2009. *Zhongguo moshi: jiedu renmin gongheguo liushinian* (China Model: Interpreting 60 Years of People's Republic). Beijing: Zhongyang bianyi chubanshe.

Pearson, M. 1997. *China's New Business Elite: The Political Consequences of Economic Reform*. Berkeley, CA: University of California Press.

Peerenboom, Randall. 2002. *China's Long March toward Rule of Law*. Cambridge: Cambridge University Press.

Perry, E. 1994. "Shanghai's Strike Wave of 1957." *The China Quarterly* 137: 1–27.

Perry, E. 1994. "Trends in the Study of Chinese Politics: State–Society Relations." *The China Quarterly* 139: 704–13.

Perry, E. 1995. "Labor's Battle for Political Space: The Role of Worker Associations in Contemporary China." In Deborah S. Davis *et al.*, eds., *Urban Spaces in Contemporary China: The Potential for Autonomy and Community in Post-Mao China*. Washington, DC and Cambridge: Woodrow Wilson Center Press and Cambridge University Press, pp. 302–25.

Perry, E. and Li Xun. 1997. *Proletarian Power: Shanghai in the Cultural Revolution*. Boulder, CO: Westview.

Pu, Xingzu, ed. 1995. *Zhonghua renmin gongheguo zhengzhi zhidu* (The Political System of the People's Republic of China). Hong Kong: Sanlian shudian.

Qi, Dongtao. 2010. "Chinese Working Class in Predicament." *EAI Background Brief 528*, East Asian Institute, National University of Singapore.

Qian, Yingyi. 1999. "The Institutional Foundations of China's Market Transition." Paper prepared for the World Bank's Annual Conference on Development Economics, Washington, DC.

Qin, Shaoxiang and Jia Ting. 1993. *Shehui xin qunti tanmi: Zhongguo siqing qiyezhu jieceng* (A Study of a New Social Group: China's Private Enterprise Class). Beijing: Zhongguo fazhan chubanshe.

Ramo, Joshua Cooper. 2004. *The Beijing Consensus*. London: The Foreign Policy Centre.

Riskin, C. 1987. *China's Political Economy: The Quest for Development since 1949.* Oxford: Oxford University Press.

Rossabi, Morris, ed. 2004. *Governing China's Multiethnic Frontiers.* Seattle and London: University of Washington Press.

Saich, T., ed. 1990. *The Chinese People's Movement: Perspectives on Spring 1989.* Armonk, NY: M. E. Sharpe.

Saich, T. 2000. "Negotiating the State: The Development of Social Organizations in China." *The China Quarterly* 161: 124–41.

Saich, T. 2004. *Governance and Politics of China.* New York: Palgrave Macmillan.

Schram, S. R., ed. 1985. *The Scope of State Power in China.* Hong Kong: The Chinese University of Hong Kong Press.

Schram, S. R., ed. 1987. *Foundations and Limits of State Power in China.* Hong Kong: The Chinese University of Hong Kong Press.

Schurmann, Franz. 1968. *Ideology and Organization in Communist China.* Berkeley, CA: University of California Press.

Shambaugh, D. 2002. *Modernizing China's Military: Progress, Problems and Prospects.* Berkeley, CA: University of California Press.

Shambaugh, David. 2008. *China's Communist Party: Atrophy and Adaptation.* Washington, DC and Berkeley, CA: Woodrow Wilson Center Press and University of California Press.

Shan, Wei. 2010. "Grievances of China's Ethnic Minorities: Analyzing Their Political Attitudes." *EAI Background Brief 515.* East Asian Institute, National University of Singapore.

Shen, Simon. 2007. *Redefining Nationalism in Modern China: Sino-American Relations and the Emergence of Chinese Public Opinion in the 21st Century.* New York: Palgrave Macmillan.

Shi, Tianjian. 1997. *Political Participation in Beijing.* Cambridge, MA: Harvard University Press.

Shirk, Susan. 1993. *The Political Logic of Economic Reform in China.* Berkeley, CA: University of California Press.

Shue, V. 1988. *The Reach of the State: Sketches of the Chinese Body Politics.* Stanford, CA: Stanford University Press.

Shue, V. 1994. "State Power and Social Organization in China." In J. S. Migdal, A. Kohli, and V. Shue, eds., *State Power and Social Forces: Domination and Transformation in the Third World.* Cambridge: Cambridge University Press, pp. 65–88.

Simon, Roger. 1991. *Gramsci's Political Thought: An Introduction.* London: Lawrence and Wishart.

Solinger, D. J. 1999. *Contesting Citizenship in Urban China: Peasant Migrants, the State, and the Logic of the Market.* Berkeley, CA: University of California Press.

Song, Qiang, Zhang Zangzang, and Qiao Bian. 1996. *Zhongguo keyi shuobu* (China Can Say No). Beijing: Zhongguo zhonghua gongshang lianhe chubanshe.

Song, Xiaojun, Wang Xiaodong, Huang Jisu, Song Qiang, and Liu Yang. 2009. *Zhongguo bu gaoxing: dashidai damubiao jiqi women de neiyouwaihuan* (Unhappy China: Grand Age, Grand Goal and Our Internal Trouble and External Disturbance). Nanjing: Jiangsu renmin chubanshe.

Spence, J. D. 1990. *The Search for Modern China.* London: Hutchinson.

Steinfeld, E. S. 1998. *Forging Reform in China: The Fate of State-Owned Industry.* Cambridge: Cambridge University Press.

Su, Xiaokang and Wang Luxiang. 1988. *Heshang* (River Elegy). Beijing: Xiandai chubanshe.

Sun, Yan. 1995. *The Chinese Reassessment of Socialism, 1976–1992.* Princeton, NJ: Princeton University Press.

Sun, Yat-sen. 1986. *Sun Zhongshan quanji* (Collected Works of Sun), vol. 9. Beijing: Zhonghua shuju.

Tang, Jun. 2010. "Chengxiang dibao zhidu: lishi, xianzhuang yu qianzhan" (Urban and Rural MSLS: History, Present Status and Future Prospects). Beijing: Institute of Sociology, Chinese Academy of Social Sciences.

Tang, Wenfang and W. L. Parich. 2000. *Chinese Urban Life under Reform: The Changing Social Contract.* Cambridge: Cambridge University Press.

Tanner, Murray Scot. 1998. *The Politics of Lawmaking in Post-Mao China: Institutions, Processes, and Democratic Prospects.* Oxford: Oxford University Press.

Teiwes, F. C. 1990. *Politics at Mao's Court: Gao Gang and Party Factionalism in the Early 1950s.* Armonk, NY: M. E. Sharpe.

Teiwes, F. C. 1993. *Politics and Purges in China: Rectification and the Decline of Party Norms, 1950–1965.* Armonk, NY: M. E. Sharpe.

Tong, Yanqi and Lei Shaohua. 2010. "Large-Scale Mass Incidents in China." *EAI Background Brief 520.* East Asian Institute, National University of Singapore.

Tong, Yanqi and Lei Shaohua. 2010. "Creating Public Opinion Pressure in China: Large-Scale Internet Protest." *EAI Background Brief 534.* East Asian Institute, National University of Singapore.

Tsai, Kellee. 2007. *Capitalism without Democracy: The Private Sector in Contemporary China.* Ithaca, NY: Cornell University Press.

Tsou, T. 1986. *The Cultural Revolution and Post-Mao Reforms: A Historical Perspective.* Chicago, IL: University of Chicago Press.

Unger, J. 2002. *The Transformation of Rural China.* New York: M. E. Sharpe.

Unger, J. and A. Chan. 1996. "Corporatism in China: A Developmental State in an East Asian Context." In B. L. McCormick and J. Unger, eds., *China after Socialism: In the Footsteps of Eastern Europe or East Asia.* Armonk, NY: M. E. Sharpe, pp. 95–129.

Vogel, Ezra. 2011. *Deng Xiaoping and the Transformation of China.* Cambridge, MA: Harvard University Press.

Walder, A. 1986. *Communist Neo-Traditionalism: Work and Authority in Chinese Industry.* Berkeley, CA: University of California Press.

Walder, Andrew. 1991. "Workers, Managers and the State: The Reform Era and the Political Crisis of 1989." *The China Quarterly* 127: 467–92.

Walder, Andrew and Zhao Litao. 2007. "China's Social Protests: Political Threat or Growing Pains?" *EAI Background Brief 357.* East Asian Institute, National University of Singapore.

Wang, David. 1998. "The East Turkestan Movement in Xinjiang: A Chinese Potential Source of Instability?" *EAI Background Brief 7.* East Asian Institute, National University of Singapore.

Wang, Feiling. 2005. *Organization through Division and Exclusion: China's Hukou System.* Stanford, CA: Stanford University Press.

Wang, Gungwu. 1995. *The Chinese Way: China's Position in International Relations.* Oslo: Scandinavian University Press.

Wang, Hui. 2003. *China's New Order: Society, Politics, and Economy in Transition,* Theodore Huter, ed. Cambridge, MA: Harvard University Press.

Wang, Kan. 2008. "A Changing Arena of Industrial Relations in China: What Is Happening after 1978." *Employee Relations* 30 (2): 190–216.

Wang, Shaoguang and Hu Angang. 1999. *The Political Economy of Uneven Development: The Case of China.* Armonk, NY: M. E. Sharpe.

Wang, Ying, *et al.* 1993. *Shehui zhongjian ceng: gaige yu Zhongguo de shetuan zuzhi* (Intermediate Social Strata: Reform and Social Groups in China). Beijing: Zhongguo fazhan chubanshe.

Wedeman, Andrew. 2007. *From Mao to Market.* Cambridge: Cambridge University Press.

Wei, Y. Q. and X. M. Liu. 2001. *Foreign Direct Investment in China.* Cheltenham, UK and Northampton, MA: Edward Elgar Publishing.

White, G. 1994. "Prospects for Civil Society: A Case Study of Xiaoshan City." In D. S. G. Goodman and B. Hooper, eds., *China's Quiet Revolution: New Interactions between State and Society.* Melbourne: Longman Cheshire, pp. 194–218.

White, Gordon, Jude Howell, and Shang Xiaoyuan. 1996. *In Search of Civil Society: Market Reform and Social Change in Contemporary China.* Oxford: Oxford University Press.

Whiting, S. 1991. "The Politics of NGO Development in China." *Voluntas* 2 (2): 16–48.

Whitney, Joseph B. R. 1970. *China: Area, Administration, and Nation Building.* Chicago, IL: Department of Geography, The University of Chicago.

Whyte, M. K. 2010. *Myth of the Social Volcano: Popular Responses to Rising Inequality in China.* Stanford, CA: Stanford University Press.

Whyte, M. K., ed. 2010. *Rural–Urban Inequality in Contemporary China.* Cambridge, MA: Harvard University Press.

Wibowo, Ignatius. 2001. "Party Recruitment and the Future of the Chinese Communist Party." Unpublished manuscript, East Asian Institute, National University of Singapore.

Williamson, John, ed. 1990. *Latin American Adjustment: How Much Has Happened.* Washington, DC: Institute for International Economics.

Womack, B., ed. 1991. *Contemporary Chinese Politics in Historical Perspective.* Cambridge: Cambridge University Press.

Wong, Christine and Richard Bird. 2008. "China's Fiscal System: A Work in Progress." In Loren Brandt and Thomas G. Rawski, eds., *China's Great Economic Transformation.* Cambridge: Cambridge University Press, pp. 429–66.

World Bank. 1994. *China: Internal Market Development and Regulations.* Washington, DC: World Bank.

World Bank. 1997. *Sharing Rising Incomes.* Washington, DC: World Bank.

World Bank. 2009. *From Poor Areas to Poor People: China's Evolving Poverty Reduction Agenda: An Assessment of Poverty and Inequality in China.* Washington, DC: World Bank, Poverty Reduction and Economic Management Department.

Wu, Guoguang. 1997. *Zhao Ziyang yu zhongguo zhengzhi gaige* (Political Reform under Zhao Ziyang). Hong Kong: The Pacific Century Institute.

Wu, Guoguang. 1997. *Zhulu shiwuda* (Power Competition for the Fifteenth Party Congress). Hong Kong: The Pacific Century Institute.

Wu, Guoguang and Helen Lansdowne, eds. 2008. *Zhao Ziyang and China's Political Future.* London and New York: Routledge.

Wu, Jiaxiang. 2004. *Lianbang hua: Zhonghua desan gongheguo zhilu* (Federalization: The Road to the Third Republic of China). Hong Kong: The Mirror Press.

Wu, Xiang. 2001. *Zhongguo nongcun gaige shilu* (Veritable Records of China's Rural Reform). Hangzhou: Zhejiang People's Publishing House.

Wu, Xu. 2007. *Chinese Cyber Nationalism: Evolution, Characteristics, and Implications.* Lanham, MD: Lexington Books.

Xiao, Donglian. 2008. *The History of the People's Republic of China*, vol. 10. *Turning Point in History: Re-examination of the Cultural Revolution and the Policy of Reform and Opening (1979–1981).* Hong Kong: Research Center for Contemporary Chinese Culture, The Chinese University of Hong Kong.

Xie, Lei. 2009. *Environmental Activism in China.* London: Routledge.

Xing, Y. Q. 2010. "China's High-tech Exports: Myth and Reality." *EAI Background Brief 506.* East Asian Institute, National University of Singapore.

Yan, Jiaqi. 1992. *Lianbang Zhongguo gouxiang* (The Conception of a Federal China). Hong Kong: Minbao chubanshe.

Yang, Dali. 1996. *Calamity and Reform in China: State, Rural Society and Institutional Change since the Great Leap Famine.* Stanford, CA: Stanford University Press.

Yang, Dali. 1997. *Beyond Beijing: Liberalization and the Regions in China.* New York: Routledge.

Yang, Dali. 2004. *Remaking the Chinese Leviathan: Market Transition and the Politics of Governance in China.* Stanford, CA: Stanford University Press.

Yang, Guobin. 2009. "Historical Imagination in the Study of Chinese Digital Civil Society." In Xiaoling Zhang and Yongnian Zheng, eds., *China's Information and Communication Technology Revolution: Social Changes and State Responses.* London and New York: Routledge, pp. 17–33.

Yang, Jishen. 1998. *Deng Xiaoping shidai* (The Deng Xiaoping Era). Beijing: Central Compilation and Translation Press.

Yang, Jishen. 2004. *Zhongguo gaige niandai de zhengzhi douzheng* (Political Struggle in China's Reform Era). Hong Kong: Excellent Culture Press.

Yang, Jisheng. 2008. *Tombstone* (Mu bei – Zhongguo liushi niandai dajihuang jishi). Hong Kong: Cosmos Books. English translation by Stacy Mosher and Guo Jian, *Tombstone: The Great Chinese Famine, 1958–1962.* New York: Farrar, Straus and Giroux, 2012.

Yang, Lijun and Lim Chee Kia. 2010. "Three Waves of Nationalism in Contemporary China: Sources, Themes, Presentations and Consequences." *International Journal of China Studies* 1 (2): 461–85.

Yang, Lijun and Zheng Yongnian. 2012. "Fen Qings (Angry Youth) in Contemporary China." *Journal of Contemporary China* 21 (76): 1–17.

Yang, Yongzhi and Yang Zhigang. 2007. *Zhongguo caizheng zhidu gaige 30 nian* (Thirty Years of China's Fiscal Reform). Shanghai: People's Publishing House.

Yao, S. and K. Wei. 2007. "Economic Growth in the Presence of FDI: The Perspective of Newly Industrializing Economics." *Journal of Comparative Economics* 35: 211–34.

Yep, R. 2000. "The Limitations of Corporatism for Understanding Reforming China: An Empirical Analysis in a Rural County." *Journal of Contemporary China* 9 (25): 547–66.

Yew, Chiew Ping. 2011. "How Property Boom Generates Social Tension in China." *EAI Background Brief 651*. East Asian Institute, National University of Singapore.

You, Ji. 1996. "Jiang Zemin: In Quest of Post-Deng Supremacy." In Maurice Brosseau, Suzanne Pepper, and Tsang Shu-ki, eds., *China Review 1996*. Hong Kong: The Chinese University of Hong Kong Press, pp. 1–28.

Young, Ernest P. 1977. *The Presidency of Yuan Shih-K'ai: Liberalism and Dictatorship in Early Republic China*. Ann Arbor, MI: University of Michigan Press.

Yueh, Linda. 2010. *Economy of China*. Cheltenham, UK and Northampton, MA: Edward Elgar.

Zhang, K. H. 2000. "Why Is U.S. Direct Investment in China so Small?" *Contemporary Economy Policy* 18 (1): 82–94.

Zhang, Xiaodan. 2009. "Trade Unions under the Modernization of Paternalist Rule in China," *Working USA: The Journal of Labor and Society* 12: 193–218.

Zhang, Zhenlong, ed. 1989. *Jundui shengchan jingying guanli* (Management of Military Production). Beijing: Jiefangjun chubanshe.

Zhao, Dingxin. 2001. *The Power of Tiananmen: State–Society Relations and the 1989 Beijing Student Movement*. Chicago, IL: University of Chicago Press.

Zhao, Litao and Huang Yanjie. 2009. "China's Moves to Reform its Healthcare System." *EAI Background Brief 486*. East Asian Institute, National University of Singapore.

Zhao, Suisheng. 1993. "Deng Xiaoping's Southern Tour: Elite Politics in Post-Tiananmen China." *Asian Survey* 33 (8): 739–56.

Zhao, Yang and Zhou Feizhou. 2000. "Nongmin fudan he caishui tizhi" (Peasants' Burdens and Fiscal System). *Hong Kong Journal of Social Sciences* 17: 67–85.

Zhao, Zhongwei. 2006. "Income Inequality, Unequal Health Care Access, and Mortality in China." *Population and Development Review* 32 (3): 461–83.

Zhao, Ziyang. 2009. *Prisoner of the State: The Secret Journal of Premier Zhao Ziyang*. New York: Simon & Schuster.

Zheng, Yongnian. 1994. "Perforated Sovereignty: Provincial Dynamics and China's Foreign Trade." *The Pacific Review* 7 (3): 309–21.

Zheng, Yongnian. 1999. *Discovering Chinese Nationalism in China: Modernization, Identity, and International Relations*. Cambridge and New York: Cambridge University Press.

Zheng, Yongnian. 2000. *Zhu Rongji xinzheng* (The New Deal of Zhu Rongji). Singapore and London: World Scientific.

Zheng, Yongnian. 2001. *Zhengzhi jianjin zhuyi* (Political Gradualism). Taipei: Chinese Eurasian Education Foundation.

Zheng, Yongnian. 2004. *Globalization and State Transformation in China*. Cambridge and New York: Cambridge University Press.

Zheng, Yongnian. 2005. "Institutional Economics and Central–Local Relations in China: Evolving Research." *China: An International Journal* 3 (2): 240–69.

Zheng, Yongnian. 2006. *De Facto Federalism in China: Reforms and Dynamics of Central–Local Relations*. Singapore and London: World Scientific.

Zheng, Yongnian. 2008. *Technological Empowerment: The Internet, State, and Society in China*. Stanford, CA: Stanford University Press.

Zheng, Yongnian. 2012. "China in 2011: Anger, Political Consciousness, Anxiety, and Uncertainty." *Asian Survey* 52 (1): 28–41.

Zheng, Yongnian and Pan Rongfang. 2012. "From Defensive to Aggressive Strategies: The Evolution of Economic Nationalism in China." In Anthony P. D'Costa, ed., *Globalization and Economic Nationalism in Asia*. Oxford: Oxford University Press, pp. 84–108.

Zhong, Yang. 2012. *Political Culture and Participation in Rural China*. London: Routledge.

Zhou, K. 1996. *How the Farmers Changed China: Power of the People*. Boulder, CO: Westview Press.

Zhou, Xiaohong, ed. 2006. *Zhongguo zhongchan jieceng diaocha* (Survey on Chinese Middle Class). Beijing: Zhongguo shehui kexue chubanshe.

Zhou, Y. P. and S. Lall. 2005. "The Impact of China's FDI Surge on FDI in South-East Asia: Panel Data Analysis for 1986–2001." *Transnational Corporations* 14 (1): 41–65.

Zhu, Guanglei, *et al.* 1998. *Dangdai Zhongguo shehui ge jieceng fenxi* (An Analysis of Social Strata in Contemporary China). Tianjin: Tianjin renmin chubanshe.

Zong, Fengming. 2007. *Zhao Ziyang ruanjin zhong de tanhua* (Zhao Ziyang: Captive Conversations). Hong Kong: The Open Press.

Zweig, D. 1997. *Freeing China's Farmers: Rural Restructuring in the Reform Era*. Armonk, NY: M. E. Sharpe.

Index

Contemporary China: A History since 1978, First Edition. Yongnian Zheng.
© 2014 John Wiley & Sons, Ltd. Published 2014 by John Wiley & Sons, Ltd.